Young Women, Girls and Postfeminism in Contemporary British Film

Library of Gender and Popular Culture

From *Mad Men* to gaming culture, performance art to steampunk fashion, the presentation and representation of gender continues to saturate popular media. This series seeks to explore the intersection of gender and popular culture, engaging with a variety of texts – drawn primarily from Art, Fashion, TV, Cinema, Cultural Studies and Media Studies – as a way of considering various models for understanding the complementary relationship between 'gender identities' and 'popular culture'. By considering race, ethnicity, class, and sexual identities across a range of cultural forms, each book in the series adopts a critical stance towards issues surrounding the development of gender identities and popular and mass cultural 'products'.

For further information or enquiries, please contact the library series editors:

Claire Nally: claire.nally@northumbria.ac.uk
Angela Smith: angela.smith@sunderland.ac.uk

Advisory Board:

Dr Kate Ames, Central Queensland University, Australia
Dr Michael Higgins, University of Strathclyde, UK
Prof Åsa Kroon, Örebro University, Sweden
Dr Andrea McDonnell, Emmanuel College, USA
Dr Niall Richardson, University of Sussex, UK
Dr Jacki Willson, University of Leeds, UK

**Library of Gender
& Popular Culture**

Young Women, Girls and Postfeminism in Contemporary British Film

Sarah Hill

BLOOMSBURY ACADEMIC
LONDON • NEW YORK • OXFORD • NEW DELHI • SYDNEY

BLOOMSBURY ACADEMIC
Bloomsbury Publishing Plc
50 Bedford Square, London, WC1B 3DP, UK
1385 Broadway, New York, NY 10018, USA
29 Earlsfort Terrace, Dublin 2, Ireland

BLOOMSBURY, BLOOMSBURY ACADEMIC and the Diana logo are trademarks
of Bloomsbury Publishing Plc

First published in Great Britain 2021
This paperback edition published 2022

Cover design: Charlotte Daniels
Cover image: Maisie WIlliams and Florence Pugh in The Falling (2014)
(© Cannon and Morley Pictures / Collection Christophel / ArenaPAL)

A catalogue record for this book is available from the British Library.

Library of Congress Cataloging-in-Publication Data
Names: Hill, Sarah (Lecturer in media studies) author.
Title: Young women, girls and postfeminism in contemporary British film / Sarah Hill.
Description: London; New York: Bloomsbury Academic, 2020. | Series: Library of
gender and popular culture | Based on the author's dissertation (doctoral)–
University of East Anglia, 2012. | Includes bibliographical references and index. |
Identifiers: LCCN 2020005802 (print) | LCCN 2020005803 (ebook) |
ISBN 9781788310369 (hardback) | ISBN 9781350120310 (pdf) |
ISBN 9781350120327 (epub) | ISBN 9781350120334
Subjects: LCSH: Girls in motion pictures. | Teenage girls in motion pictures. |
Femininity in motion pictures. | Motion pictures–Great Britain–History–21st century.
Classification: LCC PN1995.9.G57 H55 2020 (print) | LCC PN1995.9.G57
(ebook) | DDC 791.43/65342–dc23
LC record available at https://lccn.loc.gov/2020005802
LC ebook record available at https://lccn.loc.gov/2020005803

ISBN: HB: 978-1-7883-1036-9
PB: 978-1-3501-9169-3
ePDF: 978-1-350-12031-0
eBook: 978-1-350-12032-7

Series: Library of Gender and Popular Culture

Typeset by Deanta Global Publishing Services, Chennai, India

To find out more about our authors and books visit www.bloomsbury.com
and sign up for our newsletters.

Contents

Figures

Series Editors' Introduction

One of the legacies of postfeminism could be said to be the way in which young women perceive themselves, and in how popular culture in turn perceives them. As Sarah Hill's monograph shows, in the first part of the twenty-first century, there was a blossoming of films showing young women as the protagonist, and many of these films proved to be commercially successful. This is a neat counterpoint to the parallel increase in films and television shows offering positive depictions of central characters who are older, as explored in Niall Richardson's *Ageing Femininity on Screen* (2019). Set against the traditional Hollywood films, British films have often been seen as lacking such glamour and aspiration. The can-do attitude that is embedded in postfeminism is something that, Hill argues, informs British films featuring girls and young women in the early part of the twenty-first century. While Hill focuses on British film output, other books in this Library show this is not a specifically British phenomenon (see Melanie Kennedy's *Tweenhood* (2019) which explores femininity in popular culture in the United States, and Victoria Cann's *Girls Like This, Boys Like That* (2018) which explores the lived experience of British girls). Postfeminism brought into popular consciousness the notion of choice and empowerment for women of all ages, but perhaps most habitually in the case of young women, such as those who feature in the films Hill examines. As many theorists of postfeminism have argued, the body is at the centre of postfeminism, and bodily maintenance is key to female success, often through the 'makeover'. However, as Hill suggests here, the consumerist slant on the makeover in US popular culture is largely eschewed in British film, where friendship and relationships are the currency on the road to self-discovery and authenticity. Hill explores the ambivalent, particularly British approach to the makeover in the films under discussion in this book, ranging from the revisionist *St Trinian's* (Parker and Thompson 2007) to films derived from contemporary books and novels, such as *The Duchess* (Dibb 2008). The inclusion of a chapter on historical films offers a link with Julia Erhart's *Gendering History on Screen* (2018), where Hill provides a different perspective on this popular genre.

In focusing on British film, Hill is able to explore issues of class and race in a context where the former is at the heart of national identity, and the latter only recently receiving concentrated critical attention. What Hill shows here is that, while British films are often characterized by 'grit' and a lack of glamour, what the postfeminist films offer is an ambivalence to these polar opposites, with 'naturalness' favoured in place of glamour, and 'respectability' prized without necessarily being associated with grit. This ambivalence in the British films Hill explores is a theme that she returns to time and time again throughout the book, offering a nuanced view of British cinema which provides a counterpoint to the unquestioned Hollywood glamour examined in other books in this Library.

The films in this book are taken from a very specific period of production when, as Hill convincingly argues, postfeminist sensibilities were in the ascendancy and before the startling arrival of the #MeToo movement.

Angela Smith and Clare Nally

Acknowledgements

Parts of the discussion of *Chalet Girl* in Chapter 2 were originally published in 'The Ambitious Young Woman and the Contemporary British Sports Film', *Assuming Gender*, 5:1 (2015), pp. 37–58. I thank the editors for their kind permission in allowing me to include that work here.

The research for this book originated as my PhD thesis undertaken at the University of East Anglia, and I am hugely grateful to Melanie Williams for her guidance, support and enthusiasm during the supervision process. Thank you also to Yvonne Tasker and Vicky Ball who provided very generous and helpful feedback on that earlier work. I am also grateful to the anonymous peer reviewers for their constructive and thoughtful feedback on an earlier draft of this manuscript.

I am indebted to the friends I made during my time at UEA, who supported this research in the form of many stimulating conversations. I am especially thankful to Marie-Alix Thouaille for her insightful and supportive comments on earlier drafts of this work, and for all our conversations about postfeminism.

Thank you to my colleagues in Media, Culture, Heritage at Newcastle University for their support and encouragement, particularly Karen Ross for taking the time to read drafts of this work. I am also grateful to the NU Women's Writing Group for providing the much-needed time and space that enabled me to complete this project.

I thank Anna Coatman, Camilla Erskine and the editorial team at Bloomsbury for all their hard work and patience.

I am immensely grateful for Jack's unwavering support and encouragement – thank you.

Finally, the biggest, and most important, thank you must go to my family. Thank you to Becky for always being there and believing in me, and to my parents for their unconditional love and support in everything I do.

Introduction

Girlhood and contemporary British cinema

This book presents a study of young femininity in contemporary British cinema. Girls and young women – whether they be fictional characters, celebrities or 'real-life' people – have become ubiquitous across all areas of twenty-first-century media culture, including pop music, adverts, television, young adult literature, social media and, of course, film. Some of the most successful recent films are films with a young woman protagonist, which Sarah Projansky terms 'girl films'.[1] These include films such as *Frozen* (Buck and Lee 2013), *The Hunger Games* trilogy (Ross 2012, Lawrence 2013, 2014, 2015) and *Fifty Shades of Grey* (Taylor-Johnson 2015), which span a variety of genres and intended audiences, from Disney animations and adaptations of young adult novels to erotic literature. The huge success of these films has led to a number of popular press articles proclaiming that women are 'taking over' the box office that has long been thought of as the domain of blockbuster-watching young men.[2]

British cinema also experienced a proportionate increase in films with a young woman protagonist between 2000 and 2015, as part of a concerted effort to attract youth audiences. Analysis of the film magazine *Sight & Sound* during the period revealed three such films produced in 2000, rising to a peak of fourteen in 2008.[3] In 2007, Ealing Studios revived the *St Trinian's* series (Parker and Thompson 2007), which earned over £12 million at the UK box office and was followed by a sequel in 2009.[4] The British film industry also produced its first film in 3D with *StreetDance 3D* (Giwa and Pasquini 2010) starring Nichola Burley, which made £11 million in the first five weeks of its release.[5] Alongside this, the period also witnessed the development of the careers of a number of British women filmmakers, including Andrea Arnold,

Amma Asante, Carol Morley and Lynne Ramsay, all producing films with young women protagonists, although these filmmakers did not necessarily seek to specifically attract young audiences. The success of these films reinforces Melanie Bell and Melanie Williams' assertion that female-centred British films are not 'cuckoos-in-the-nest or exceptional observations but rather form the very core of popular national cinema'.[6] However, British cinema is often thought to be 'far more at ease with masculine stories and imagery', which means that contemporary British cinema's girl films have remained largely overlooked.[7]

This book offers the first comprehensive study of how young femininity has been constructed in British cinema since the millennium. Certain films in this corpus have been written about previously – either as a single case study like Lucy Bolton's examination of *Fish Tank* (Arnold 2009) as a phenomenology of British girlhood[8] or as part of a generic cycle, such as Louise Wilks' examination of British 'tween' films *St Trinian's, Wild Child* (Moore 2008) and *Angus, Thongs and Perfect Snogging* (Chadha 2008).[9] There has also been a tendency to focus more on British art-house cinema as explicitly feminist, such as So Mayer's exploration of British cinema's 'runaway girl' in films such as *Movern Callar* (Ramsay 2002) and *The Unloved* (Morton 2009).[10] By contrast, this monograph takes into account a range of British girl films produced during this period through a variety of genres and modes of production, and intended audiences, in order to capture the state of British cinema's representations of girlhood by tracing the commonalities and differences between the films and their constructions of young femininity, as well as showcasing the dynamism and diversity of British film production during this period.

In mapping the construction of young femininity in contemporary British cinema, this book seeks to make the case for a nationally specific articulation of postfeminism by examining how postfeminism is modified and articulated in a British context. Postfeminism is a 'pervasive phenomenon of contemporary culture' that has been the focus of a wealth of academic attention,[11] although more recently its continued relevance has been questioned.[12] Since the 1980s, postfeminism has variously been thought of as a 'historical shift within' feminism, a 'backlash' against feminism and an 'epistemological break' from feminism. I use the term here to signify the period 'after' second-wave feminism, while acknowledging that the wave metaphor is highly contentious as 'feminism ebbs and flows within generations, with various issues resurfacing in a cyclical fashion'.[13] As with Angela McRobbie's 'double entanglement',[14] Rosalind Gill's 'sensibility'[15] and Sarah Projansky's 'cultural *discourse*' (original emphasis),[16] I understand postfeminism as defined by a complex and contradictory set of characteristics. As Gill argues, 'postfeminism is a critical analytical term that refers to empirical regularities or patterns in contemporary cultural life'.[17] This includes the incorporation of feminist gains, which are then filtered through a grammar of 'choice', empowerment and individualism which work to relegate feminism to the past; an entanglement of feminist and anti-feminist ideas that allows for a reinvestment in traditional markers of heterosexual femininity; an imperative of self-monitoring – both of the body and of one's psychological interior; and the dominance of the makeover paradigm.[18] In postfeminist culture, the body is seen as the key to a woman's identity and must be subject to constant self-monitoring and discipline in order to maintain a suitably feminine identity that closely resembles the kind of 'heterosexual male fantasy found in pornography'.[19] It is this notion that women in particular are compelled to enact physical and psychological self-monitoring and transformation, and that this is achieved primarily through consumption, which is seen to account for the dominance of the makeover paradigm within postfeminist culture. The imperative to monitor and work on the self is indicative of late modern theories of identity that purport that the self must be reflexively constructed through a range of choices in order to construct a coherent narrative of the self as part of an authentic identity.[20] This mode of self-making is situated within the context of neoliberalism, whereby the free-market economics and privatization that characterized the Conservative governments in the 1980s – led by Margaret Thatcher in the UK and Ronald Regan in the United States – constructed the individual as entrepreneurial, autonomous and self-governing. Rosalind Gill has noted the synergy between the freely choosing, self-monitoring postfeminist woman who must transform herself through consumption and the autonomous and self-regulating subject of neoliberalism. Like neoliberalism, postfeminism has been 'taken for granted' in its everyday ability to speak to 'meaning-making' about gender so that it 'operates as a kind of gendered form of neoliberalism'.[21] It is neoliberalism, therefore, that has enabled the hegemonic spread of postfeminism.[22]

Although postfeminism is regarded as a transnational concept, very little attention has been paid to how postfeminism is discursively engaged in a British context. As Justine Ashby argues, 'We should not assume that these discourses can simply be grafted onto the rather different contours of British political and popular culture'.[23] Where British incarnations of postfeminism have been thought about, it is often in relation to singular texts such as Angela McRobbie's (2004, 2007) examination of *Bridget Jones' Diary* (Maguire 2001). Although considered an emblematic postfeminist text, we need only to think about the differences between the hapless, clumsy and ordinary Bridget (Renee Zellweger) and her glossy and fashionable American counterparts such as the women from *Sex and the City* (HBO 1998–2004) and *Ally McBeal* (20th Century Fox 1997–2002) to see that, although they are all considered to be canonical transit texts,[24] their articulations of postfeminism differ according to national context. This book seeks to map how postfeminism is modified in a British cultural context by examining how young femininity is constructed in contemporary British cinema. A key point of distinction is in the films' ambivalent engagement with the postfeminist makeover. Postfeminist culture constructs women as autonomous 'empowered consumers' who must continuously work on themselves to ensure appropriate femininity and subsequently reveal their authentic self.[25] As Diane Negra argues, the postfeminist makeover allows for the kind of 'transformative consumption so valued by postfeminism' and is the 'key ritual of the female coming into being' that allows for the 'revelation of the self that has "been there all along"'.[26] British girl films, however, eschew the overt consumption inherent within the Hollywood makeover, instead swapping clothes with friends or buying them second-hand. Rather than enabling the revelation of the 'authentic' self, the makeovers in these films are frequently presented as inauthentic and false, providing only temporary respite in the protagonists' quest for the 'perfect' feminine self. Where makeovers are successful, such as in *St Trinian's* (Parker and Thompson 2007) and *Wild Child* (Moore 2008), which I analyse in Chapter 1, the revelation of the authentic self is linked to the revelation of a distinctly British feminine identity. British cinema's ambivalence towards the postfeminist makeover can be situated, I argue, within the broader history of British cinema's (and Britain more broadly) ambivalent relationship to glamour and consumption. Although the meaning of glamour has shifted over time, 'connotations of charm, artifice and allure still remain'.[27] As Melanie Williams argues, British cinema has frequently struggled to accommodate glamour, and glamour has often been used as a marker of differentiation between British films (and its female stars) and Hollywood.[28] Furthermore, Jackie Stacey's study of British women's film spectatorship in the 1940s and 1950s placed Britain and America's relationship to glamour in opposition with one another, with British stars being described as having natural beauty, talent and charm in comparison with the 'cheap' and 'artificial' glamour offered by Hollywood stars. This equating of British femininity with 'natural' beauty goes some way to explaining British cinema's ambivalence towards the postfeminist makeover, as although the makeover facilitates the revelation of the authentic self, it nevertheless draws attention to the process and the products used to achieve this via the prolonged makeover scene, which is the 'scene par excellence of postfeminist identity making', troubling the idea of naturalness.[29] Classed discourses are evident within this too: the 'assertion of "respectable" British femininity becomes an assertion of middle-class norms: "true" *British* femininity is middle class and is not "painted" or glamorous, and by implication, not explicitly sexual' (original emphasis).[30] As I argue in the following chapters, this positioning of British femininity as 'natural' and classy persists in these contemporary British girl films, in both the films themselves and the extra-textual discourses that circulate around them and the young women who star in them.

The ideal postfeminist subject is young, white, able-bodied and middle class, and at the heart of the postfeminist makeover is the idea that 'the right clothes, worn properly, have the power to shatter class boundaries and allow characters to climb social ladders', allowing the subject to occupy the ideal middle-class position.[31] A focus on class continues to be a defining feature of British cinema,[32] and class plays a key role in how postfeminism is articulated within a British context. Class occupies a tricky position within these films given that contemporary postfeminist girlhood is ideally middle class. Working-class protagonists are repeatedly required to transcend class boundaries and become appropriately feminine, usually via a makeover, but are ultimately unsuccessful because class barriers remain insurmountable, such as in *Kicks* (Heymann 2008) and *My Summer of Love* (Pawlikowski 2004), which I discuss in Chapter 3. Occasionally, the working-class protagonist is able to transcend her classed identity in accordance with meritocratic neoliberal and postfeminist discourses, such as in the sports films *Chalet Girl* and *StreetDance*, which I explore in Chapter 2.

Postfeminist girlhood

Youthful femininity is key to postfeminist culture, and the figure of the girl has become increasingly visible in popular culture in the twenty-first century. This has coincided with the development of girl studies as an academic discipline. Developing out of disciplines such as psychology and sociology, as well as film, media and cultural studies, girl studies combines feminist and critical youth studies to explore the variety of ways in which the girl functions as a representational figure in popular culture, while also capturing how girls' subjectivities are constructed in various cultural, social and historical contexts through studying girls' lived experiences.[33] While young people have always carried a peculiar 'burden of representation' as indicators of the sign of the times,[34] young women in particular have had to carry most of the weight of this burden in modernity.[35] As Sarah Projansky suggests, in the twenty-first century the 'convenient figure of the girl' resurfaces to work through contemporary issues such as neoliberalism and postfeminism.[36] As has been well established, postfeminist culture of the 1990s and 2000s privileged individualized and celebratory discourses of girlhood. Confident, successful, sexy, assertive and independent 'can-do girls' were made ubiquitous through the idea of 'girl power'.[37] Girl power was associated with a number of iconic female characters within popular culture such as Buffy (Sarah Michelle Gellar) in *Buffy the Vampire Slayer* (20th Century Fox 1997–2003) and Lara Croft from the *Tomb Raider* video game series, while in the UK, the language of girl power was popularized by 1990s girl pop group Spice Girls. As Ashby notes, girl power all at once seemed to 'link being sexy with being ballsy, to celebrate female camaraderie while privileging individualism'.[38] Girl power was, therefore, inherently contradictory and depoliticized. As Rosalind Gill states, can-do girlhood and girl power were about individual achievement, not feminism.[39] Postfeminist 'can-do' girlhood, then, put forth a narrow version of 'acceptable' girlhood that encapsulated neoliberal ideologies via the 'fantasy promise' that girls can achieve anything as long as they work hard enough,[40] and failure to succeed is due to an individual lack of effort and character rather than structural inequalities.

The figure of the 'can-do' girl embodies Western neoliberal ideals around hard work, success and social mobility. In the UK, the figure of the 'top girl' emerged to exemplify New Labour's desire to present the UK as an aspirational meritocracy by making the most of their new-found 'freedom' and 'equality', by being highly productive in work and education and displaying their success by investing in consumer culture. Education was central to New Labour's campaign to raise the aspirations of the nation, and young women were at the forefront of New Labour's expansion of higher education. 'Top girls', as Angela McRobbie argues, are hard-working, high-achieving, white, middle-class girls destined for elite universities such as Oxford and Cambridge,[41] as young women were 'marked by the possession of grades, qualifications and occupational identities', more so than their male peers.[42] New Labour missed their target to get 50 per cent of young people into higher education by 2010, but, as of 2017–18, this target has now been reached, with young women's participation in higher education exceeding that of young men at 57 per cent.[43] At the same time that girls' successes, along with their new confidence and resilience, were being celebrated, research, journalism and government policy articulated and reinforced anxieties around young women, including concerns about eating disorders, low self-esteem and 'mean girl behaviour'.[44] Jessica Ringrose has identified these gender-specific concerns as 'postfeminist panics'. Such panics, she argues, position girls as 'overly successful', 'overly aggressive' and 'overly sexy' as a direct consequence of feminist gains; a sign of 'girl power taken too far'.[45]

The (hyper-)visibility afforded to girls means that they have become 'luminous',[46] 'sparkling'[47] and 'spectacular'.[48] This 'luminosity' has been thought of as regulatory – a moving spotlight that works to soften and disguise the regulatory dynamics[49] – but it is literal as well as symbolic. As Mary Celeste Kearney argues, sparkle is ubiquitous, dominating 'girlhood's visual landscape' and 'making our world twinkle and shine as if it is bedazzled by pixie dust'.[50] Unlike earlier forms of sparkle, such as the magical creation of the dress in *Cinderella* (1950), in the twenty-first century sparkle operates as a specific form of postfeminist glamour, signifying 'empowerment, visibility and independent wealth' in a manner that is easily accessible to girls.[51] Despite the dominance of sparkle in contemporary girl culture, British cinema's ambivalent relationship to glamour means that incorporating sparkle is sometimes difficult for a national cinema associated with realist modes of filmmaking. As Justine Ashby and Andrew Higson argue, British cinema 'has always been promoted in terms of cultural value, pitting the authentic, indigenous culture of "ordinary people" against the Americanised culture of glamour, spectacle, commercialism and mere entertainment'.[52] British cinema's close association with social realism means that British films are often referred to as 'gritty', which has connotations of greyness and discomfort, along with implicitly aesthetically unambitious filmmaking in comparison with Hollywood spectacles.[53] British cinema's ambivalence towards sparkle is also driven by financial as well as cultural concerns, given that budgets for British film are significantly lower than their Hollywood counterparts, limiting Britain's ability to produce sparkling spectacles. Nevertheless, contemporary British cinema's girl films have made some deliberate attempts to incorporate sparkle as part of wider efforts to attract youth audiences. In 2015, Kenneth Branagh directed a fantasy live-action remake of Disney's *Cinderella* – the exemplar figure of girlhood – starring Lily James who sparkled in a series of dazzling costumes by Oscar-winning costume designer Sandy Powell. In addition, as I argue in Chapter 2, the sports film *StreetDance* offered sparkle and spectacle through its incorporation of teen dance film aesthetics and its presentation of London as a city full of glittering skyscrapers akin to New York. The amazed reactions of the film's reviewers here suggest that sparkle is occasionally welcomed, even if it is not considered typically British. The incorporation of sparkle in this way is also further evidence of the continuous 'push and pull of influence and distinction' that characterizes British cinema's relationship with Hollywood.[54]

British girlhood and celebrity

The increased visibility of girls and girlhood is closely intertwined with contemporary celebrity culture, both of which are intensely public.[55] Celebrity culture is also recognized as a 'key site in which the "successful girl" discourse of neoliberalism is reproduced' through an emphasis on 'compulsory success', self-monitoring and transformation and social mobility.[56] At the same time, there is increasing concern about girls' relationship to celebrity culture in both governmental and media discourses that express concern about girls' 'inappropriate' ambitions that entail foregoing hard work for quick and easy fame.[57] It is worth considering, then, the young women who have emerged as stars of British cinema during this period, whose stardom exists within the wider celebrity culture.[58] These include Emma Watson, Carey Mulligan, Lily James, Keira Knightley and Felicity Jones. As Melanie Williams argues, these stars are all indicative of a 'reiterative white middle class femininity' that is perpetuated by the 'stranglehold of the "English rose" ideal in relation to British femininity, which is tied to nostalgic visions of the past'.[59] The star discourse that circulates around Emma Watson and Felicity Jones in particular, positions them as British postfeminist 'top girls' through an emphasis on their elite education (both attended Oxford University, although Watson as a visiting student), along with hard work and the fact that they began their careers at an early age. I discuss the significance of Jones' 'top girl' persona in Chapter 2 in relation to her role in *Chalet Girl*. In their study of the role that celebrities play in young people's aspirations, Heather Mendick et al. highlight Watson as a celebrity whom young people frequently referred to as an example of an 'achieved' celebrity whose hard work makes her deserving of fame, and it is Watson's middle-class femininity that enables her to occupy this position.[60] I would further add that Watson's *Britishness* also plays a role here, particularly as British femininity is consistently defined by notions of middle-class respectability in opposition to artificial American glamour and overt self-display.[61] Britain, and British cinema, has always had a deeply ambivalent relationship with stardom and celebrity due to connotations of promoting glamour at the expense of talent and an emphasis on self-display, which sits uneasily with a national culture that has frequently been represented in terms of restrained respectability.[62] This ambivalence is also apparent within contemporary British cinema's girl films, which both acknowledge contemporary girlhood's investment in discourses of celebrity and display unease, with occasional attempts to distance themselves from a celebrity culture that is closely associated with America. This British ambivalence towards celebrity culture is inherent within a number of the films I analyse in the following chapters. The schoolgirl films *St Trinian's* and *Wild Child*, which I discuss in Chapter 1, suggest that

Britain needs to be taught the codes and requirements of celebrity culture from America, as British girls learn about celebrity from their American peers, while *Kicks* in Chapter 3 presents a more overt parable about the risks of girls' investment in celebrity culture.

British girlhood and 'post-postfeminism'

This book examines the mediation of young femininity in British cinema in films produced between 2000 and 2015. This fifteen-year period experienced a series of significant political, economic and socio-cultural shifts that prompted questions about the continued relevance of postfeminism. As a result of the 2008 financial crash, which triggered a global economic crisis, the UK entered a period of austerity led by the Conservative–Liberal Democrat coalition, which continued under Theresa May's Conservative government. Heather Mendick et al. conceptualize this cultural moment as an 'austere meritocracy', which works to capture the tension between the simultaneous intensification of meritocratic ideals at the very time that opportunities for upward social mobility are being diminished due to austerity and the decimation of the welfare state.[63] Although the self-responsible neoliberal subject remains constant, the context of austerity gave rise to a specific set of regulative discourses, such as an intensified emphasis on 'hard work', 'optimism' and 'resilience', along with the 'regulation of consumption through discourses of "(un)deserving wealth" and "thrift"'.[64] This, in turn, prompted a renewed interest in the British class system in a recessionary media culture that is characterized by themes of wealth and inequality.[65] These shifting discourses reflect how, as Diane Negra and Yvonne Tasker argue, postfeminism 'reads differently now the economic bubble has burst'[66] because the celebratory image of the postfeminist consumer now looks like a 'luxury that can no longer be afforded'.[67] Instead, postfeminism's emphasis on choice and empowerment takes the form of female resourcefulness that draws on British wartime notions of 'pluck' and 'making do' as a way of managing and adapting to precarity,[68] as exemplified by the image of the female cupcake baker who signifies a comfortably gendered form of entrepreneurialism.[69]

While postfeminism 'reads differently now' post-2008, I argue that it remains highly relevant as a critical term. As Rosalind Gill argues, far from receding, postfeminism has 'spread out and intensified' across all aspects of contemporary culture and it is now much more difficult to identify postfeminism's distinctive characteristics because 'its "edges" have become blurred'.[70] In addition to its individualized emphasis on the body, postfeminism has become increasingly dependent on a psychologicalized register that is 'built around cultivating the "right" kinds of disposition' necessary to survive in the neoliberal society, such as aspiration, confidence, resilience, happiness and a positive mental attitude.[71] The intense 'spread' of postfeminism means that we can no longer assume that white, middle-class young women are its sole subjects, and more recent work has explored postfeminism's racialized contours and how it interpellates women of colour,[72] while also acknowledging that postfeminist discourses are intertwined with post-racial discourses, which both work to relegate gender and race inequality to the past, while historicizing the political struggles into a linear narrative that comfortably explains how we arrived at the contemporary 'post' moment.[73] Postfeminism's classed dynamics have also been explored.[74] As well as adopting intersectional approaches, others have also identified specific features of postfeminism, such as Alison Winch's concept of 'the girlfriend gaze', which I utilize in an analysis of British cinema's depictions of girls' friendships in Chapter 3.[75] The sheer range and reach of postfeminism in contemporary culture therefore demonstrate that a nationally specific postfeminist framework is more urgent than ever, into which this book seeks to make an intervention.

The intensification of postfeminism exists alongside an increased visibility of feminism in popular culture, particularly in online spaces, such as Laura Bates' Everyday Sexism Project,[76] which Nicola Rivers argues characterizes the 'fourth wave' of feminism.[77] Celebratory discourses praising the potential that online spaces offer for feminist activism, however, often obscure the fact that women are frequently subjected to intense violence and misogyny in these spaces.[78] Feminism's new visibility online also co-exists with the intensification of (self-) surveillance and regulation via self-determined goals in pursuit of 'the good life' which McRobbie refers to as 'the perfect'. For young women in particular, social media sites such as Instagram offer images of 'the virtual good life', as users regulate their posts in the goal of perfection. 'The perfect', and the harsh scrutiny that constitutes part of its apparatus, consequently evokes forms of suffering that have become commonplace – a 'space of everyday femininity' – such as cyberbullying.[79] Celebrity culture is another key site in which feminism has become increasingly visible, perhaps best demonstrated by Beyoncé's 2014 MTV Video Music Awards performance which saw her perform in front of a giant illuminated sign stating 'feminist', along with *Harry Potter* star Emma Watson's role as a UN Goodwill Ambassador where she advocates for gender equality as part of her #HeForShe campaign.[80] In interviews, Watson has described how she equates feminism with 'choice' for women,[81] indicating a neoliberal imperative that is key to celebrity feminism.[82] This 'neoliberal feminism', Catherine Rottenberg argues, ties individualized mainstream feminism with the market values of neoliberalism.[83] The neoliberal feminist acknowledges inequalities between men and women but not the social, economic and cultural forces that produce these inequalities; rather, she internalizes this by setting goals and taking responsibility for her own self-care.[84] Contemporary feminist visibilities are, subsequently, highly uneven.[85] The chapters that follow will trace how contemporary British cinema mediates and responds to these shifting discourses through its representations of young femininity.

Contemporary British cinema

British cinema has 'always been a complex site of representation';[86] both an industry with economic structures and particular methods of classification and a cultural practice that establishes 'nationhood as a distinct, familiar sense of belonging', defined through comparison with other national cinemas.[87] Any attempts to define Britishness itself, however, are beyond the scope of this book. While it is naive to assume that British cinema simply 'reflects' British society, it is possible to trace how British cinema mediates contemporary discourses of young femininity, as well as the wider political, social and cultural context in which films are produced and received. When *Bend It Like Beckham* was released in 2002, Prime Minister Tony Blair reportedly enthused that he and his wife Cherie loved the film because 'this is my Britain'.[88] The postfeminist 'girl power' film revolves around two teenagers Jess (Parminder Nagra) and Jules (Keira Knightley), who dream of becoming professional footballers but must first overcome the obstacle of discrimination. Justine Ashby notes how this 'girl power movie' frames 'questions of racial and sexual identity within an upbeat, postfeminist idiom',[89] and the film's feel-good ending, in which Jess and Jules depart for their new footballing careers in the United States, assuages a number of social issues, such as racism and sexism, in keeping with its 'upbeat postfeminist message' and presents Britain as an unproblematically multicultural nation that glosses over continuing problems of racial discrimination in line with New Labour rhetoric.[90]

Contemporary British cinema's girl films are symptomatic of the British film industry's organizational structures during this period, which were characterized by attempts to make British cinema more mainstream while also remaining culturally British with a distinctive identity. Efforts to make British film more mainstream began in the 1990s, where film played a key part in a shift towards the 'creative industries', which included a more neoliberal 'market-savvy and business-minded approach to film' that combined mainstream appeal and commercial success while maintaining a culturally British film culture.[91] The New Labour government introduced a number of changes as part of this mainstreaming of film culture, including a tax rebate scheme for production and National Lottery funding. Most significantly, perhaps, was the introduction of the UK Film Council (UKFC) in 2000, overseen by the Minster for Culture, Media and Sport,

Chris Smith. The UKFC was 'intended as a single well-funded entity' that consolidated a number of single organizations such as the British Film Institute (BFI), which was responsible for the cultural and educational promotion of British film.⁹² These changes were part of Labour's broader 'Cool Britannia' campaign that sought to rebrand the UK as a modern, multicultural, youthful and creative country, which included focusing on films that had mainstream appeal while being distinctly British that were attractive to younger audiences. Elements of this approach are evident in Gurinder Chadha's *Angus, Thongs and Perfect Snogging* – the follow-up to her earlier British girl film *Bend It Like Beckham*. Based on the Confessions of Georgia Nicholson series of young adult novels by Louise Rennison, *Angus* is narrated by its fourteen-year-old protagonist Georgia (Georgia Groome) as she attempts to get a 'sex god' boyfriend with the help of her 'ace gang' of girlfriends within the confines of the seaside town of Eastbourne. When she was approached to make the film, Chadha saw an opportunity to 'make a British high school teen movie in a way that we don't make them here'.⁹³ The teen film – a Hollywood construct – is at odds with perceived notions of British cinema, and yet Chadha was determined to make a culturally specific teen film. For the *Daily Mail*'s Baz Bamigboye, Chadha achieves her aim as she 'takes on Hollywood's teenage girl genre movies, like *Mean Girls* and *Clueless*, and gives them a perfect English pitch.⁹⁴ The *Times*' Kevin Maher also references Hollywood girl teen film *Clueless* (Heckerling 1995) in his assertion that the world of *Angus* is 'half Clueless, half Byker Grove'.⁹⁵ Maher's comments reflect the tension between the desire to create a mainstream British film that is influenced by (and seeking to compete with) Hollywood while also remaining recognizably British. Contemporary British girl films are therefore part of a long history of 'cross Atlantic flows' of culture between Britain and the United States.⁹⁶ *Angus* incorporates key elements of the American teen high school film, such as the pursuit of heterosexual romance and a prom-style moment of visibility for the heroine in the form of a birthday party at the end of the film. The film is also presented as distinctly British, which here is configured through its use of

British slang, and an emphasis on 'natural' beauty. Georgia is, as the *Guardian*'s Peter Bradshaw claims, a 'realistically not-conventionally-pretty heroine'.[97] This emphasis on 'realistic' and 'natural' beauty is indicative of British cinema's ambivalent relationship with glamour, which is a key characteristic of how postfeminism is modified and articulated in a British context. This more mainstream approach is particularly evident in Chapter 1, where, I argue, *St Trinian's* and *Wild Child* attempt to emulate teen high school film conventions while remaining distinctly British. Similarly, the influence of the Hollywood sports film is evident in *StreetDance*, *Chalet Girl* (Traill 2011) and *Fast Girls* (Hall 2012), which I discuss in Chapter 2.

While a more market-driven approach to British film was clearly evident, the policies introduced in this period 'typically possessed implicit cultural underpinnings' that sought to distinguish the British film industry.[98] In 2007, a new tax rebate scheme was launched for films with a budget of under £20 million; British films could claim 25 per cent of their UK expenditure if they passed the 'cultural test'.[99] Films had to score at least sixteen out of a possible thirty-one points, with an emphasis on films with themes that evidenced a national cultural heritage.[100] The cultural test, therefore, represented an attempt to create a specifically British national cinema that was distinct from Hollywood's production practices. In practice, the test proved to be largely arbitrary, meaning that films often considered Hollywood blockbusters, such as the *Harry Potter* franchise, could be considered British via their British themes (the public school system) and their source material. Indeed, this Britishness is often key to their marketing and appeal.[101]

The symbiotic relationship between British cinema and television continued during this period, with public service broadcasters (PSBs) Channel Four and the BBC becoming 'key players in the commercialised British film culture at the turn of the twenty-first century'.[102] Channel Four, in particular, is noted for its support of British film culture, having focused on making 'uniquely British films' for budgets under £10 million throughout the 1980s and 1990s.[103] Led by the increased emphasis on a more commercialized film culture, in 1998 Channel Four consolidated its filmmaking operations into a 'single, semi-vertically integrated mini-studio' in the form of FilmFour.[104] By 2002, FilmFour had scaled back its operations after a number of expensive disappointments, with production re-integrated into Channel Four's Drama department under Tessa Ross before becoming Film4, a free-to-air digital channel, in 2006.[105] The limited success of FilmFour is, according to Hannah Andrews, indicative of the tension between its commercial ambitions and its raison d'être: 'to produce innovative, non-mainstream work' for Channel Four.[106] Like Channel Four, the BBC supported films intended for the mainstream, initially focusing on 'middle-budget features' via co-production or distribution deals with Hollywood studios. Notable examples include *Becoming Jane* (Jarrold 2007), in which Hollywood star Anne Hathaway plays a young Jane Austen opposite James McAvoy, co-produced by BBC Films and distributed by Miramax in the United States. Similarly, the middle-budget film (£13.5 million) *The Duchess* (Dibb 2008), starring Keira Knightley (discussed in Chapter 4), was co-produced by BBC Films and the French company Pathé, as well as Paramount Vantage.[107]

The BBC has also aided efforts to attract youth audiences, particularly via the various 'micro-budget schemes' established in recent years, which address the BBC's public service remit through an emphasis on finding new talent. Micro-budget film schemes such as Digital Departures support films with budgets of under £1 million and ensure that a certain percentage of the budget is spent on training and skills development.[108] Digital Departures supported three films that were developed, filmed and produced in Liverpool in order to celebrate the city's status as Capital of Culture 2008: *Of Time and City* (Davies 2008), *Salvage* (Gough 2008) and *Kicks* (Heymann 2008). *Kicks* depicts the friendship between teenagers Nicole (Kerrie Hayes) and Jasmine (Nichola Burley) who bond over their love for Liverpool footballer Lee Cassidy (Jamie Doyle), as discussed in Chapter 3. A 'low-budget, slightly edgier film' like *Kicks* is more contemporary than BBC Film's usual output, and is suggestive of attempts by the BBC to attract a more youthful audience.[109] Similarly, Film London's Microwave scheme, established in 2006 to provide first-time filmmakers with funding, training and support, produced micro-budget films aimed at younger and under-represented groups that created more localized representations of Britain.[110] This included films such as *Freestyle* (Lee 2010), a film about two teenagers who fall in love on the basketball court, and *Ill Manors* (Drew 2012), written and directed by the rapper Plan B and starring Riz Ahmed.

Following the departure of New Labour, the incoming Coalition government sought to make its own mark on British film policy, most notably via the dramatic and unexpected closure of the UKFC. Following the global banking crash of 2008, the UKFC was viewed as a quango that could no longer be justified within the context of austerity.[111] Despite concerns about the quality of some of the films supported by the UKFC, overall it was considered successful. Its closure came as a shock to many in the industry, particularly because the announcement of the closure in 2010 came off the back of a 'record-breaking year' for the British box office, which took £944 million. Furthermore, Culture Minister Ed Vaizey's speech following the announcement highlighted British cinema's recent successes, including women-centred films such as *Made in Dagenham* (Cole 2010) – about the women workers at the Dagenham Ford factory and their fight for equal pay – and the Gemma Arterton vehicle *Tamara Drewe* (Frears 2010), both of which received funding from the UKFC. Nevertheless, the majority of the UKFC's operations were consolidated into the BFI, which was now responsible for distributing Lottery money and the certification of the new cultural test introduced in 2014. Now films had to score eighteen points out of a possible thirty-five. The criteria were expanded to include characters from the whole of the EU, as long as the dialogue was in English, and an increase in the number of points available for special effects produced in the UK. The Regional Screen Agencies in their current form were also deemed 'no longer sensible or sustainable' and reconfigured into a single national body in Creative England, with 'hubs' in the north, Midlands and south of England.[112] This was all part of the government's plan to make the British film industry more 'sustainable' and mainstream, to create 'more films that people want to watch', as Prime Minister David Cameron said.[113] Overall, the Coalition's film policy was more or less consistent with New Labour. However, as Hannah Andrews observes, attempts to make British cinema more commercialized have manifested through British cinema's relationship with PSBs. These include an increased keenness to produce with foreign investors, which has resulted in a number of films that deal with American themes, stories and characters, but with 'British personnel at the helm' that are more international in scope rather than 'straightforwardly British' such as Lynne Ramsay's *We Need to Talk about Kevin* (2011).[114]

While multiculturalism and diversity were held up as markers of contemporary British cinema in the New Labour period,[115] there is still a considerable lack of diversity in British cinema, and I argue that this is intensifying. As Melanie Williams suggests, a lack of black, Asian and ethnic minority (BAME) representation 'seems to have been a particular problem of British cinema.'[116] Indeed, in 2017, the BFI's Black Star research found 59 per cent of British films released in the last ten years did not feature a single black actor.[117] The 'accelerating gentrification of British cinema stardom' via the rise of public school–educated stars such as Benedict Cumberbatch and Eddie Redmayne is highly noticeable,[118] prompting older working-class actors like Julie Walters to remark that the British film industry seems to be 'going back the other way' now, and how, in this period of austerity, there are very limited opportunities in the British film industry for those working-class young people who lack cultural and economic capital.[119] This lack of diversity is not just limited to male actors, however, as demonstrated through this chapter's consideration of the young (white and middle-class) female stars who have made considerable contributions to contemporary British cinema. Of course, there are exceptions, such as Gugu Mbatha-Raw who plays the titular *Belle* (Asante 2013), discussed in Chapter 4. Mbatha-Raw won the British Academy of Film and Television Arts (BAFTA) Rising Star award in 2015 for her performance, and her image was used to promote the BFI's new 'three ticks' model aimed at promoting on- and off-screen diversity, as well as creating opportunities for 'new entrants from diverse backgrounds'.[120] According to So Mayer, the BFI's 'three ticks' model is an example of 'representational justice in action' that has led to the increase of women of colour behind the camera in the UK.[121]

Outline of the book

The key aim of this book is to explore contemporary British cinema's construction of young femininity in the period 2000–2015. The fifteen-year cycle functions to create manageable research boundaries, although many of the sociopolitical, cultural and industrial factors I discuss throughout this book both precede and exceed this periodization. In particular, I explore how contemporary British cinema mediates postfeminist discourses of girlhood. Discourses are a way of 'constructing knowledge about a particular topic or practices: a cluster (or formation) of ideas, images and practices' which 'provide ways of thinking or talking about topics, groups or institutional sites within society',[122] and I am interested in how British cinema discursively (re) produces British young femininity.

I conceive of youth as a social construct that is contextually dependent rather than a biologically fixed category that implies a 'natural' state of being.[123] The period characterized as youth is also seen to have extended under neoliberalism due to increased participation in higher education, and increasingly precarious employment practices which make traditional markers of adulthood, such as home ownership, more difficult to obtain.[124] Youth is also increasingly defined as a commercial marketing category, which places the limit of the age of youth at twenty-five.[125] Although these age-based distinctions are problematic, they are nevertheless useful in providing manageable research parameters, and as such I define 'young' as protagonists who are between fifteen and twenty-five years old. Similarly, I refer to characters as 'girls' and 'young women' as appropriate, given that girlhood is also not a 'natural, fixed state of being'.[126] This fluidity is also indicative of what Tasker and Negra refer to as 'the "girling" of femininity' in postfeminist culture as part of its celebration of young women, with the effect of treating women as girls.[127]

Both the films themselves and their critical reception function as primary sources, and I have afforded them equal status as far as possible. The film reviews analysed here are all from UK newspapers obtained via the Nexis UK newspaper database. These film reviews act as types of 'social discourse' that contribute to the mediation of young femininity in contemporary British cinema, showcasing how postfeminist discourses of girlhood circulate around the films in the wider media culture.[128] This is supplemented by extra-textual or paratextual materials such as interviews, production notes and press books, where available, in order to provide a thorough understanding of how these films are both informed by, and contribute to, ideas about young British femininity in the twenty-first century. The range of case study films is diverse, encapsulating a variety of genres, intended audiences and production trends and yet they all sit together comfortably within their thematic clusters, indicating the dynamism and variety of British film production during this period, as well as the pervasiveness of these discourses that work to produce British cinema's mediation of young femininity. The book is made up of four thematic case study chapters – schooling and education, ambition, friendship, and the search for identity or 'becoming' – with four case studies in each. These themes are common in cultural texts produced for and about young people, particularly young women, and are not specific to British cinema. What I am interested in is how British cinema specifically explores these themes in relation to its mediation of young femininity. After identifying every British film with a young woman protagonist released in this period, the films I analyse in the following chapters exemplify the thematic concerns of each chapter. Every case study film has been identified as a UK production using the classification provided by the BFI's *Sight and Sound* magazine, with the occasional UK-US co-production, such as *Wild Child* and *The Other Boleyn Girl* (Chadwick 2008), both of which are thematically British.

This book also seeks to identify how postfeminism is modified and articulated within a British context. Two key components are present throughout the chapters. First, class plays a prominent role in these representations. While class is a defining feature of British cinema more broadly,[129] it occupies a tricky position within these films given that contemporary postfeminist girlhood is ideally middle class. Working-class protagonists are frequently expected to undergo a makeover in order to become appropriately feminine and thus transcend class boundaries, but are ultimately unsuccessful. The second distinction lies within the use of the postfeminist makeover trope. In postfeminist culture, the makeover works to 'reveal the self that has been there all along'.[130] The expression of an 'authentic' self is a moral imperative; in contemporary culture 'we must know – and express – who we really are'.[131] This is particularly important for young people, as developmental discourses of youth characterize it as a critical period of identity formation in which young people undergo an often turbulent search for the 'true' self.[132] However, British cinema's articulation of the makeover trope is complicated as it is closely tied to its aforementioned ambivalence towards glamour and sparkle, and consumer culture. As such, not only is the self revealed by the makeover temporary within this development of identity but it is also deemed to be not 'authentic', and attention is frequently drawn to the artificiality of the makeover, particularly for working-class characters.

I first examine how contemporary British girl films discursively engage with the postfeminist makeover in order to construct a British postfeminist identity in Chapter 1 via an analysis of schoolgirl films *St Trinian's* and *Wild Child*. This chapter takes up the theme of schooling and education by examining how the British girls' school functions as a site through which to explore ideas and concerns related to the 'sexualization' of teenage girls. The chapter begins with an examination of two contemporary-set films – *St Trinian's* and *Wild Child* – both of which are aimed at young girls. The schools in these films are presented as relics from a past era, but often inherent within this is a critique of twenty-first-century schooling and the limitations of the national curriculum. While both of these films engage with ideas about girls' sexualization, I argue that the characters are not as sexually knowing or experienced as they wish to be, or as the 'sexualization' discourse suggests, and films' critical reception discourses similarly demonstrate that the films are not viewed as colluding with these moral panics. The second section of this chapter discusses two girls' school films set in the 1960s: *An Education* (Scherfig 2009) and *The Falling* (Morley 2014). These films explore girls' sexuality in relation to the changing mores of the 1960s, and concerns about promiscuity and increased female sexual autonomy. Despite their period setting, I demonstrate how a number of parallels can be drawn between these concerns in the 1960s and the contemporary discourses surrounding girls' sexuality discussed in this chapter.

Chapter 2 uses the British girl-centred sports film to explore how discourses of aspiration are mediated. This is primarily achieved via a focus on more mainstream, commercially orientated films like *StreetDance 3D* (2010), *Chalet Girl* (Traill 2011) and *Fast Girls* (Clarke 2012). While the girl protagonist's working-class identity is presented as a significant barrier to success in these films, this is easily overcome in keeping with meritocratic discourses of aspiration and an emphasis on feel-good optimism. The production and critical reception discourses of these films also contribute to the films' mediation of aspiration by highlighting the ambition of the British film industry itself through emphasizing the films' deliberately glossy aesthetics as a distinct move away from British realist traditions. The chapter begins, however, with a discussion of *Fish Tank* (Arnold 2009). Although, as a social realist text, *Fish Tank* seems like an anomaly, when considered along with these other films, *Fish Tank* and its mediation of girls' ambitions functions as part of a dialogue about what it means to be a British ambitious girl.

Class is also a significant concern in Chapter 3, which is concerned with ambivalent and ambiguous depictions of girl friendship, and the impact friendship has upon the formation of identity, drawing on the notion of the 'postfeminist sisterhood'.[133] I argue that British cinema's girlfriends most often come in pairs, with one working-class and one middle-class girl. In *Me Without You* (Goldbacher 2001), *Kicks*, *Albatross* (MacCormick 2011) and *My Summer of Love* (Pawlikowski 2004), the girlfriends support each other in their quest for visibility and their 'authentic' self. The makeover trope is key here but rather than producing the ideal postfeminist self by revealing the 'true self', these makeovers are deemed to be temporary and inauthentic and fail to lead to the postfeminist 'perfect self'.[134] This is particularly the case for the working-class characters, such Nicole (Kerrie Hayes) in *Kicks* and Mona (Natalie Press) in *My Summer of Love*, who are shown to *know* that they will not achieve this, despite their best efforts.

The final chapter takes on the British historical films that are 'filtered through the lens of the postfeminist movement' through depictions of four aristocratic and royal young women – Anne Boleyn, Queen Victoria, Georgiana, Duchess of Devonshire and Dido Elizabeth Belle.[135] I explore the production discourses of these films that emphasize a deliberate move away from the Merchant Ivory–style of British heritage films as part of the films' attempts to construct these well-known historical figures as twenty-first-century British girls. Overall, these films raise pertinent questions about young women's freedom and power, and the idea that attempting to maintain postfeminist ideals leads to anxiety and a fragmented sense of identity. However, these become depoliticized through being either subsumed into a love story or merely accepted. Finally, I conclude by summarizing how the depictions of young femininity in these films help us to understand postfeminism within a specifically British context.

Education and 'sexualization' in the British girls' school film

In the introduction, I argued that British cinema has seen a significant increase in the number of girl films in the twenty-first century as part of a more concerted engagement with girl culture and an increased effort to attract youth audiences. One of the ways in which this is apparent is through the increase in girls' school films during this period. These films, I argue, function in part to explore contemporary postfeminist anxieties about girls' sexualities and 'sexualization' (Ringrose 2013). The school film has always been considered a quintessentially British genre. As Stephen Glynn argues, 'the school film constitutes part of the DNA of British cinema and society',[1] its narrative allowing filmmakers to 'comment on explicit education and broader socio-cultural issues'.[2] Films such as *Goodbye, Mr Chips* (Wood 1939) presented the boarding school as a safe and unchanging world that 'promoted the wisdom of the traditional value system'.[3] British cinema's interest in the school film intensified during the 1950s, along with an increased desire to attract youth audiences in the face of competition from television and other leisure activities.[4] By the 1960s, the Labour government was making plans to introduce comprehensive secondary education that moved away from selection. By 1965, the boarding school film had virtually disappeared, with Lindsay Anderson's *If* (1968) signalling a violent end to the boarding school film through post-war rebellion against public school order and tradition as the school is literally blown up.[5] Historically, girls have largely been absent from the British school film genre, except for notable examples such as the *St Trinian's* series (1954–66, 1980) and *The Prime of Miss Jean Brodie* (Neame 1969), which centred around the charismatic Jean Brodie (Maggie Smith) and her select group of pupils at a school in the 1930s. There is a much richer tradition of British girls' school stories in literature, however, through the work of Angela Brazil and Enid Blyton's *Mallory Towers* series.

British cinema's renewed interest in the school film was undoubtedly fuelled by the phenomenal international success of the *Harry Potter* film franchise, which offered not just magical fantasy but also a nostalgic fantasy version of the past and traditional notions of Britishness.[6] The cultural influence of *Harry Potter* on perceptions of the British boarding school and the British school film is evident in the two contemporary-set school films discussed in this chapter – *St Trinian's* (Parker and Thompson 2007) and *Wild Child* (Moore 2008) – as both ironically draw attention to its legacy. On arriving at Abbey Mount boarding school, *Wild Child's* Poppy (Emma Roberts) remarks, 'What is this place, Hogwarts?', while the ramshackle St Trinian's is disparagingly deemed 'Hogwarts for pikeys'.[7] The girls' school film has been a key feature of this increased interest in the British school film, encompassing a variety of genres and intended audiences, including *St Trinian's*, *Wild Child* and the horror film *The Hole* (Hamm 2001). A number of recent girls' school films have also been set in the past, such as *An Education* (Scherfig 2009), *Cracks* (Scott 2008) – centred around a charismatic Jean Brodie-esque teacher Miss G (Eva Green) in a remote girls' school in the 1930s – *The Falling* (Morley 2014) and (more ambiguously) *Never Let Me Go* (Romaneck 2010). In a number of these films, girls' education takes place within the confined and highly regulated space of the single-sex school, where tensions, passions and jealousies destabilize the school's order. This has historically been a key feature of the British girls' school film and one to which it continues to return. The British school film also continues to be 'most unyielding in its depiction of social class', with an emphasis on upper-middle-class hegemony.[8] The films analysed in this chapter – *St Trinian's*, *Wild Child*, *An Education* and *The Falling* – all tend towards depictions of middle-class girlhood, or at least, not overtly working class. Even *St Trinian's*, which has historically provided an antidote to this by featuring shabbier gentile girls or nouveau-riche girls, has moved towards depicting the characters as middle class in line with dominant discourses of postfeminist girlhood, which present white, middle-class femininity as the default ideal.[9] Although still presenting a more ambiguous class status, the characters in the revived *St Trinian's* were considered to have 'gone posh' in comparison with the girls from the original films of the 1950s and 1960s.[10]

This chapter explores how the same-sex school functions in British cinema as a representational site through which to explore contemporary anxieties about girls' sexuality and sexualization. As Stephen Glynn notes, in the British school film 'burgeoning female sexuality has been a constant source of quasi-terror and demonised as corrosive to a fully functioning society'.[11] The contemporary British girls' school film is therefore ideally placed to explore 'postfeminist panics' over girls' sexuality and sexualization, which have emerged alongside girls' increased visibility within educational discourses via the figure of the 'top girl'.[12]. As Angela McRobbie has argued, since the 1990s, young women have been cast as the key beneficiaries of social change and offered a notional form of equality in the guise of 'the new sexual contract'. Education is a key site in which this new sexual contract is mobilized, where young women are encouraged to use their newly acquired 'freedom' to gain qualifications and earn enough money to enable them to participate in consumer culture.[13] Here, girls, more so than boys, are marked by their grades and occupational identities, with a particular 'luminosity' on the 'top girl', a figure mobilized on the values of the new meritocracy promoted by New Labour that coincided with a period of expansion of higher education.[14] The 'top girls' are hard-working, high achieving – usually white and middle class – and destined for Oxford or Cambridge.[15] This increased focus on girls' educational success has, somewhat inevitably, led to a backlash in the form of a moral panic about boys' failure that is centred around white working-class boys in particular.[16] This concern is exemplified by comments made by the Conservative minister for Universities and Science, David Willetts, in 2011, when he claimed that feminism was the 'key factor' contributing to the economic decline in the UK, as the increase in education and employment opportunities for women since the 1970s had led to a lack of social mobility for working-class men.[17]

The rise of the 'top girl' has occurred simultaneously with a moral panic over girls' sexuality and 'sexualization', particularly the idea that girls are being 'adultified' and sexualized before they are ready. This panic reached fever pitch in the 2000s via a 'consistent stream of newspaper headlines',[18] government reviews such as the 'Review on the Sexualization of Young People'[19] and campaigns such as Mumsnet's 'Let Girls be Girls', which was concerned that 'an increasingly sexualised culture was dripping toxically into the lives of children'.[20] This concern over the sexualization of girls in particular exists alongside the rise of what journalist Ariel Levy has termed 'raunch culture', a strand of postfeminism that emerged in the early years of the twenty-first century, promoting a 'pornified' version of female sexuality that encourages women to make sex objects of themselves in order to feel empowered.[21] Younger girls were also incorporated into this raunch culture through media imagery and consumer culture, such as clothing with 'sexy' slogans, which fuelled concern that girls were being encouraged to become sexually active at a (too) young age. As Jessica Ringrose argues, this concern over sexualization is a specifically postfeminist panic because sexualization is poisoned as a result of 'too much and too early sexual liberation on the back of feminist gains'.[22] Girls' sexuality is therefore simultaneously presented as 'at-risk' from sexualization via media and consumer culture and 'risky' through their supposed participation in such a culture.

This chapter examines how young femininity is constructed within recent British girls' school films via the mediation of the postfeminist 'sexualization' discourse, as well as educational discourses more broadly, beginning with two contemporary-set boarding school films: *St Trinian's* and *Wild Child*. I analyse these films in relation to the ways in which they engage with contemporary discourses around girls' education and sexuality, and also how they utilize the postfeminist makeover trope to construct a nationally specific postfeminist feminine identity as the ideal. *St Trinian's* and *Wild Child* are two examples of British tween films. As Melanie Kennedy has theorized, the tween is a gendered, aged, raced and classed subject engaged in a transitional process of 'becoming' from girlhood to young womanhood. Emerging in the 1990s, the tween is a discursive construct of the postfeminist context, 'marked by the distinct coming together of the rhetoric of choice and authenticity, together with the themes of makeover, princesshood and celebrity'.[23] Tween popular culture grew exponentially during the 2000s, dominated by Disney, via texts such as the *Hannah Montana* television series (2006–2011) and the *High School Musical* film franchise (2006, 2007, 2008). These texts construct and address the tween as needing to build and maintain an appropriate 'authentic' feminine identity through a rhetoric of choice that presents a postfeminist identity as the ideal and 'natural' choice.[24] While, on the one hand, the tween (and tweenhood) is a discursive construct, on the other hand, it is also a consumer demographic consisting of girls aged between nine and fourteen years. *St Trinian's* and *Wild Child* represent British cinema's attempts to address this audience within an area of popular culture that has been dominated by the United States. In doing so, I argue, these films construct a *British* postfeminist identity as the ideal.

Following this, I discuss two girls' school films set in the 1960s: *An Education* and *The Falling*. The 1960s setting is significant here because it marked another period when concerns and anxieties around young women's sexuality came to the fore. This was the decade that witnessed key moments of political and social change, such as the introduction of the contraceptive pill in 1961, although initially only for married women, and the legalization of abortion in 1967. The idea of the 'swinging sixties' dominates cultural representations of the period, particularly via the figure of the 'single girl', a youthful, liberated and mobile figure as depicted in British cinema by Julie Christie in films such as *Billy Liar* (1963) and *Darling* (1965). The figure of the 'single girl' chimes closely with the 'empowered' young woman of postfeminist culture, so it is unsurprising that texts set in the 1960s function as a site of, what Lynn Spigel terms, 'postfeminist nostalgia'. Using the US television series *Mad Men* (2007–2015) as an example, Spigel argues that this postfeminist nostalgia offers a reimagining of the past, where urbane and cosmopolitan women have a certain amount of power and mobility but do not yet have feminism.[25] However, *An Education* and *The Falling* trouble this idea of postfeminist nostalgia via the confined space of the British girls' school where the 1960s are yet to swing.

Postfeminist (school)girl power in *St Trinian's* (2007) and *Wild Child* (2008)

In 2002, Ealing Studios announced that it was reviving the iconic *St Trinian's* films as part of a £50 million redevelopment plan. Based on the cartoons of Ronald Searle, the *St Trinian's* series began in 1954 with *The Belles of St Trinian's* (Launder 1954). The original series consisted of five films produced between 1954 and 1980 and dealt with the exploits of the unruly pupils of the infamous St Trinian's School for Young Ladies. As Emma Bell notes, the films 'play[ed] on the postwar decline of the British upper class' with its depiction of a crumbling relic of a boarding school, the elitist 'cradle of the British class system'. More importantly, the films depicted young womanhood as unruly, offering the pleasure of the 'spectacle of the destructive female group that challenged established social order'.[26] The legacy of the films and their depictions of law-breaking schoolgirls who liked to drink, smoke and gamble mean that 'St Trinian's has become shorthand for anarchic female subordination'.[27]

The *St Trinian's* films are associated with a 'peculiarly British' representation of girlhood,[28] so it is unsurprising that this iconic girl-centred series should be revived during a period when British cinema showed a significant interest in girls and young women, and made a concerted effort to attract youth audiences. *St Trinian's* (2007) was directed by Oliver Parker and Barnaby Thompson and produced by Ealing Studios with support from the UKFC, with a budget of £7 million. The film stars Rupert Everett as headmistress Camilla Fritton and

Talulah Riley as new girl Annabelle Fritton, who arrives at St Trinian's as an ex-pupil of the prestigious boarding school Cheltenham Ladies' College. In order to revive the school's finances and prevent its closure, the girls devise a heist to steal Johannes Vermeer's *Girl with a Pearl Earring* from the National Gallery. The film was a surprise success, making around £12.5 million at the UK box office.[29] Producer Barnaby Thompson attributes the film's success in part to the fact that the film targeted girls aged between ten and sixteen, which he highlights as an underserved demographic within British cinema: 'For them to see other girls up on screen leading the story was something they found thrilling that they could relate to.'[30] With the redevelopment of Ealing, and its reputation hinging on *St Trinian's*, it was hugely important that the revival was a success not only at home but also internationally. Ealing's Head of Sales, Natalie Brenner, was fully aware of the challenges of selling a very 'British' film series that 'has a history of being successful only in the UK' to international audiences.[31] It was therefore crucial that the film included a mix of this 'peculiarly British' representation of girlhood that *St Trinian's* is known for, along with transatlantic elements that are usually found in American high school movies, such as the division of girls into cliques and a postfeminist makeover, which I discuss later. Actress Talulah Riley best sums up the approach by describing the film as 'Hogwarts meets *Mean Girls*'.[32]

In this revival, the rebellious and anarchic spirit of the earlier films has been subsumed into the language of 'girl power'. Girl power is part of the postfeminist lexicon of female success and empowerment that, in the UK, was closely associated with the 1990s girl group Spice Girls. As Justine Ashby argues, the 'boisterous' language of girl power presented a logic that 'somehow managed to link being sexy with being ballsy, to celebrate female camaraderie while privileging individualism'.[33] The film's emphasis on girl power can be attributed, in part, to the fact that Barnaby Thompson was also the producer of *Spice World* (Spiers 1997). The aesthetic similarities between the two films are also highlighted in reviews of the film, with the *Daily Mail*'s Chris Tookey noting how 'the movie it most resembles is not any of the *St Trinian's* movies of the Fifties and Sixties, but *Spiceworld* [*sic*]: *The Movie*, which had very much the same mixture of high spirits, camp and cheerful trashiness'.[34] The boisterous attitude of girl power therefore dovetails with the figure of the fearless and assertive St Trinian's girl, as Gemma Arterton, who plays Head Girl Kelly, explains in an interview in the *Evening Standard*: 'Our film is more about girl power. It's the message we really want to push. I don't think there's a point in the film where the girls aren't in control: they're doing the trampling rather than being trampled on'.[35]

However, due to the prevalence of the girl power discourse in contemporary media culture, St Trinian's girls are no longer viewed as anarchic or subversive. As Damon Smith writes in the *Herald Express*, 'Unlike the naughty hockey-stick wielding minxes' of the original films, the new St Trinian's girls 'don't seem fearsome at all'.[36] The spectacle of girls behaving in such an incongruously aggressive way was one of the main attractions of the original films, but this kind of 'unladylike' behaviour is now considered commonplace through the evocation of girl power. Throughout the film reviews, there is a strong sense that not only have the St Trinian's girls lost their shock value but the behaviour of the characters on screen also could not be any worse than some real-life girls today. As Smith writes, 'keeping in mind the nightmarish headlines about drugs, violence and bullying in our classrooms, the pranks of these girl cliques are now rather tame'.[37] Similarly, the *Daily Mail*'s Chris Tookey claims that the original girls were a 'refreshing corrective to the straight-laced image of British public schoolgirls; now, they merely look like girls at any inner-city comprehensive, but with fewer knives and pregnancies'.[38] These kinds of comments draw on and perpetuate the 'postfeminist panics' within the media around girls and their education that suggest that girl power has 'gone too far'.[39] This includes panic around the so-called 'mean girl' behaviour and bullying, as well as concerns about the 'at-risk' working-class girls who leave school without qualifications and are more likely to become pregnant at a young age.[40] This discourse of girl power 'gone too far' is discussed not just within education but also in relation to society more broadly. In his review for the *Sunday Times*, Cosmo Landesman claims the original films were a 'celebration of English eccentricity [and] non-conformity' but the remake is *St Trinian's* for the 'Bratz/Girls Aloud generation. That is, girls who think getting drunk and acting like a moronic ladette is a form of female empowerment . . . . We see St Trinian's excess all over England, and it's not a pretty sight.'[41] In his criticism, Landesman evokes the media panic around young women's behaviour that coalesced around the figure of the 'ladette', which emerged in the UK in the 1990s. As McRobbie argues, the ladette – or to use her term, 'phallic girl' – is the product of the imagined equality offered by postfeminism that bore the marks of boldness and aggression, and allowed for the emulation of typically masculine behaviour, such as heavy drinking and casual sex, while at the same time, foregoing any critique of hegemonic masculinity to ensure that power relations are maintained.[42] However, as Louise Wilks argues, the question of how far the St Trinian's girls can adhere to this is significant because as teenagers, they do not have a large amount of freedom with which to pursue this hedonistic lifestyle of casual sex and heavy drinking, as their transgressions are mostly confined to the boarding school.[43]

Comparisons between St Trinian's and real-life classrooms are often evoked to criticize the UK education system under New Labour. While the comments by Damon Smith and Chris Tookey draw on broader media panics about the seeming lawlessness of British classrooms, the reviews of *St Trinian's* also function to critique New Labour's education policy and the national curriculum. The lessons offered at St Trinian's are highly unorthodox; the girls make counterfeit alcohol in Science and learn how to talk their way out of drug smuggling in Spanish. Also, the plot largely revolves around the girls fighting to keep the school open as it is under threat of closure from the Department of Education. As Miss Fritton (Rupert Everett) passionately argues, 'St Trinian's is a place for girls who find shelter nowhere else . . . we refuse to let you strangle us with your limited curriculum.' Mainstream education polices are therefore presented as stifling and detrimental to girls' creativity, which is a recurring theme throughout the school films discussed here. Writing in the far-left newspaper the *Morning Star*, Jeff Sawtell views the film's representation of schooling as 'a direct attack on New Labour's idea of academy schools and being subjected to soul-destroying excessive exams and league tables designed to dull the creative mind'.[44] Similarly, Henry Fitzherbert writes for the *Sunday Express* that the film is a 'good-natured celebration' of British traditions like the public school system, suggesting that British education was better before the introduction of the comprehensive system.[45] While opinions on *St Trinian's* differ, critics from both left- and right-wing publications are united in their criticism of New Labour's education policies.

A key difference between the original *St Trinian's* series and the recent films is that the girls are now divided into tribes or cliques, including geeks, chavs, emos and 'posh totty'. This went largely underappreciated by reviewers who felt that the division of the characters in this way produced a 'series of social cliches'[46] and 'over-familiar caricatures'[47]. It was, however, important to the filmmakers, who claim that they visited schools, including 'posh public schools and comprehensives' and found that 'Girls at modern schools today are divided into gangs and cliques. By visiting a number we were able to plug into the mindset of today's girls.'[48] The decision to carry out research in both comprehensive and public schools aligns with the original series' more democratic approach to class, where the girls have a more ambiguous class status than is typical of the British boarding school film. It also points to the filmmakers' desire to make the films relevant to girls today. More significantly perhaps, the use of cliques acts as a mechanism to give the film international appeal and relevance by drawing on the conventions of the American high school movie. At the start of the film, Kelly introduces Annabelle (and us) to the cliques of St Trinian's, which is reminiscent of the way Cady (Lindsay Lohan) learns about 'The Plastics' in *Mean Girls*, which St Trinian's is likened to in promotional discourses. Unlike its Hollywood counterparts, however, the cliques in *St Trinian's* are not hierarchical. In *Mean Girls*, 'The Plastics' rule the school with celebrity-like status, with ultimate Plastic Regina George (Rachel McAdams) as queen bee, but in *St Trinian's* no one group is in charge and each group has its own strengths and characteristics. Instead, all the girls, regardless of which clique they belong to, look up to (but do not worship) Head Girl Kelly, who exists outside of a particular group. Kelly does not exhibit a particular subcultural identity; rather, she is styled like a femme fatale of film noir with a blunt dark bob and red lips. Dress is a key signifier of 'tribal' identity in the film, but this is largely depoliticized. Some of the St Trinian's belong to the 'chav' clique, a term that became ubiquitous in the UK media in the 2000s to signify 'class disgust' at the poor, white, working class.[49] In *St Trinian's*, however, the chav clique is situated within the broader reclamation of the term as an 'affirmative subcultural identity' that took place particularly in the music industry via working-class rappers like Lady Sovereign, who features on the film's soundtrack.[50] When 'chav' is evoked as an insult in the film, it is not an expression of class disgust but rather a way of signifying rivalry between the various groups. The girls use clothes and accessories to adopt the markers of chav identity to create a sense of belonging; it is not necessarily evoked as an explicit comment on their working-class status.

St Trinian's also uses the postfeminist makeover trope that is a staple of the Hollywood teen film as part of attempts to make the series relevant to contemporary audiences. The makeover scene marks a pivotal point in Annabelle's character development. The scene begins with a sinister soundtrack as Kelly and the other girls lean menacingly over Annabelle's bed while she sleeps. They drag her out of bed, tie her to a chair and shine a lamp in her eyes like an interrogation. Kelly whispers, 'You've had this coming since the day you arrived', but when the camera zooms in it becomes clear that the 'weapons' they are brandishing are actually beauty implements such as tongs and eyelash curlers. The mood then changes as Kelly cheerfully announces that they are going to 'Give you a makeover, silly!' and members of each clique take it in turns to style Annabelle in their own image. The shift in tone encapsulates the sensibility of the *St Trinian's* revival as the beginning of the scene nods at the figure of the wild and dangerous St Trinian's girl before becoming a celebration of the teen makeover. In a music video–style sequence, the girls take turns to transform Annabelle into a member of each clique. The results of each makeover are captured as a fashion Polaroid photo with a thematically appropriate background reminiscent of a glossy magazine photo shoot. The sequence is highly stylized and provides a moment of glamorous visibility that is key to the contemporary girl teen film. Samantha Colling highlights another moment of glamorous visibility later on in the film with what she terms 'the St Trinian's strut'. In this similarly stylized sequence, the girls strut up the steps in Trafalgar Square. The scene is filmed in slow motion, offering glamorous visibility as a spectacle for pleasure rather than for narrative purposes. For Colling, the 'St Trinian's strut' is an 'interesting example because, being British, the mise-en-scène is conspicuously greyer in comparison to its Hollywood counterparts. However, the film still employs the same techniques that make visibility a glamorous surface'.[51] Colling's comment points to British cinema's prevailing identity as grey and gritty, with implications of realism and the sense that British cinema is somehow less than its Hollywood counterparts. However, as I argue more fully in Chapter 2, British girl films during this period made a concerted effort to avoid associations with 'grey' and 'grittiness' by promoting deliberately glossy and aspirational aesthetics of which the highly stylized *St Trinian's* makeover scene is part. When Annabelle's final makeover is revealed, she is not dressed as belonging to any particular group, and when Kelly asks her how she feels, she replies 'like a St Trinian', causing all the girls to cheer. As Kennedy argues, the makeover is central to tween popular culture and works to construct and reinforce appropriate femininity, while also ensuring the revelation of the *authentic* (original emphasis) self in line with the broader context of the postfeminist makeover, which, according to Diane Negra, is the 'key ritual of female coming into being' that 'allows for the revelation of the self that has been there all along'.[52] The makeover has seemingly revealed Annabelle's authentic self, as she is not dressed as belonging to a particular clique. This also ensures that her individual visibility, which is deemed essential to postfeminist girlhood, is reinforced and maintained through the contrast between Annabelle and the other girls, who are all wearing pyjamas. Annabelle's makeover also ensures that her 'authentic' self conforms to the ideal postfeminist femininity via an attractive appearance that includes big hair, glossy lips and a dress that draws attention to a slim figure. It is also indicative of British cinema's ambivalence towards glamour. While Annabelle's appearance may seem at odds with the idea that British femininity, as Jackie Stacey argues, 'is not "painted" or glamorous, and, by implication, not explicitly sexual',[53] as I discussed in the introduction, it is configured as a *British* postfeminist identity through Annabelle's assertion that she 'feels like a St Trinian', placing her image within the lineage of the British St Trinian's girl, which has featured throughout the history of the series.

The *St Trinian's* series has engaged with moral panics about girls' sexuality throughout its history via the figure of the sexy St Trinian's girl. The original films were produced during the 1950s and 1960s amid concerns about the permissive society and female sexual autonomy, while the recent films were produced during a period of increased concern over the 'sexualization' of girls. However, as Louise Wilks argues, British tween films like *St Trinian's* engage in debates about sexualization in contradictory ways by both critiquing the empowerment supposedly offered to girls in postfeminist raunch culture while also celebrating

Figure 1.1 *St Trinian's* (2007) Annabelle (Talulah Riley) becomes a St Trinian.

the 'commodified young woman's body'.[54] While the girls in these films may appear sexualized, this does not usually equate to sexual experience, which media panics about the sexualization of girls often fail to take into account.[55] This is most evident in the characterization of the 'posh totty' girls who wear sexy underwear and feather boas within the confines of their dressing room at the girls' boarding school. It appears as if the posh totty girls are running a sex chatline as sexy schoolgirls. The educational lexicon is deployed as innuendo as Chelsea says, 'I did really well in my last oral, although I did find it a bit of a mouthful at first.' It seems that Chelsea wants to titillate her caller, but it becomes clear this was not her intention when she innocently ends her conversation by explaining how much she likes Greek lessons. A similar scene occurs in *Wild Child* when posh Harriet (Georgia King) is unaware that Poppy has advertised her phone number as a chatline with 'naughty schoolgirls' and she cannot understand why the caller is so keen to hear about her uniform. As the conversation continues, Harriet asks the caller 'are you okay?', which implies that the caller has reached sexual climax but she does not recognize this. Both these scenes use innuendo as humour for the (presumably older) viewer, but the characters remain innocent. The issue of the sexy schoolgirl is also addressed in the critical reception of *St Trinian's*, with reviewers seeing this as simplistic and ultimately harmless. Writing in the *Sunday Mirror*, Mark Adams notes: 'Of course, it's all good-natured fun, but at times the film does lapse into a bit of simplistic salaciousness with lingering shots of short skirts and suspender belts.'[56] The *Times'* James Christopher is similarly unconcerned, saying, 'Despite the micro-skirts, fishnet stockings, and catwalk models, including Lily Cole, the raunch factor rarely exceeds a Carry On tease.'[57] The review discourse, then, suggests that the film's construction of girlhood sexuality is simplistic and dated. Christopher's allusion to the *Carry On* films (1958–1978) is particularly telling. As Steven Gerrard explains, the *Carry On* films were 'bawdy, smutty, innuendo-laden farces' that embodied the peculiarly British traditions of saucy seaside postcards and music hall acts, along with a fondness for innuendo and double entendre like the kind uttered by Chelsea as described earlier.[58] The depiction of the sexy schoolgirl in *St Trinian's* is, therefore, located within a particular kind of British humour, and a tradition within British cinema that the original films were also part of, which placates any contemporary concerns about the sexualization of girls in raunch culture. This also contributes to the overall sense within the film's critical reception that the contemporary St Trinian's girls could not possibly be more troublesome than real-life girls.

The posh totty girls offer a particular image of upper-middle-class British femininity; that is, the slightly comical, posh, blonde girl who is not particularly intelligent, a role that Tamsin Egerton, who plays Chelsea, will reprise in *Chalet Girl* (2011), which I discuss in Chapter 2. The glamorous and fun image portrayed by the posh totty girls makes them the perfect pupils to represent St Trinian's on the fictional television quiz show, School Challenge. As the girls progress through the competition, they seek advice on how to manage their growing celebrity status from ex-head girl and PR guru J. J. French (Mischa Barton). French advises the girls that if done properly, their appearance on School Challenge could lead to them appearing on a reality TV show 'and before you know it you've married a footballer and bought the Bahamas'. This line alludes to the UK's 'WAG' culture, a specific aspect of British celebrity culture during this period that is characterized as an illegitimate source of 'fame by proxy' that promotes fame over talent, and is at the centre of concerns about girls' supposed desire to be celebrities.[59] (I discuss WAG culture more fully in Chapter 3 in relation to *Kicks* (Heymann 2008).) The girls are stunned by J. J.'s plan, and their lack of knowledge of PR and celebrity culture stands in marked contrast to *Kicks'* Jasmine, who knows how to strategically plan her route to fame. While the girls in *St Trinian's* are not entirely removed from media culture, their limited knowledge is indicative of British cinema's representation of the same-sex school as a hermetically sealed environment. The girls' limited awareness of celebrity culture is also presented as nationally specific, as indicated by the casting of American Mischa Barton. The film capitalizes on Barton's reputation from her role as Marissa Cooper in *The O.C.* (Fox 2003–2007), a series about affluent teenagers in California's Orange County. Barton's image is therefore associated with affluence, fashion and consumption, which is the aim of the posh totty girls. Barton plays the only identifiably American character within the film, and the fact that she is brought in to tutor the girls hints at Britain's ambivalence towards celebrity culture as it implies that celebrity culture and self-branding is something that Britain has had to learn from America, which is presented comparatively as more overtly capitalist, consumerist and celebrity driven.

As comical characters, the posh totty girls adhere to the stereotype of the 'dumb blonde' girl, and rely on communicating with the geek girls like Polly (model Lily Cole, deliberately playing against type) who feed them the correct answers. When the technology fails, Miss Dickinson (Lena Headley), who is coded as a typical feminist sinister teacher through her plain clothes and dark-rimmed glasses, convinces them to believe in their own ability because 'smart is sexy'. It is suggested that knowledge leads to empowerment, as the girls win the quiz without assistance, but their knowledge is specifically gendered. Chelsea correctly guesses that Aztec women were banned from consuming chocolate because it was thought to have aphrodisiac properties (appropriately alluding to the idea of 'dangerous' female sexuality), while another girl only knows the capital of Brazil because she once had a boyfriend who was from Brasilia. Their knowledge is acquired from women's magazines and heterosexual relationships, suggesting that maintaining a postfeminist feminine identity is more beneficial than an academic education. Although *St Trinian's* seemingly celebrates freedom and creativity within education, ultimately the film upholds the notion that success and empowerment can only really be gained from investment in ideal, normative (postfeminist) femininity.

The success of *St Trinian's* led to a 2009 sequel, *St Trinian's 2: The Legend of Fritton's Gold* (Parker and Thompson 2009). The film is very much in the same vein as its predecessor so I shall discuss it only briefly here. In *The Legend of Fritton's Gold*, the girls must retrieve the lost gold of Miss Fritton's (Rupert Everett) pirate ancestor. In order to get their fortune, they must outwit Lord Pomfrey (David Tennant), head of the AD1 Brotherhood, a misogynistic secret society that believes 'women are cattle'. During their quest, the girls discover a number of secrets, including that Miss Fritton's ancestor wrote the plays of William Shakespeare – and Shakespeare was a woman. Unlike *St Trinian's*, the sequel was poorly received by the majority of critics, who viewed the film as 'clunky'[60] and 'laboured'.[61] The sequel retains many of the key elements from the first film, such as references to British film history, a strong girl power ethos and cliques. New cliques are added, such as the ecos and the flammables, while the chavs have evolved into rude girls, who are closely associated with ska culture. These changes were once again apparently made on the basis of 'market research' with teenage girls, this time carried out by the costume designer's niece, who told the filmmakers about how school cliques had changed since the previous film.[62] *St Trinian's 2* also responds to more recent shifts within postfeminist culture. Describing how the characters have changed, Barnaby Thompson explains, 'The girls are more empowered. They know what they want and will go out to get it, but they still all have push-up bras, iPods, mobile phones, curling tongs and hair straighteners.'[63] There is a continued commitment to postfeminist 'empowerment' and identity making through consumption, but there is also a more overt fight back against sexism and lad culture that is indicative of feminism's renewed visibility within popular culture. This is depicted symbolically when the girls need to defend the school from AD1 intruders. Chelsea lounges on the stairs and greets them with a seductive 'Hello, boys', and as the stunned men stare at her, the other girls take the opportunity to pour gunge over them from the upstairs landing. The scene evokes the iconic 'Hello, boys' Wonderbra advert from the 1990s, which, for Angela McRobbie, exemplifies postfeminism's ironic 'undoing' of feminism and critiques of the male gaze.[64] However, here there are consequences and the men are depicted as foolish for thinking that they can look upon this image and objectify Chelsea without repercussions. Similar reproaches of sexism take place in later films such as *Chalet Girl* (2011) and *Fast Girls* (2012), which are discussed in Chapter 2.

This fight back against sexism is embedded within the film's battle-of-the-sexes narrative, as the girls must go undercover at the boys' school to retrieve the priceless ring that has been stolen from the Fritton archives. This involves passing for boys by dressing up in Eton-style uniforms. The slow-motion St Trinian's strut is utilized once again, but the glamorous visibility offered in the earlier film is undercut as the strut offers up the spectacle of cross-dressing that mocks a particular kind of upper-class male privilege. This mockery of the upper classes acts as a link to the original *St Trinian's* films, and as a reminder that the privileged upper classes are far from being in decline in Britain today. The figure of the Etonian male became increasingly prominent with the election of a Conservative–Liberal Democrat coalition in 2010 and was heavily critiqued in Lone Scherfig's film *The Riot Club* (2014), which is centred around a thinly veiled version of Oxford's exclusive Bullingdon Club. The issue of male privilege is also evoked through the girls' discovery that the plays of Shakespeare were written by a woman, who was also Miss Fritton's ancestor. This raises questions of women's authorship and the need for a revisionist history of women's work. The narrative resolution celebrates the girls' success against the AD1, with Lord Pomfrey's misogyny exposed by the media, while acting as a reminder to the girls (and the viewer) that women have struggled to claim their authorship throughout history, and the battle for equality might not be as confined to the past as they thought.

'What is this place? Hogwarts?': *Wild Child* (2008)

With its UK cinema release in August 2008, *Wild Child* (Moore 2008), along with *St Trinian's* and *Angus, Thongs and Perfect Snogging*, is part of a trio of schoolgirl films that emerged within months of each other. *Wild Child* is the first Working Title film made specifically for teenage girls.[65] It is rather fitting, then, that the screenplay was written by Lucy Dahl, daughter of children's author Roald Dahl. The film marks Nick Moore's directorial debut, having previously worked as an editor on

Working Title productions, such as *Notting Hill* (Michell 1999) and *Love Actually* (Curtis 2003). The film stars American actress Emma Roberts (niece of *Notting Hill* star Julia Roberts) as Poppy, a spoilt sixteen-year-old, who lives in Los Angeles with her widowed father. When Poppy's latest prank aimed at preventing her father's girlfriend from moving in goes wrong, his patience is pushed to the limit and he sends her to an English boarding school. Poppy immediately clashes with her sensible British classmates and plans her escape by getting expelled for kissing the headteacher's son, Freddie (Alex Pettyfer). However, with the help of her new friends, she comes to realize that life in an English boarding school is not as bad as she thought; in fact, it is the best place for her.

Like *St Trinian's* (and *Angus*), *Wild Child* represents another attempt by the British film industry to draw on the conventions of the American teen film while remaining identifiably British in order to appeal to an international audience through a 'culture clash' comedy. As such, reviewers position *Wild Child* as a blend of *St Trinian's* and *Mean Girls*, but notably less sophisticated than either.[66] Unlike the ramshackle St Trinian's, Abbey Mount is a traditional conservative boarding school that is distinctly middle class. The slightly quaint and conservative image of Abbey Mount is in keeping with its status as a Working Title film, along with the familiar trope of the American young woman as an outsider in this very particular version of England seen in films like *Four Weddings and a Funeral* (Newell 1994), *Notting Hill* and *About Time* (Curtis 2013). National tensions between the United Kingdom and the United States are key to the film and are exemplified by the contrast between Poppy and her British peers. On her arrival at Abbey Mount, Poppy is viewed as ridiculous due to her display of overt consumption via her bleached blonde hair, designer clothes and oversized sunglasses which contrast sharply with the grey British setting and her peers who are wearing school uniforms and are distinctly unimpressed by Poppy's 'emphasised femininity'.[67] Poppy's emphasized femininity and overt consumption are attributed to her American identity. This is particularly evident in the film's production notes, in which Poppy is described as 'selfish', a 'fake-tanned, bleach-blonde brat',[68] while Abbey Mount is an English boarding school that produces 'fine young lad[ies]'.[69] Long-held ideas about the relationship between national identity and femininity are evident here, with the suggestion that British femininity is associated with ideal middle-class respectability while American femininity is seen as glamorous but ultimately fake and unnatural.[70] The Abbey Mount girls' lack of overt consumption is indicative of the subtly different ways in which postfeminism is articulated in a British cultural context that recur throughout this book. Key to this is how the film evokes the postfeminist makeover trope. When Poppy suggests that they get dressed up for an upcoming dance, the girls take her to the local charity shop, much to Poppy's disappointment as she thinks they are going to Oxford Street in London. In another music video–style montage, the girls try on a variety of outfits while Poppy rearranges material and casts her expert eye over them. Like the makeover scene in *St Trinian's*, the use of split screen simultaneously highlights the girls as a collective while also making each girl visible individually in keeping with ideas of postfeminist individualism. The girls achieve their makeover using second-hand clothes, a recurring trope throughout British girl-centred films from this period. While this highlights the characters' lack of spending power as teenagers, it is more specifically indicative of a British articulation of a key postfeminist trope that sees British films and their girl protagonists eschew branded consumption in their pursuit of ideal postfeminist femininity. In many of the films analysed in this book, with the exception of the historical films featuring royal or aristocratic young women discussed in Chapter 4, characters are depicted undergoing a makeover via clothes they have been given by friends or, in the case of *Wild Child*, at low cost from a charity shop. As well as helping her friends, Poppy also undergoes a makeover – or rather, a make-under – when the local hairdresser (Nick Frost) is unable to offer Poppy the high maintenance look she asks for and suggests something 'a bit more natural' instead. This involves removing Poppy's hair extensions and transforming her from blonde to brunette (Figure 1.2). As Samantha Colling argues, this kind of make-under occurs in millennial girl teen films when 'characters'

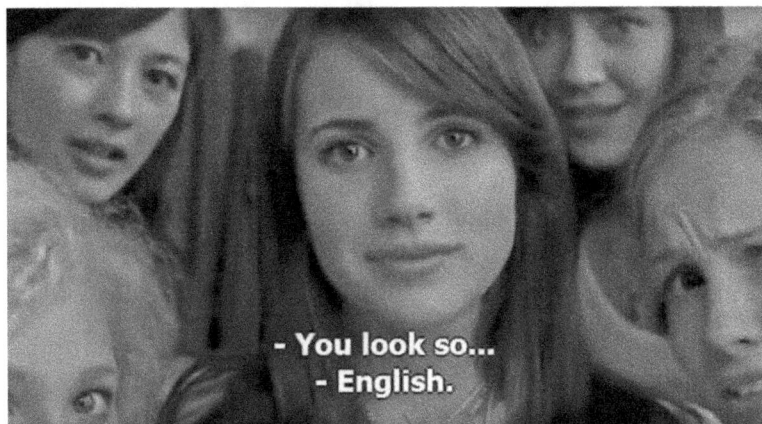

Figure 1.2 *Wild Child* (2008) Poppy's (Emma Roberts) make-under is revealed.

excesses are toned down or stripped away' because their current level of 'glitz is found to be unsustainable and corrupting'.[71] For Kennedy, Poppy's makeover represents the removal of the fake and unnatural elements of her inappropriate femininity, and is indicative of how the makeover trope in tween texts – and postfeminist culture more broadly – functions to ensure appropriate femininity and the revelation of the authentic self.[72] I would further add that this authenticity is specifically mediated as British, as indicated by the girls' reaction to Poppy's new appearance:

> Drippy: You look so . . .
> Kate: English!

Kate's reaction is indicative of a discourse within British cinema that has continuously linked British femininity with 'naturalness'. As Jackie Stacey argues in her study of female spectatorship of Hollywood cinema in the 1940s and 1950s, British actresses and, by extension, British femininity are associated with talent, charm and natural beauty as opposed to the artificial glamour possessed by American stars. This discourse is perpetuated in *Wild Child*'s production notes, which describe the importance of being able to find an American actress who could 'convincingly carry off a gradual transformation into a considerate fresh-faced English school girl', suggesting that this could be a challenge for the producers and for the American actress (Roberts) who is required to perform distinctly British femininity with which American actresses are not typically associated.[73]

Wild Child's specifically British articulation of postfeminist girlhood is also constructed through its mediation of postfeminist raunch culture. The Abbey Mount girls are convinced that Poppy, unlike them, is not a virgin because she is from LA, and they can supposedly tell by her hips, reinforcing the idea that British femininity is implicitly not sexual in comparison with glamorous American femininity. As Louise Wilks argues, the Abbey Mount girls have apparently internalized elements of postfeminist raunch culture, while at the same time, they are comically misinformed about sex.[74] This is exemplified by the character Drippy (*St Trinian's* Juno Temple), who, when describing the kind of outfit she would like for the dance, says: 'I want something that says "elegant", but at the same time, incredibly slutty and available. In fact, I'm not that bothered about elegant.' While the girls may sound like they are sexually empowered, they appear comically misinformed about sex and admit they are all virgins and talk euphemistically about 'doing it'. It is clear that, as in *St Trinian's*, adopting a 'sexy' image does not equate to sexual activity as the sexualization panic suggests. Despite this, the film's critical reception demonstrates a moral anxiety about girls' sexuality in keeping with the postfeminist 'sexualization' panic, with reviewers suggesting that the surprising number of sexual references in the film is inappropriate given the young age of the tween audience to which it is most likely to appeal. Writing in the *Derby Evening Telegraph*, Damon Parkin refers to *Wild Child* as a film with a 'big heart and a foul mouth. . . . Because this tale, which bears the hallmarks of a fun teenage Disney flick in the *Lizzie McGuire* mould, is liberally littered with swear words and sexual references. And that's a real shame because it could be perfect family fodder for the school holidays.'[75] The *Daily Mail*'s Chris Tookey similarly agrees that 'were it not for some sexual references which might easily have been omitted and probably should have been – its target audience would be ten and eleven-year-olds'.[76] For reviewer Gary Beckwith, however, this anxiety is assuaged by the 'pleasantly chaste' relationship between Poppy and Freddie.[77] This points to the paradox within *Wild Child* – and tween culture more broadly – where the girl characters retain their innocence but the tween girl in the audience is assumed to have enough knowledge to understand the jokes, which causes concern among the adult critics.[78]

The characters' lack of knowledge is in keeping with the hermetically sealed boarding school environment, which limits access to the outside world and the media that could potentially teach the girls about sex. The school's attitude towards sex is depicted as highly regulatory, with the school's 'honour court' acting as a means of regulating and punishing the most unacceptable behaviour. When Poppy wants to get expelled so that she can go back home, the girls inform her that she must do something bad enough to get summoned to the honour court. They tell her that getting caught kissing Freddie would guarantee this, suggesting that expressions of female sexuality are the ultimate transgression. Moreover, the Abbey Mount honour court is regulated by pupils as well as teachers. This peer-to-peer regulation is indicative of how, as Emma Renold and Jessica Ringrose argue, 'girls are socially sanctioned' to directly and indirectly regulate other girls' sexuality as a way of constructing idealized femininity.[79] This regulatory meanness is almost always expressed in relation to sexuality and this is evident within the film, such as when Harriett (Georgia King) aggressively insults Poppy by telling her to 'remember that the school's motto is scholarship, fellowship, loyalty, not be a slutty whore-y shitbrain'. Poppy does eventually discover an aptitude for fellowship and loyalty as she overcomes her individualistic and selfish attitude to lead the lacrosse team to victory. In taming the worst of her postfeminist excess, such as overt consumption and (hyper-)sexuality, Poppy discovers her authentic self as she proudly declares: 'In my heart I have discovered that I am an Abbey Mount girl after all.' Poppy has discovered the false empowerment on offer from the more overtly consumerist postfeminist femininity and found her appropriately feminine, authentic self.

Ultimately, it is Poppy's ability to be an Abbey Mount girl – a *British* girl – that cements her authenticity.

Not so 'swinging sixties': *An Education* (2009) and *The Falling* (2015)

British cinema's interest in the girl school film in this period also manifested in a return to the past – the 1960s in particular – with Lone Scherfig's *An Education* (2009) and Carol Morley's *The Falling* (2014), set in 1961 and 1968, respectively. Unlike the school films discussed earlier, *An Education* and *The Falling* are not specifically targeted at girls. *An Education* can be understood as a prestigious heritage film, while *The Falling* is framed as an art-house film in the poetic realism mode. The 1960s has been characterized as a decade of intense social and political change, particularly in relation to ideas around sex and morality. Key moments of progress in the period included the introduction of the contraceptive pill; the legalization of homosexuality and abortion; and the Chatterley trial of 1960 during which D. H. Lawrence's novel, *Lady Chatterley's Lover*, was absolved of all charges after being banned under the Obscene Publications Act. As cultural historian Dominic Sandbrook notes, the trial 'caught the mood of a society on the brim of a new era of hedonism, liberation and excitement'.[80] The post-war period was also concerned with the newest emerging youth demographic, including increasing moral anxiety about young people's sexuality. As Christine Geraghty has highlighted, the late 1950s saw a shift away from concerns about delinquent young men and their supposedly anti-social, often violent, behaviour and towards debates and anxieties around premarital sex, which brought the figure of the young woman to the fore.[81] Changing sexual politics and the opening up of education and employment opportunities for women during this period, along with an emphasis on consumption, gave rise to a set of sociological discourses that suggested that young women were more powerful and confident than ever before.[82] British cinema recognized the importance of the figure of the young, liberated woman as a means of attracting crucial youth audiences, and as such provided new, youthful, liberated and mobile heroines epitomized by Julie Christie in films such as *Billy Liar* (1963) and *Darling* (1965).[83]

As discussed earlier, it is perhaps unsurprising that contemporary media culture – both in the United Kingdom and the United States – is so enamoured with the cultural image of the 'swinging sixties' given that the figure of the 1960s' single girl chimes so closely with the 'empowered' young woman of postfeminism, creating what Lynn Spigel terms 'postfeminist nostalgia'. Spigel argues that 1960s-set texts such as the US television series *Mad Men* (2007–2017) offer a reimagining of the past, where urbane and cosmopolitan women have a certain amount of power and mobility but do not yet have feminism.[84] These texts, Spigel argues, chart a 'teleology of postfeminism' where women are 'already hoping to be postfeminists: independent, career-focused, yet hyperbolically "feminine" in their embrace of fashion, shopping and dating', without acknowledging feminism as a political struggle.[85] For the 1960s schoolgirls in this chapter, however, this kind of glamour and mobility eludes them, or is at best, temporary, troubling this idea of postfeminist nostalgia. It is glamour and mobility that Jenny (Carey Mulligan) dreams of in *An Education*. Set in 1961, *An Education* tells the story of sixteen-year-old Jenny who looks set to go to Oxford. That is until she meets David (Peter Sarsgaard), an older man who introduces Jenny to a culture of art galleries and classical music about which she has always dreamed. When David asks her to marry him, Jenny must decide whether her academic education is more important to her than the seemingly cultured education offered by David and his glamorous friends. *An Education* was directed by Lone Scherfig and produced by Amanda Posey and Finola Dwyer in association with BBC Films. The screenplay was adapted by Nick Hornby from journalist Lynn Barber's essay for literary magazine *Granta*. Barber's essay details her time as a pupil at the Lady Eleanor Holles School, an independent day school for girls, and she reflects on her teenage affair with a duplicitous older man.[86]

An Education is set during the post-war years when Britain was still experiencing austerity and had not yet started to swing. For the film's producers, this very specific setting was crucial to telling the story of a young girl being seduced by an older man. Discussion of the film's period setting dominates the production and critical reception discourses, with frequent references to Phillip Larkin's 'Annus Mirabilis' (1967) and it's assertion that 'Sexual intercourse began/ In nineteen sixty-three . . . / Between the end of the *Chatterley* ban/ And the Beatles' first LP'.[87] Jenny's home environment is presented as a microcosm of the film's pre-swinging world. Much of the film's comedy arises from the generational clash between Jenny and her parents. Jenny's father, Jack (Alfred Molina), is determined that his daughter should have a good education and go to Oxford University even though, as he often reminds her, it costs him a lot of money. For Jenny's parents, an Oxford education presents a broadening of opportunity in the post-war period, while Jenny views it as an opportunity to escape her suffocating and uncultured surroundings. Jenny searches for escapism via the Juliette Greco records she listens to in her bedroom, her foot tapping as she swoons to the music while the tap of the rain on the window is a constant reminder of reality.

The school environment is depicted as equally stifling for Jenny. In an opening montage set to Floyd Cramer's 'On the Rebound' (1961), we see Jenny and her friends learning to balance books on their heads in etiquette class, learning ballroom dancing and baking cakes in Home Economics. It is dull and monotonous, serving to demonstrate the limited education offered to girls in the 1960s that emphasized traditionalism and domesticity. Career prospects are also limited, as Jenny is informed that possible graduate positions for women consist of teaching or the civil service. Within the school environment, Jenny is presented as remarkable and more intelligent than her peers. The idea that Jenny is distinctive is furthered by Barber herself who, in the film's press kit, refers to her own group of school friends as her 'disciples', suggesting that she took on the role of leader who the other girls looked to learn from and emulate.[88] Jenny's status as an individual, a girl who rises above all others, makes her attraction to David – his lifestyle in particular – all the more understandable. David opens up a new world for Jenny, including trips to classical concerts and jazz clubs, and this is reflected by a changing mise en scène, which becomes brighter. Consumption is key in this new environment, and David's glamorous friend Helen (Rosamund Pike) exemplifies female consumption within the film. Seemingly lacking intelligence, Helen is portrayed as the opposite of Jenny. She does not understand why Jenny wants to go to university because she thinks female students are 'ugly'. Helen's attitude, combined with Pike's performance, presents Helen as a comical figure; the implication being that the audience can laugh at Helen and her stereotypical femininity because girls today seemingly have more options available to them than simply being a girlfriend.

As Jenny becomes more involved with David and his friends, her changing identity is, in typical fashion, indicated by a makeover as Helen transforms her into the image of Audrey Hepburn in *Breakfast at Tiffany's* (Edwards 1961). The use of Hepburn's image serves to further the film's sense of period and, at the same time, as Rachel Mosley argues, the image of a tiara-clad Audrey Hepburn has emerged as a key site of the Cinderella motif that permeates postfeminist culture.[89] Hepburn represents a 'democratic standard of beauty' which 'produced her as a star whose looks and style were potentially available to and achievable by any young woman',[90] making Hepburn the ideal icon for Jenny to emulate as a schoolgirl who borrows her friend's clothes in order to adopt a more sophisticated image. This particular image of Audrey Hepburn is also understood within the mode of postfeminist nostalgia, as it allows women in the audience to experience the pleasures offered by this iconic presentation of conventional feminine beauty without relinquishing their 'equality'.[91] David takes the made-over Jenny to Paris, which is captured in a montage of images around various Parisian landmarks (Figure 1.3). This highly stylized montage, which is not in keeping with the rest of the film, evokes stereotypical Parisian images, such as sweeping camera movements that capture the Eiffel Tower set to accordion music as David and Jenny create the impression that they are

Figure 1.3 *An Education* (2009) Jenny (Carey Mulligan) and David (Peter Sarsgaard) in Paris.

a glamorous couple who are in love. The montage also has a noticeably comic tone as David and Jenny pose for photos, which are captured in monochrome stills. This works to undercut the glamorous image and suggests that Jenny's new identity is false and temporary.

David and Jenny's trip to Paris also provides an opportunity for Jenny to lose her virginity, which she has carefully considered and has decided must take place after she turns seventeen. Unlike the girls in *Wild Child*, Jenny and her friends are depicted as more knowing in matters of sex. When Jenny's friends imply that David will expect sex in exchange for their dinner dates, Jenny denounces their attitude as 'Victorian'. Jenny displays a mature attitude towards sex, as she decides when and where she will lose her virginity. Reviewers also highlight Jenny's maturity as being at odds with the film's period setting. In his review of the film for the *Times*, Toby Young describes Jenny as 'sexually self-confident', adding, 'She has a down-to-earth, matter-of-fact attitude to sex that is more like that of a contemporary teenage girl than someone born in the 1940s.'[92] The idea that Jenny is sexually self-confident is indicative of the mediation of postfeminist discourses, which address women as sexually 'empowered' and agentic subjects within a historical setting (which I return to in Chapter 4).[93] Certainly, Jenny's attitude towards sex does seem modern when positioned in relation to the male characters, who all seem to uphold the notion that sex had not yet been invented. For all his charm and cultural sophistication, David displays an immature and peculiar attitude towards sex, such as when he initiates sex by presenting Jenny with a banana and suggesting that they 'get the messy bit over with' first. He also insists on using child-like pet names, all of which clearly make Jenny uncomfortable and make David look ridiculous. When it comes to sex, David is just as naive as the teenage Graham (Matthew Beard), Jenny's hapless suitor, who stutters and stumbles through their interactions. Jenny's attitude towards sex is also presented as out of step with the school's stance on girls' sexuality. In both of the 1960s-set films in this chapter, fear of changing sexual mores underpins the schools' approach to education, and girls' sexuality is both covertly and overtly regulated in an attempt to ensure 'appropriate' feminine behaviour. Jenny's relationship with David acquires legendary status within the conservative school, and she is called to the headmistress (Emma Thompson). In a euphemistic speech, the headmistress describes how there has been the 'odd sixth-former, who has lost part of herself – perhaps the best part of herself – while under our supervision, regrettably' and if the school is made aware of this happening then the girl must take her A-levels elsewhere, 'if she even has any further use for them'. Here, girls' sexuality is presented as a risky burden that the institution assumes a great deal of responsibility in regulating because pregnancy would mean the end of a girl's ambitions and confine her to the role of wife and mother, so virginity and innocence must be kept as long as possible, not least of all to uphold moral standards and avoid scandal.

The early 1960s setting is key to *An Education*'s mediation of girlhood sexuality, as it neatly sidesteps any anxiety about girls' vulnerability by safely confining to the past the story of a girl who gets seduced by a much older man. According to director Lone Scherfig, 'We all believed that the story could *only* take place then if audiences were expected to identify with it now' (original emphasis).[94] This concern over whether audiences would be able to identify with the story is indicative of the postfeminist context in which the film was produced and released, where girl power discourses continuously construct and address girls and young women as the savvy and confident beneficiaries of feminism who would unlikely be fooled by someone like David. Alison Rowat, writing for the *Glasgow Herald*, also places the incident within the context of the 1960s as a way of sidestepping the moral panic, as she says, 'to misquote Hartley, the past is a foreign country: they viewed dodgy behaviour differently there', acknowledging that the incident would be taken more seriously today.[95]

This emphasis on the importance of the 1960s setting also works to situate *An Education* alongside the 'social problem' films of the 1960s, which often explored anxieties about the dangers posed by older men, further relegating such concerns to the past. As Janet Fink and Penny Tinkler argue, films such as *Don't Talk to Strange Men* (Jackson 1962) featured girls who were at risk of predatory men whose reach was extended by the new technologies of the time, such as the phone and the car, just as when Jenny first meets David and he offers her a lift home in the rain.[96] The *Guardian*'s Peter Bradshaw similarly positions the film within the context of the 1960s because 'the story, as it is played out, is not too far from the kitchen-sink dramas from the 60s', such as *A Taste of Honey*, in which working-class Jo (Rita Tushingham) unintentionally gets pregnant.[97] In *An Education*, however, Jenny is a middle-class girl, and as such the repercussion of her relationship is not pregnancy but the potential loss of her education, which is in keeping with the postfeminist context in which education serves as a key site in which the figure of the 'successful girl' is discursively produced.[98] Lone Scherfig also highlights the importance of education when she describes what she hopes young women would gain from watching the film, saying, 'I hope they come away from it knowing that if they're in doubt about what they should do, they should have an education!'[99] Although Jenny is sceptical about the value of an academic education after experiencing a more cultural life with David, the way that the film inherently values education is in keeping with twenty-first-century discourses surrounding girls' education, and it is possible to view Jenny as having 'top girl' attributes as the middle-class, high-flying girl headed for Oxford.[100] Jenny's teachers also encourage this 'can-do' ethos, as Miss Stubbs (Olivia Williams) reminds her, 'You can do anything, be anything. You know that', and the headmistress informs her that 'no-one does anything without a degree'. However, Jenny's retort that 'no woman' does anything *with* a degree serves as a reminder that in the pre–second wave era of the film, girls' opportunities were more limited than they are for educated girls today. The lack of opportunities for educated women in the 1960s is also highlighted in *Made in Dagenham* (Cole 2010), a film about the strike led by the women workers at the Dagenham Ford factory as they fought for equal pay. Rosamund Pike plays Lisa, who, in sharp contrast to Helen, has a degree from Cambridge and yet she is confined in the role of wife and mother, and as such is not expected to convey her opinions to her husband's colleagues.

Jenny's 'can-do' attributes are further emphasized when, after discovering David's deceit, she goes to Miss Stubbs for help, having left the school without taking her exams. This is a significant departure from Barber's original memoir, in which her father goes to the headteacher to beg for his daughter's place at the school. In the film, Jenny takes charge of the situation herself by going to see Miss Stubbs and asking for tuition, which further serves the construction of Jenny as an agentic 'top girl'. Jenny's changed, more determined attitude is most apparent in a montage of Jenny reading and studying as she prepares for her exams. This is in direct contrast to the earlier montage in Paris, as it is not romanticized and stylized. Rather, it is dull and grey, filmed as through rain-soaked windows. While it is not as exciting, it is realistic, reflecting the idea that Jenny must work hard to succeed. She also returns to more muted clothing, in contrast to the earlier image of glamorous femininity. The final scene shows Jenny in Oxford, cycling alongside a boy as the camera lingers on Oxford's spires with a sweeping orchestral score, an idyllic image that suggests Jenny is exactly where she should be as a typical student, having relationships with boys rather than men, but her experience has made her wiser. It is, therefore, the combination of an academic education and wisdom that is deemed most valuable. This emphasis on education is in keeping with the postfeminist context in which the film was released and offers a kind of postfeminist nostalgia where prefeminist girls of the 1960s can take advantage of increased educational opportunities that exist as a result of feminist gains, and explore their sexuality without narrative punishment typically found in the British cinema of the 1960s. Moreover, *An Education* demonstrates that glamour is fleeting, and success is obtained via hard work and wisdom.

'Standards of behaviour must be kept': *The Falling* (2015)

Carol Morley's *The Falling* is also set in the 1960s, this time at the tail end of the decade in 1968. The film was produced by BBC Films and the BFI. Despite following the so-called 'Summer of Love', the era of free love has yet to arrive at the strict English girls' school in which the film is set. At the centre of this closed world are two best friends: charismatic Abbie (Florence Pugh) and the more serious Lydia (Maisie Williams). The steady rhythm of the school is shattered when a seemingly pregnant Abbie dies following a seizure. As the girls try to come to terms with Abbie's sudden death, an outbreak of mass hysteria consumes the school, characterized by twitching, fainting and vomiting. Director Carol Morley 'seeded through various possibilities' as to the cause of the hysteria, most of which are related to the girls' increasing sexuality, such as pregnancy, masturbation and sexual intercourse, and incestuous feelings and behaviour.[101] *The Falling* is characterized by a preoccupation with sexuality and sexual guilt, from the curious schoolgirls to the seemingly repressed teachers who desperately try to maintain a strict school order while the world around them changes. Setting *The Falling* in the 1960s was an obvious choice for Morley, as it was a period in which girlhood hysteria was made visible via Beatlemania and the frenzied and hysterical reactions of the Beatles' teenage girl fans. Morley was fascinated by the abundance of research into hysteria among girls that suggested a preoccupation with sexual matters as a cause: 'I felt it would be an interesting way of looking at the complexity of young female identity and sexuality and the changing nature of sexual morality for women in particular, so the outbreaks could be linked to cultural and social stresses.'[102] Such examinations of the female experience are key to Morley's work. In addition, *The Falling*'s largely female production crew is notable at a time when gender equality in the film industry is under scrutiny and Morley views this deliberate decision as 'a political act'.[103] This includes Morley as writer-director, Cairo Cannon as one of the producers, cinematographer Agnès Godard and Tracey Thorn as the sole soundtrack composer.

Intense, passionate and mysterious, *The Falling* can be placed within the context of British girl school films like Jordan Scott's *Cracks* (2009), which, like *The Prime of Miss Jean Brodie*, is set in a boarding school in the 1930s. *Cracks* tells the story of the mysterious Miss G (Eva Green) and her select group of favourite pupils. *The Falling*'s dreamlike otherworldliness positions Morley as a contemporary of Lynne Ramsay, a filmmaker who can, according to the film critic Mark Kermode, 'combine the authentic grit of British realism with the heady ambition of European experimentalism'.[104] While emphasizing the film's uncanniness, there is a simultaneous realist discourse as review and publicity discourses also highlight Morley's attention to detail and extensive research into outbreaks of mass psychogenic illness. In an article for the *Observer*, Morley details how she obsessively researched suspected cases from the period, as well as more recent examples such as the mysterious illness that struck girls in El Carmen de Bolívar, northern Colombia in 2014, which included symptoms such as fainting, nausea and convulsions that were publicly attributed to the Gardasil HPV vaccine.[105] Comparisons are also drawn between *The Falling* and Morley's earlier documentary-based films, *The Alcohol Years* (2000) and *Dreams of a Life* (2011), which used interviews and archive footage to recreate the life of Joyce Carol Vincent, whose body was found in her flat three years after she had died. Morley also reinforces this realist discourse by describing how writing the script for *The Falling* was like 'writing a documentary reconstruction of something that had happened. I felt I was rescuing part of their lives by bringing them to the screen.'[106] This poetic realist discourse is perhaps best summarized by Mark Kermode, who, in his review of *The Falling*, describes how even though it contains 'near-subliminal flashes', it also 'grounds itself in the firm terrain of the everyday'.[107] The opening scene of the film perfectly encapsulates its aesthetic qualities. Dispensing with an opening credit sequence, the film begins as Mary Hopkins' 'Voyage to the Moon' (1968) plays over the BBC Films and BFI logos, immediately drawing the viewer into the enclosed world of the film. This is followed by a shot of trees reflected in water and the ambiguous sound of someone breathing that implies both sex and fear, along with an extreme close-up of (Abbie's) long blonde hair and a bruise as Abbie, through voice-over, reads Wordsworth's *Ode: Intimations of Mortality From Recollections of Early Childhood* (1807), which draws on images of 'meadows, groves and streams' and 'celestial light' that are all present within the sequence and are suggestive of a rite of passage. This series of mostly abstract, flashing images and sounds encapsulates the film, establishing the period setting through music and highlighting themes such as sex and nature in a disjointed, disorientating manner.

By contrast, the school is a drab, brown, crumbling institution with woodchip peeling off the walls, which Abbie and Lydia pick at during various points in the film, adding to the film's haptic quality. Here, feelings and individuality are repressed as the girls travel around in straight lines and the strict teachers strive to maintain order. Despite the mini skirt – a signifier of female sexuality and freedom – being the height of fashion during this period, the girls are told that their school skirts must be 'no more than two inches off the floor when kneeling'. This strict monitoring of school skirt hemlines is presented as part of the school's attempts to regulate the teenage girls' behaviour more broadly and keep burgeoning sexualities at bay. Within the repressive school environment, Abbie and Lydia's friendship is constructed as particularly intense and formative in a way that is typical of depictions of teenage girl friendship, as I discuss in Chapter 3. Abbie and Lydia spend all of their time together, smothering each other in hugs and kisses and sharing the same piece of chewing gum. They are depicted as binary opposites, a common trope within films centred around girl friendship. Clever, blonde and middle class, Abbie has the outward appearance of ideal femininity that is only slightly marred by her rebellious nature. She is the founder of the 'alternative school orchestra' and enthrals her classmates with her impassioned reading of Wordsworth's *Ode*. Abbie is a source of fascination as she is the only girl with any sexual experience after she has sex with Lydia's brother, Kenneth (Joe Cole) – her loss of virginity is depicted in flashbacks in the film's opening scene – which is valuable currency within the repressed school environment. Her descriptions of sex and references to 'le petit mort' are intended to make her sound intriguing and sophisticated, but her reliance on vague clichés betrays the limits of her sexual experience. Lydia, by contrast, is depicted as repressed, dismissive of Abbie's constant talk of feelings and proudly asserts her status as a virgin. She doesn't understand why 'doing it' is so important to Abbie. Their respective differences create tension within their friendship and Lydia feels she is being left behind now that Abbie is more interested in boys. As Abbie tells Lydia: 'There's a real world out there, Lamb', to which Lydia replies, 'Yeah and you're the centre of it.' 'Lamb' is Abbie's nickname for Lydia, as her surname is Lamont, but lamb also has connotations of innocence that reinforces Lydia's status in relation to Abbie. Lydia's assertion that Abbie is at the centre of the world highlights the elevated position she occupies within the school and acts as an explanation for the way in which her death triggers the outbreak of mass hysteria.

The Falling is another film set in a world where the 1960s has yet to start swinging, but sex is seeping into the repressive school environment. Myths about sex are shared and dispelled, as the girls seek to establish each other's 'status', that is, virginity. Abbie's unconfirmed pregnancy is discussed in ways that were typical of the period – it is a 'situation' that can be solved with 'gin and a knitting needle'. Although abortion was legalized in 1967, Abbie reminds the girls that it is not available to girls like them. Despite the availability of the contraceptive pill, access to services was still highly restricted and sex was predominantly conceived as taking place within a marriage. The physical signs of Abbie's pregnancy, such as vomiting and fainting, mark her body out as unruly, particularly when she vomits over Miss Mantel as she is admonishing Abbie. Vomiting and fainting are also symptoms of the subsequent hysteria, which heightens the ambiguity. Abbie's pregnancy also evokes the aforementioned trope of unintended pregnancy that was common in British cinema in the 1960s, which served to contain the threat of female sexual autonomy. As Carrie Tarr argues, films such as *Sapphire* (Dearden 1959) and *Darling* (Schlesinger 1965) foregrounded young, single women who were contained within the 'boundaries of permitted pleasure' as the 'problem' of permissiveness was displaced onto the 'terrain of female sexuality'.[108]

Although *The Falling* positions the concern over teenage female sexuality as a part of the changing morality of the 1960s, comparisons can be drawn with contemporary moral panics about girls' sexuality. As I have discussed, this postfeminist panic positions girls and young women as the beneficiaries of feminist gains while simultaneously constructing young female sexuality as a source of anxiety. Contemporary concerns about morality are continuously mapped onto the terrain of young female sexuality, and *The Falling* engages with the positioning of girls' sexuality as both risky and at-risk through the suggestion that young female sexuality is the cause of the hysteria. One girl starts displaying symptoms after a brief shot of her masturbating, while Lydia's symptoms worsen as her relationship with her brother Kenneth shifts. The sexual undertones to their relationship are first hinted at through the holding and touching of hands, but it is suggested that rather than being overtly sexual, this touching allows Lydia in her grief to feel closer to Abbie, as Abbie also had a sexual relationship with Kenneth. This sexual exploration seemingly stems from Lydia's confusion and emotional distress, as well as her desire to feel closer to Abbie. The film does not blame Lydia for this as Kenneth is presented as someone who preys on teenage girls.

Through its exploration of girlhood hysteria, the film draws on the Ophelia narrative, which re-emerged in the late 1990s alongside girl power as a symbol of femininity in crisis. As Catherine Driscoll notes, 'Ophelia has become an icon of feminine adolescence repeatedly invoked as emblematic of girlhood difficulties and passions.'[109] Elizabeth Marshall argues that contemporary Ophelia narratives echo the 'late-nineteenth century fascination with the definition of hysteria as manifestations of psychological trauma written on the bodies of adolescent girls', but here this femininity in crisis is seemingly brought about by the girl's failure to be a normative can-do girl.[110] Texts such as Mary Pipher's (1994) *Reviving Ophelia* and Peggy Orenstein's *Schoolgirls* (1994) are indicative of this, as they employ a psychological discourse positioned as feminist intervention, arguing that girls are increasingly vulnerable and suffering from low levels of confidence and self-esteem in comparison with boys in a world where eating disorders and promiscuity are the norm. In Ophelia narratives, 'the school surfaces as one of the primary sites in which bodies are regulated through the inculcation of gendered competencies which train and discipline the body until an "identity" is etched below the surface.'[111] This is certainly the case in *The Falling*, where the school is presented as a highly regulatory institution that works to inscribe ideal femininity onto its pupils through emphasizing their domestic role and limiting expressions of creativity and individuality. As Miss Mantel reminds the girls, 'standards of behaviour must be kept'. As such, it is suggested that the hysteria is a manifestation of the attempts to resist normative femininity. Significantly, the hysteria reaches a crescendo when the girls attend an assembly led by a woman from the Stockshire Women's Circle, a group akin to the Women's Institute, who is keen to teach the girls about accidents in the home. At the start of the scene, Lydia is outside the hall, having been isolated from the other girls for being a bad influence. Lydia's status as a hysteric means she is removed from the school body, and the conformity within it, further enabling her to rebel. She watches from outside, tapping her foot against the door to create disruption. Girls then start to faint en masse, stopping

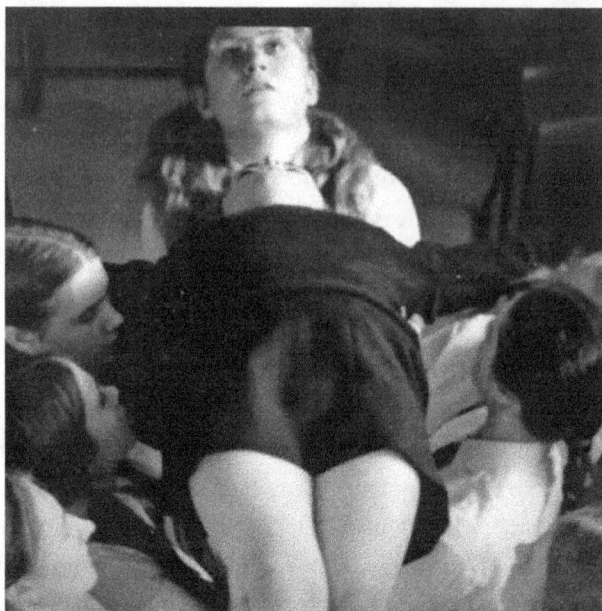

Figure 1.4 *The Falling* (2015) Lydia (Maisie Williams) as an icon of rebellion.

the woman in her tracks. The scene then takes on the qualities of a theatrical performance, as the girls faint slowly and gracefully like dancers as the camera swoops over them. Lydia then enters the hall to survey the scene and walks down the centre aisle. As she faints, she is lifted upwards with her arms outstretched in a Christ-like formation, an image that further inscribes her as a leader and an icon of rebellion for the girls (Figure 1.4).

There is a sudden jarring and disorientating cut to a close-up of a girl gasping for air as the girls are hospitalized as a result of the hysteria. The soundtrack contributes to this sense of delirium by featuring a mix of sounds and voices, including lines from the aforementioned speech on accidents in the home. Most prominent, however, is a Jean Brodie-esque voice saying, 'Now girls, let's talk about the devil. The devil can enter in many ways, so please cross your legs.' This line not only hints at the possibility of hysteria caused by possession but also reinforces the idea of girls' sexuality as making them both vulnerable and dangerous and highlighting the need for abstinence. The instruction for girls to 'cross their legs' further renders sexual activity as a burden for girls for which they must take full responsibility. The link between hysteria and sexuality is further explored when a male psychologist, whose voice is heard off-screen for the majority of the scene, interviews the girls about their sexual experience. With the psychologist as a largely disembodied voice, the girls directly address the camera, asserting their presence, with the psychologist unable to infiltrate their closed world. Here, as throughout the film as a whole, the power belongs to the girls. Although they experience hysteria, the film demonstrates that they are not really victims and they are not mad, they are simply too creative and rebellious for the confined roles into which the school tries to force them. As film critic Kate Muir writes in the *Times*, *The Falling* is 'a tale of grrl power long before the term existed'.[112] Muir's use of the term 'grrl power' rather than *girl* power is suggestive of the riot grrl movement and their DIY, feminist punk philosophy rather than the normative femininity promoted by postfeminist girl power discourses that emerged during the late 1990s and into the 2000s, highlighting the film's radical potential.

The film's rejection of the girl-as-victim is cemented in its final scene when Lydia discovers that the reason her mother is so distant with her is because Lydia was conceived through rape. Lydia then runs to the oak tree by the river, shouting 'What's wrong with me? Who am I?', throwing herself in the river in an image reminiscent of the drowning Ophelia, lit by the full moon as a symbol of female madness. However, Lydia is saved from drowning by her mother, who overcomes her fear of the outside world to rescue her. As she pulls Lydia from the water, she reassures her: 'There's nothing wrong with you.' In saving Lydia, she saves herself and their relationship is seemingly restored as mother and daughter rescue each other. Although *The Falling* hints at the many typical discourses surrounding girls' hysteria, the film never fully commits to any of these, refusing to entirely construct the girls as weak and vulnerable, examples of failed femininity. It refuses to let Ophelia drown.

Sex and repression in the British girls' school film

Contemporary British cinema has demonstrated a renewed interest in the girls' school film, where the school functions as a site through which to explore ideas about girls' sexuality and postfeminist panics around sexualization. In all the films analyzed in this chapter, the school is a source of confinement, with girls' sexuality in particular seen as needing to be repressed. In contemporary tween films *St Trinian's* and *Wild Child*, the school is a relic of the past with approaches to education that are also presented as out of step with the twenty-first century, both within the films themselves and in their critical reception. Unsurprisingly, it is these films that most fully engage with discourses of sexualization while allowing the characters to remain reassuringly innocent. *St Trinian's* draws on the figure of the sexy schoolgirl, which, conforms to an ideal of heterosexual femininity promoted by postfeminist raunch culture, though the film's critical reception discourses did not perpetuate this sexualization panic and the film's representation of girls' sexuality was deemed harmless. Instead, the figure of the raunchy St Trinian's girl was positioned in line with the broader history of *St Trinian's* films and the saucy *Carry On*–style British humour that was indicative of the earlier films. *Wild Child*, on the other hand, more overtly engages with the sexualization panic that views girls' sexuality as being both risky and at-risk because even though the characters are similarly represented as naive with regard to sex, the critical reception discourse suggests that the tween-age audience *will* understand the sexual references and are therefore at risk of being further 'adultified' through exposure to inappropriate content. These British girls' school films also further our understanding of how postfeminist girlhood is articulated within a specifically British context through and within their focus on girls' sexuality and education via their blending of postfeminist (British) girl power and the Hollywood teen film. The production and critical reception discourses that circulate around *St Trinian's* and *Wild Child*, as well as the films themselves, acknowledge a desire to emulate the Hollywood high school teen film through the use of tropes such as the clique and the makeover, while also remaining characteristically British. These national tensions help to further demonstrate the specificities of British representations of postfeminist girlhood. In *Wild Child*, hyper-sexuality and postfeminist excess are presented as distinctly American, while *St Trinian's* highlights Britain's ambivalence towards postfeminist celebrity culture by suggesting that British girls are unaware of the nuances of postfeminist celebrity culture in which these ideas around consumption and hyper-sexuality are mediated and reinforced until they are taught by the American J. J. French. Overt consumption is also eschewed, and the make-under in *Wild Child* is deployed to reveal the authentic self, but to do so in a way that suggests that authenticity and naturalness are defining features of British girlhood specifically.

This chapter also examined how two British girls' school films set in the 1960s – *An Education* and *The Falling* – explored ideas around girls' sexuality and sexualization. The 1960s setting was significant here as a period in which sociopolitical and cultural shifts prompted increased concern about young women's sexuality, and the 1960s figure of the independent, confident and sexually liberated 'single girl' chimes with discourses of postfeminist femininity. Both films trouble the 'swinging sixties' discourse that dominates cultural representations of the period as the protagonists are confined within a highly regulated school system. This also complicates the notion of 'postfeminist nostalgia', in which contemporary texts set in the 1960s seemingly depict young women who are already postfeminist in their pursuits of glamorous careers and sexual freedom. *An Education* offers a certain degree of postfeminist nostalgia by presenting Jenny as a postfeminist 'top girl' and evoking the image of Audrey Hepburn which features prominently as a Cinderella motif within postfeminist culture. However, the glamour inherent in this image is only offered temporarily and is ultimately seen as false. This is in keeping with contemporary British cinema's mediation of the makeover trope more broadly and its inherent ambivalence towards glamour. Mobility and sexual pleasure are also limited as Jenny discovers that sex – like education – is less fun than she imagined. Although the school is represented as a site in which girls' sexuality is highly regulated, Jenny is attributed with a confident and pragmatic attitude to sex that is deemed modern, and while sex is risky in the sense that Jenny's education is jeopardized, this is neatly resolved due to her 'can-do' characteristics.

The Falling examines the idea of unruly female sexuality via an outbreak of hysteria at another conservative girls' school at the tail end of the 1960s. In doing so, it draws on the Ophelia narrative, which re-emerged in the late 1990s as a symbol of femininity in crisis. However, the film refuses to uphold the idea of girl-as-victim. Instead, the school is presented as an institution that stifles female creativity and rebellion. The regulation of girls' sexuality is also seen as detrimental to their sense of identity. Fear of girls' emerging sexuality has always been a defining feature of the British girls' school film, which has re-emerged in this period to explore contemporary anxieties around sexuality and sexualization. Ultimately, however, the concerns are shown to be largely unfounded. It is the repressive school environment, not sex, that causes the most harm to the girls it seeks to protect.

The ambitious girl and the British sports film

Since the millennium, British cinema has witnessed an increase in the number of sports films featuring young women protagonists, such as *Bend It Like Beckham* (Chadha 2003), *Freestyle* (Lee 2010), *Fast Girls* (Hall 2012), *Chalet Girl* (Traill 2011) and *StreetDance* (Giwa and Pasquini 2010) as part of a broader mainstreaming of British film culture during this period, which included attempts to emulate contemporary Hollywood sports films such as *Blue Crush* (Stockwell 2002), *Stick It* (Bendinger 2006) and *Step Up* (Fletcher 2006) in order to attract young audiences. As Katharina Lindner argues, the increasing visibility of the Hollywood female sports film is a response to the 'increased visibility of female athletes in the media landscape and the emergence of postfeminist discourses'.[1] Lindner and Leslie Heywood highlight how the figure of the female athlete is the perfect representative agency for neoliberal postfeminist discourses of self-monitoring and self-discipline, with sport offering the potential for female 'empowerment' via a consumer lifestyle through the purchasing of sports clothing and equipment, along with the opportunity for the spectacularization (and sexualization) of the female body.[2] Sports film narratives, meanwhile, reinforce meritocratic ideals, where the young woman protagonist can achieve success through hard work and determination, with sport presented as a means through which to overcome structural inequality. These discourses extend beyond film and media culture, as Heywood argues in her examination of US government sports programmes, which, she argues, present sport as a means through which young women can develop self-responsibility through caring for their bodies, which can lead to better health and 'success', while preventing the development of 'risky' behaviours such as the consumption of drugs and alcohol, and pregnancy. As such, 'the ideal image of the female athlete perfectly incorporates the ideal of the new, can-do, DIY, take-responsibility-for-yourself subject'.[3]

This chapter examines how contemporary British sports films construct young femininity through their mediation of postfeminist neoliberal discourses of aspiration, which suggest that success can be achieved through hard work, self-responsibility and authenticity. In the four films I analyse here – *Fish Tank* (Arnold 2009), *StreetDance*, *Chalet Girl* and *Fast Girls* – class is presented as a barrier to the young woman's success, which is in keeping with a focus on class being a defining characteristic of British cinema more broadly. However, *StreetDance*, *Chalet Girl* and *Fast Girls* suggest that participation in sport can eradicate class inequalities because these films seek to be aspirational and attract young audiences in line with the Hollywood sports film. This aspiration is mostly constructed through the films' glossy aesthetics, which – as the films' production and critical reception discourses suggest – work to represent not only the characters' aspirations but also the aspirations of the British film industry itself.

'Aspiration nation'

With their focus on ambition and determination, it is possible to see why British cinema turned to the girl-centred sports film during a period which saw an increasing concern with young people's aspirations. A focus on aspiration has been a key feature of UK government discourse since New Labour and its emphasis on education, particularly increasing young people's access to and participation in higher education. This was followed by Conservative prime minister David Cameron's calls for an 'aspiration nation', encouraging those who want to 'rise from the bottom to the top'.[4] This discourse constructs aspiration within middle-class norms and enables a further entrenchment of neoliberal forms of governance that emphasize individual self-management.[5] Such discourses fail to take into account the structural inequalities that prevent upward social mobility; instead, these are reconfigured as indicative of a lack of effort and aspiration.[6] Working-class youth in particular are deemed to be lacking ambition, despite a wealth of evidence to the contrary.[7] This concern is typified by the phrase 'broken Britain', which was continuously employed by Conservative Party leader David Cameron in the lead up to the 2010 general election and then again as prime minister following the summer riots of 2011. 'Broken Britain' is characterized by perceived social ills such as teenage pregnancy, binge drinking, violence and knife crime, which are attributed to a lack of aspiration among working-class young people.[8]

These discourses of aspiration are gendered as well as classed. As Angela McRobbie argues, 'young women . . . have replaced youth as a metaphor for social change [and] are now recognised as one of the stakes upon which the future depends'.[9] During the 1990s, the figure of the girl as a beneficiary of equal opportunities was mobilized as the embodiment of the values of New Labour's new meritocracy.[10] These 'top girls' function as the ideal neoliberal subject who is hard-working, productive and self-managing.[11] Since the global financial crash of 2008 and subsequent recession, discourses of aspiration have intensified. Heather Mendick et al. define the cultural moment post-2008 financial crash as 'austere meritocracy' – a form of 'cruel optimism' (Berlant 2011) that calls on young people to aspire while the opportunities for social mobility are being eroded.[12] In the era of austerity, neoliberal economic, political and social policies have accelerated and tightened their grip. Although effort has always been prominent within meritocratic discourses, in this era of austerity hard work has taken on greater significance as key to how success is 'evidenced, achieved and legitimised'.[13] This intensified emphasis on neoliberal discourses of hard work and self-responsibility works to position a lack of success as due to the individual's personal failings, which allows for the dismantling of traditional support structures such as the welfare state under 'austerity measures'. It is significant then that these deliberately aspirational girl sports films emerged during a period of austerity when incitements for young people to aspire strengthened despite growing inequality.

The British sports film

Ellis Cashmore has defined the sports film as films that 'use sports themes as their plot dynamic . . . and they usually end with a climactic triumph or disaster'.[14] Cashmore's definition is broad but useful as it enables us to consider a range of films that reflect the diversity of British cinema's output at this time. This chapter views the girl-centred sports film as a significant feature of contemporary British cinema's output; however, as Glen Jones argues, the British sports film has typically been considered an 'invisible genre' in comparison to its status within Hollywood cinema.[15] Of course, there are one or two notable exceptions, such as *Chariots of Fire* (Hudson 1981). The film about two young men who run to victory in the 1924 Paris Olympics was a surprise hit with audiences and critics, winning four Academy Awards in 1982 (including Best Film). *Chariots of Fire* was widely purported to have heralded a renaissance of the British film industry in the 1980s and has featured prominently in surveys of British cinema ever since.[16] Paradigmatic examples of the British sports film such as *Chariots of Fire* and the new wave film *This Sporting Life* (Anderson 1963), in which Yorkshire coal miner Frank Machin (Richard Harris) becomes a rugby league star, highlight how the British sports film – like British cinema as a whole – has been overwhelmingly concerned with men and masculinity. A 2017 feature by the BFI lists '10 great British sports films', all of which are directed by men and centred around male protagonists.[17] What separates the British sports film from its Hollywood counterpart, Jones suggests, is that 'the hero is not necessarily deserving or will achieve success'.[18] This is due to the legacy of the British new wave and, as such, the British sports film 'has never really been in the position or placed any emphasis upon . . . the "spectacularisation" of sport'.[19] However, contemporary British cinema's girl-centred sports films, particularly those aimed at youth audiences such as *Chalet Girl*, *StreetDance* and *Fast Girls*, do make deliberate attempts to spectacularize the sports on display (along with the girls who play them) via glossy and aspirational aesthetics. As Samantha Colling highlights, sport in girl teen films such as these provide the opportunity for a 'moment of celebrity, visibility and recognition' in a postfeminist culture that demands girls make themselves visible akin to celebrities.[20] As well as offering a mediation of discourses of young women's ambitions, these films also work to showcase the ambitions of the British film industry itself as part of attempts to make British film culture more mainstream during this period. This includes attempts to differentiate themselves from associations with social realist traditions that focus on 'gritty' stories of masculinity , which pervade not only the sports film but also British cinema more broadly. However, these attempts to create aspirational aesthetics are often complicated by the British film industry's inability to match Hollywood budgets, and British cinema's ongoing ambivalence towards glamour and consumption.

Glen Jones argues that the British sports film presents sport as a means through which individuals attempt to 'overcome their social situation or problems'.[21] This remains a constant within the girl-centred sports films discussed here, with sport presented as a means through which to overcome class and race inequalities – the latter to a lesser extent. All of the protagonists are coded as working (or lower middle)class and this is the biggest barrier to their sporting ambitions, although in the more aspirational films, such as *Chalet Girl*, *StreetDance* and *Fast Girls*, there is no doubt that this barrier will be overcome via the girl's hard work and talent in line with neoliberal discourses. This chapter examines four girl-centred films with sporting themes: *Fish Tank*, *StreetDance*, *Chalet Girl* and *Fast Girls* whose narratives centre around street dance, snowboarding and athletics, respectively. Like Katharina Lindner, I include dance as a form of sport because in these films, dance, like other forms of sport, is presented as a competitive endeavour.[22] The dance film – often considered a sub-genre of the sports film – has become increasingly popular during the twenty-first century, in part due to technological advancements, such as 3D film, which prioritize movement and spectacle.[23] Dance films also draw on the popularity of music videos, emulating their MTV-style aesthetics and focus on popular music genres such as R&B and hip-hop, exemplified by films such as *Step Up*. Dance is central to both *Fish Tank* and *StreetDance* in this chapter. *Fish Tank* is not a typical sports film – it certainly was not positioned or received as such – but it 'uses sports themes as a plot dynamic' in that the narrative follows Mia (Katie Jarvis), a working-class girl living on a council estate in Essex, as she develops her dancing, working up to an audition where she is placed in competition with other girls but is ultimately – and deliberately – unsuccessful. Mia's lack of success is in keeping with Jones' suggestion that a hero(ine) who is not necessarily successful is a key characteristic of the British sports film.[24] The legacy of the British new wave is also more evident in *Fish Tank* than the other films discussed in this chapter. *Fish Tank* may seem like an anomaly here, but I argue that there are a number of parallels between *Fish Tank* and the other films discussed in this chapter in relation to its mediation of discourses of girlhood ambition, particularly through the extra-textual narrative surrounding actress Katie Jarvis, which is constructed through a meritocratic discourse. Unlike the other films discussed in this chapter, however, *Fish Tank* exposes the limits of meritocratic aspirational discourses through its working-class protagonist who does not achieve the visibility demanded by contemporary girlhood. *Fish Tank*, therefore, functions as part of a dialogue about what it means to be a British ambitious girl.

Ambition and the 'at-risk' girl: *Fish Tank* (2009)

Fish Tank is the second feature film from writer-director Andrea Arnold following her critically acclaimed debut *Red Road* (2006). Both films won the Jury Prize at Cannes and draw on Arnold's key themes of lust, claustrophobia and obsession. *Red Road* and *Fish Tank* earned

Arnold a reputation as a British auteur who casts an unflinching eye over Britain's housing estates and uncritically explores the lives of the marginalized characters within them. *Fish Tank* centres on fifteen-year-old Mia Williams (Katie Jarvis) who lives on a council estate in Essex with her mother Joanne (Kierston Wareing) and younger sister Tyler (Rebecca Griffiths). Mia spends her days practising street dance in an empty flat overlooking her estate, but she lacks the necessary resources and support to cultivate her ambition. When Joanne's new boyfriend, Connor (Michael Fassbender), enters their lives, Mia finds the encouragement she has been looking for and the pair embark on a murky relationship that is at first paternal and then sexual. Mia then learns that Connor has been living a double life and he already has a wife and a young daughter, Keira. Seeking revenge, Mia coaxes the girl to the sea, where she pushes her into the water before deciding to rescue her. Mia eventually leaves for Wales with a young traveller called Billy (Harry Treadaway).

Arnold's focus on marginalized outsiders has seen her heralded as 'the successor to Ken Loach',[25] a filmmaker synonymous with British social realism. As David Forrest argues, Loach's work is characterized by a 'direct and frank means of highlighting the perceived ills of social and political institutions and concepts via emotive and authentic protagonists, while consistently maintaining a clear environmental verisimilitude'.[26] However, for Forrest, filmmakers such as Arnold, along with Shane Meadows, Pawel Pawlikowski and Lynne Ramsay, indicate developments within British realism towards a more ambiguous mode of filmmaking that prioritizes poetic aesthetics against a sociopolitical backdrop.[27] In Arnold's films, this manifests primarily in a lyrical depiction of location, which Claire Monk terms 'poetic realism'.[28] This 'poetic realism' discourse is evident in numerous reviews, where critics single out cinematographer Robbie Ryan for capturing a council estate that is indicative of 'broken Britain' and elevating it from a mundane environment to something beautiful and abstract. Mia's subjectivity is also prioritized through this more ambiguous and poetic mode of filmmaking. Lucy Bolton argues that, through giving prominence to

Mia's subjectivity, *Fish Tank* 'evokes the experience of what it is *to be* a girl in modern Britain' in contrast to the more traditional approach to social realism that prioritizes the social and cultural context (original emphasis).[29] More specifically, I argue, *Fish Tank* evokes what it is to be an *ambitious* British girl in this period, and its inclusion here forms part of a dialogue about the mediation of girls' ambitions in relation to the sports and dance films discussed later in this chapter.

Mia is characterized as an 'at-risk' girl – the 'educational failure' with 'misaligned ambitions'.[30] She has been expelled from school and, although she has dance ambitions, these are misaligned because she lacks the knowledge, information and resources needed to fulfil them.[31] Even though she practices regularly, there is little sense that this will lead somewhere. It is only with Connor's encouragement, and the use of his video camera, that Mia is able to audition. More specifically, Mia is suggestive of the figure of the 'chav'. As Imogen Tyler argues, the figure of the chav emerged in the 2000s, highlighting deepening inequalities and class antagonisms in contemporary Britain, becoming a 'ubiquitous term of abuse for the white poor'.[32] As traditional demarcations of class, such as education and access to branded consumer goods, become blurred, Tyler argues, 'the vilification of the chav can be interpreted as a symptom of a middle-class desire to re-demarcate class boundaries within the context of contemporary consumer culture'.[33] While consumption is key to neoliberal postfeminism, the figure of the chav is distinguished by the emphasis on the 'wrong' kind of consumption of branded consumer goods that is deemed vulgar and excessive, signified by items such as large gold hoop earrings, sovereign rings and branded sports clothes, which Mia also wears.[34] While the figure of the chav typically elicits cultural reactions of class disgust, Arnold's approach means that she never vilifies her protagonist in this way.

The 'at-risk' discourse circulates prominently within the film's extra-cinematic materials and paratexts, where Katie Jarvis is constructed as a 'girl as failure' who has reformed. When she took the part in *Fish Tank*, seventeen-year-old Jarvis was an 'unemployed school leaver with two GCSEs' who had never acted and was spotted by a casting director while arguing with her boyfriend at Tilbury train station.[35] This emphasis on the casting of unknown young actors is not unusual in British cinema, especially in social realist films from *Kes* (Loach 1969) to *This is England* (Meadows 2006). What is most striking about the discussions of Jarvis, however, is this classed educational discourse that emphasizes her lack of qualifications and prospects, reinforcing the centrality of education to contemporary discourses of youth aspiration. In an interview for the film's press book, Jarvis reflects on how working on the film has changed her:

> Whereas before I was doing nothing all the time, it made me learn that I could do things if I wanted to do it. It was hard, but it was fun and rewarding. Now I want to make the most of it. It shows you you don't have to go to drama school to get into it but I think I was one of a kind, [*sic*] I don't think anyone else will get picked off a train station![36]

Before the film, Jarvis is depicted as a working-class girl who was (in her own words) 'doing nothing all the time' and lacking aspiration in keeping with the discourses of youth aspiration discussed earlier which presume that working-class young people lack aspiration and drive rather than resources.[37] Moreover, her comment works to show how taking part in the film has helped to reposition her from 'girl as failure' to a girl who recognizes her own capacity for success and the benefits of working hard and seizing opportunities, discourses that have become heightened within the context of the 'austere meritocracy'.[38] In claiming that she was 'one of a kind', Jarvis is furthering the narrative constructed around her within the film's press reception that emphasizes the unusualness of her casting that was due to 'sheer luck'. The meritocratic narrative surrounding Jarvis furthers Dyer's notion of the 'success myth' where success is available to all who are willing to work for it.[39] However, in promotional articles it is noted, in a somewhat disappointed tone, that Jarvis was not able to capitalize on her success with *Fish Tank*. She missed the film's premiere at Cannes because she had recently given birth to her baby daughter at the age of eighteen and subsequently turned down further acting roles.[40] Teenage motherhood is a defining characteristic of the 'at-risk' girl and is associated with failed femininity, as postfeminism demands that women control their fertility in order to be productive.[41] As Imogen Tyler argues, the young, unmarried, working-class mother – the 'chav mum' – is vilified because she 'embodies historically familiar and contemporary anxieties about reproduction, fertility and "racial mixing"'.[42] Arnold produced a typically non-judgemental depiction of the 'chav mum' in her Oscar-winning short film *Wasp* (2003). The film follows Zoe (Natalie Press), a young, poor, working-class single mother who leaves her children unattended to go on a date and momentarily escape her situation. Young motherhood is typically seen as a barrier to success, and, as Anita Harris notes, 'at-risk' girls are set up as 'failures in making' who can never truly overcome their status as an 'at-risk' girl due to their circumstances and poor personal choices.[43] As such, Jarvis' situation is discussed in tones of inevitability. Speaking at the film's premiere, Arnold commented on Jarvis' absence, highlighting how Jarvis' life is far removed from the glamorous world of Cannes: 'I don't think she really understands what this means . . . . Festivals and things are not really part of her life . . . . I don't know if she wants to continue. I think she does but she's just had a baby and that's a whole other life.'[44]

Arnold's comments are a reminder of how difficult it is for working-class girls to transcend their background, and how discourses of aspiration construct subjects as ideally middle class, failing to take into account the structural inequalities that working-class girls in particular experience.[45] However, by the time *Fish Tank* had been released on DVD, Jarvis was able to take part in promotional interviews where she revealed that she had returned to acting because she wanted to 'chase' the opportunities that *Fish Tank* provided.[46] This is an interesting conclusion to Jarvis' personal narrative within the film's promotional discourses. It is a story of transformation, as Jarvis has seemingly gone from being an 'at-risk' girl whose fate, it was thought, was sealed, to an ambitious young woman who is determined to work hard and make the most of her talent and opportunities. Jarvis did continue to act but struggled to match the success of *Fish Tank*, with occasional roles in short films and television appearances. More recently, Jarvis joined the BBC soap opera *EastEnders* (1985–) as Hayley Slater after a hiatus. It seems Jarvis' career is yet more evidence of the continuing – and escalating – barriers faced by working-class actors in the British film industry.

Katie Jarvis was given an unexpected opportunity but it seems unlikely that Mia would be so fortunate, and Arnold shows us that there are uncultivated dreams and ambitions all over the estate. As Mia charges around the estate, swearing at anyone who gets in her way in the film's kinetic opening scene, she notices a group of girls dancing in the car park being watched by a group of boys. They dance to a self-choreographed routine that emulates the sexualized dance style of contemporary R&B music videos, a key feature of contemporary dance films. The girls perform sexualized moves and sing suggestive lyrics while wearing crop tops and shorts, all of which are in keeping with the postfeminist 'raunch culture' that characterized the 2000s.[47] Raunch culture promoted a commercially driven form of sexualization in keeping with postfeminist culture's requirement that young women must always present themselves as desiring, capitalizing on their sexual power and always 'up for it'.[48] Raunch culture promotes a supposed sexual empowerment for women but one that is hinged on heterosexual male pleasure, and the girls' performance is validated by the boys who watch them and discuss which girl they would 'have'. Although dancing as a group, the girls take it in turns to come forward in front of the boys – and the camera – and present themselves as potential objects of desire, as Mia watches scornfully. The girls' dancing and outfits are at odds with their child-like faces, suggesting that they are not as knowing as they pretend to be. The girls' performance is indicative of how, as Samantha Colling argues, visibility is part of the 'everyday' of millennial girlhood, and being in view is a key means of identity validation.[49] However, unlike the girl characters in the more aspirational films discussed in this chapter, it is evident that Mia and the girls from the estate will remain dancing in car parks that are a far cry from the glamorous cityscapes that provide the backdrop for teen girl dance films.

Aspirational US media culture is a constant presence within the film, providing a stark contrast between Mia and Tyler's lives and the girls they watch in music videos and reality television. Tyler is often lounging in front of television programmes such as MTV's *Cribs* (2000–), which takes the viewer on a tour of a celebrity's home, and *My Super Sweet 16* (MTV 2005). *My Super Sweet 16* follows affluent American teenagers as they plan extravagant 'sweet sixteen' birthday parties. The excessive consumerism within these programmes means that they are often watched ironically, as viewers simultaneously mock these unrealistic lifestyles while also aspiring to them to a degree.[50] Tyler also appears to watch *My Super Sweet 16* ironically, dismissing the girls as 'rank' while she smokes and drinks alcohol, which are the kind of 'inappropriate' consumption behaviours that characterize 'at-risk' girlhood.[51] Participation in consumer culture is mandatory within postfeminist girlhood and the sight of Tyler watching these aspirational shows serves to highlight the deep disparity between the life contemporary culture dictates she should aspire to and the life she actually has. Furthermore, the contrast between the lifestyles promoted by *My Super Sweet 16* and Tyler's dismissal of the show reinforces the ambivalent relationship between British and American girl culture that characterizes British articulations of postfeminist girlhood, where aspirational American culture is both a noticeable influence and mocked for being too gaudy and implicitly fake.

American music videos also provide Mia with inspiration, as she dances in front of the television, unaware of Connor watching her. Mia is the object of the 'male gaze'[52] as Arnold captures her swinging hips covered in girlish pyjamas adorned with strawberries, capturing the 'in-between-ness' of teenage girlhood and setting the tone for the part-paternal, part-sexual relationship between the pair. However, after Connor compliments Mia's dancing, Mia becomes the 'bearer of the look' as her gaze follows a half-dressed Connor upstairs with a mixture of curiosity and desire. This scene is singled out in a number of reviews as a positively subversive way of depicting Mia's growing sexuality. Writing in the *Times*, Kevin Maher highlights how Fassbender is shot with a 'fantastically lusty eye',[53] while Ryan Gilbey says that viewing Connor through Mia's eyes 'feels positively transgressive' and acts as a reminder of how the 'male gaze' continues to dominate what we see on screen.[54] The relationship between Mia and Connor is ambiguous; we feel Mia's confusion as her feelings for Connor shift. At first, Mia seems confused by Connor's presence and his willingness to adopt a fatherly role in this female-centric household by including Mia and Tyler on a trip to the countryside. He also encourages Mia's dance ambitions while her mother and sister scoff, and lends Mia his camera so that she can record an audition tape. Without Connor, Mia would lack the resources and the confidence needed to chase her goals. The lending of the camera marks a pivotal point in Mia and Connor's relationship. Mia tests the camera by filming Connor as he gets dressed and he leans into her and asks what she thinks of his aftershave. Mia breathes in deeply in such an extreme close-up that her breath on Connor's neck is palpable. Mia cheekily deems the aftershave 'fox piss' so Connor wrestles her over his knee and spanks her in what Lucy Bolton calls a 'parody of fatherliness', leaving Mia stunned.[55] Mia's growing feelings for Connor also impact upon her dancing. She chooses Connor's favourite song – Bobby Womack's version of 'California Dreamin'' (1968) – for her audition piece, and as we see her rehearsing, it is clear that her movements have become more graceful and sensual. Plugged into her earphones in her own private world, Mia dances slowly while looking out over the estate with only the sound of her heavy breathing (Figure 2.1). The darkened mise en scène contributes to an increasing tension and sense of danger within the film that culminates with Mia demonstrating her dance routine for Connor late at night, which inevitably leads to them having sex. Connor tells Mia not to tell anyone and is gone by the morning.

As Samantha Colling argues, in girl culture, visibility offers a key form of identity validation that is constructed through discourses of celebrity, and *Fish Tank* suggests that this visibility is crafted from a young age.[56] Connor's lies are exposed when Mia finds footage of his young daughter, Keira (Sydney Mary Nash), singing as her parents gently encourage her performance off camera. The inextricable link between

Figure 2.1 *Fish Tank* (2009) Mia (Katie Jarvis) lost in her own world.

celebrity and girlhood is overt as Keira is singing 'Bleeding Love' (2007) by UK *X Factor* winner Leona Lewis. The increase in popular talent shows such as *The X Factor*, and previously *Pop Idol* (ITV 2001–2003), in this period work to shore up these neoliberal postfeminist discourses as part of the democratization of celebrity where seemingly ordinary yet exceptionally talented people can become famous.[57] This has also led to particular moral panics about the supposed limits of girls' ambitions, which I discuss in Chapter 3. Unlike Mia, Keira is also a can-do girl in the making. When Mia tracks down Connor's family home, we see that it is in a suburban cul-de-sac that is markedly different from the council estate. As well as being middle class, Keira is also blonde and cute, and has the kind of familial support that Mia lacks. The kind of visibility on offer to Mia, however, is very different. Mia stumbles upon her potential route to visibility by chance when she walks past a window advert reading: 'Female dancers wanted. Top club seeks fresh talent.' The advert draws on talent show discourse with its emphasis on young, undiscovered 'fresh talent' with an ability to be at the 'top'. When Mia arrives at the club, she discovers that the talent required is lap dancing. As Rosalind Gill argues, in postfeminist culture women are encouraged to make sex objects of themselves in a manner that closely resembles the heterosexual male fantasy found in porn through activities such as lap dancing, which are reconfigured as fun and 'empowering', experiencing a rise in popularity in the 2000s.[58] However, whereas for middle-class girls, these activities are presented as fun leisure activities akin to going to the gym that enable the presentation and regulation of the 'sexy' body that is paramount to postfeminist culture, for working-class girls they represent illegitimate forms of employment. In an echo of the opening scene of the film, Mia is noticeably out of place among the other girls, who are all dressed in crop tops and shorts in contrast to Mia's tracksuit, highlighting the sameness and limits of acceptable 'sexy' femininity in postfeminist culture. As the music starts, Mia remains rooted to the spot before walking briskly out of the club.

Mia does not get to fulfil her dance ambitions, but she is offered a way out. Mia visits Billy and is upset to learn that the horse that she is fond of had to be put down. Billy comforts her by saying, 'She was sixteen. It was her time.' It is also Mia's 'time'; that is, to come forward and make her own future away from the constraints of her situation.[59] Mia agrees to go to Wales with Billy, but before she does she experiences an unspoken reconciliation with her mother as they dance together to Nas' 'Life's a Bitch' (1994); however, things no longer seem so futile for Mia as she has a chance to escape and start again. As Mia and Billy drive away, Arnold ends her film on a hopeful note with the romanticized image of a red balloon floating over the estate. Mia may not have become visible in line with postfeminist girlhood, but in leaving the estate she has the opportunity to make a better life on her own terms.

One in a Million: *StreetDance* (2010)

Class is also a significant barrier to aspiration in *StreetDance*, but the film offers a much more glossy and aspirational depiction of girls' dance ambitions that is more in line with the contemporary Hollywood dance film. *StreetDance* is the first UK film to be filmed entirely in 3D. The film centres around Carly (Nichola Burley) who leads a street dance crew following the departure of her crew leader and boyfriend, Jay (Ukwell Roach). Carly works in a sandwich shop and cannot afford to rent a rehearsal space, but when ballet principal Helena (Charlotte Rampling) spots Carly's choreography scribbled on a sandwich bag, she offers her a room in her ballet school – on the condition that Carly includes her ballet dancers in her routine for the street dance competition finals. The two groups are initially hostile and struggle to gel before – predictably – Carly's leadership brings them together and they are crowned street dance champions. The film also boasts the presence of former *Britain's Got Talent* (ITV 2007–) stars George Sampson as Eddie and street dance groups Flawless and Diversity. *StreetDance* was produced by Vertigo Films, previously known for producing laddish British films like *The Football Factory* (Love 2004), along with BBC Films and the UKFC. With a budget of £3.5 million, *StreetDance* went on to reach number one at the UK box office and make £11 million during the first five weeks of its release in 2010.[60] (A sequel followed in 2012.)[61] *StreetDance* was subsequently sold to almost thirty countries but was a global commercial failure.[62] Despite being released at the height of austerity and the beginning of the Conservative–Lib Dem coalition, any hint of economic recession is glossed over and the tourist board–thrilling presentation of London depicts the capital – and, by extension, the UK – as an aspirational meritocracy where hard work and talent are all that is required to succeed, regardless of class background.

As an urban dance film centred around competitions where the characters have to define themselves in opposition to one another, achieve physical proficiency through dance and develop a heterosexual romance, *StreetDance* was unsurprisingly compared to Hollywood teen dance films such as *Step Up* (Fletcher 2006) and *Save the Last Dance* (Carter 2001).[63] References to *Save the Last Dance* and *Step Up* feature throughout *StreetDance*'s critical reception, which serves to highlight how *StreetDance* formulaically adheres to the US dance film format.[64] This was part of the filmmakers' attempts to create an aspirational film, as the production discourses equate aspirational filmmaking with Hollywood. Producer James Richardson outlines his desire to make 'a dance film with the same aspirational feel of an American movie, but in a very British setting.'[65] He adds: 'Why do we (Brits) always make films where we go for the grey and miserable? . . . I'm not knocking them – I've made some of those films – but this one, *StreetDance*, is about fun.'[66] Richardson's comment raises a number of key points. First, he draws on the dominant discourse where British cinema is synonymous with social realism and stylistically unambitious filmmaking; it is 'grey and miserable'. As Justine Ashby and Andrew Higson argue, British cinema 'has always been promoted in terms of cultural value, pitting the authentic, ingenuous culture of "ordinary people" against the Americanised culture of glamour, spectacle, commercialism and mere entertainment.'[67] For Richardson, *StreetDance* is not just about entertainment but also, more specifically, about fun. As Samantha Colling argues, fun is one of the central pleasures offered by the contemporary Hollywood girl teen film.[68] In emphasizing that *StreetDance* is about fun, Richardson is further aligning *StreetDance* with such Hollywood teen films, while *StreetDance*'s status as a teen dance film is cemented by the use of promo directors Max Giwa and Dania Pasquini, who had previously directed music videos for British pop groups such as Girls Aloud. Giwa and Pasquini's experience of making music videos makes them ideally placed to direct *StreetDance* as the contemporary dance film evokes music video aesthetics through the use of fast editing and synchronicity between music and image.[69]

Key to the film's mediation of girls' ambitions is its depiction of London, which is presented as cool and glamorous, in keeping with consistent attempts to rebrand the UK as metropolitan and diverse ever since New Labour's 'Cool Britannia' campaign, which emphasized Britain's youthful popular culture.[70] The film's depiction of London is also part of an attempt to 'glocalize' the teen dance film. As Albert Moran argues, 'glocalization' recognizes that audiences identify as both global and local, but tend to prefer 'culturally proximate' films and television.

Global formats, such as the teen dance film, can be 'customised and domesticated for reception and consumption by specific audiences in local or national contexts'.[71] *StreetDance* further 'glocalizes' the dance film through its British cast, particularly their accents, a soundtrack featuring predominantly British artists and the casting of British talent show contestants Diversity, Flawless and George Sampson. *StreetDance* opens with a shot of the London skyline, where landmarks such as the Shard are bathed in the glowing red hue of the sunrise (Figure 2.2). This then leads into the opening title sequence, where we are introduced to the characters who dance at a number of key locations such as outside the Southbank Centre and on a red London bus. As Samantha Colling argues, the metropolitan city plays a crucial role in teen films as an object of glamour, exemplified by the city skyline,[72] which creates what Mary Celeste Kearney refers to as 'environmental' sparkle,[73] a 'key signifier of youthful femininity'.[74] The opening shot of the London skyline also resembles the shot of the New York skyline that is so prominent in US dance films like *Step Up*, which symbolizes the American Dream.[75] Its evocation here suggests that the UK, like America, is a meritocratic society in which anyone can potentially rise to the top, regardless of their background. While emulating the aesthetics of the US teen dance film works to position *StreetDance* as part of a transatlantic flow of

Figure 2.2 *StreetDance* (2010) The London skyline.

youth culture, the fact that the film was a global commercial failure suggests that there is a discrepancy between how Britain wants to be seen and how it is perceived elsewhere.

StreetDance's mediation of aspiration through its depiction of London is also prominent throughout the film's critical reception. There is a mix of surprise and pleasure as film reviewers discuss *StreetDance*'s atypical depiction of London. Tim Robey describes how the film is a 'shamelessly mechanical attempt' to translate the teen dance film to a London setting that is 'wiped free of grot', drawing on the positioning of the film as antithetical to British cinema's common associations with 'gritty' social realism.[76] Other reviewers are more effusive. The *Mirror*'s Mark Adams calls *StreetDance* a 'cool' film that 'makes great use of its London locations';[77] while Maria Duarte goes even further to say that 'London has never looked so good'.[78] This discourse is most overt in Henry Fitzherbert's review for the *Daily Mail*. Fitzherbert reinforces the production discourse that positions the film as a specifically British response to the contemporary Hollywood dance film that subverts expectations of British cinema while also drawing on the film's links with *Britain's Got Talent* in his review, 'Yes, we have talent'. He describes the 'huge novelty of seeing this kind of movie set in Britain, a genre thus far owned by Hollywood', suggesting that British cinema should be praised for its ambitious attempt to compete with Hollywood.[79] Although Fitzherbert, like most reviewers, acknowledges that *StreetDance* is not exactly an original film due to its adherence to the Hollywood teen dance film format, the novelty of a glossy London-set dance film elicits praise and a proud desire to assert that *StreetDance* is a *British* film. It is referred to variously as 'a very British affair'[80] and a 'homegrown hit'.[81] Referring directly to the film's depiction of London, Fitzherbert notes how 'it's a thrill to find London photographed with such appealing slickness, all gleaming skyscrapers and pink skylines, with the "street" portrayed as a place of aspiration as opposed to blood-spattered knife crime'.[82] Once again, *StreetDance* is positioned in opposition to British cinema's typical output. Here, it is contrasted with British films that present urban working-class youth as the victims of poverty and perpetrators of crime, such as *Kidulthood* (Huda 2006) and *Adulthood* (Clarke 2008). Producer James Richardson similarly highlights the desire to portray aspirational youth. He laments that 'so many British films focus on the dark, gritty side of British youth . . . when there are so many positive stories out there', citing the fact that Ashley Banjo from Diversity was studying for a postgraduate degree in physics alongside dancing.[83] Once again, British cinema is associated with grit, which functions as 'shorthand for traditions of realism', from which *StreetDance* is presented as deliberately moving away.[84] Richard Winsor, who plays Tomas, also claims that *StreetDance* represents the '90% of good kids and good youth out there in the UK who really have an aspiration and a desire and a dream to push forward and do something with their lives'.[85] *StreetDance*'s depiction of London – and by extension, Britain – as cool, fun and meritocratic – a city where young people aspire and dreams are fulfilled – is seen to be representative of the majority of young people and subsequently more authentic than the typically 'gritty' explorations of British youth mentioned previously.

As Heather Mendick et al. argue, in the post-financial crash landscape of 'austere meritocracy', neoliberal discourses of aspiration that emphasize the importance of optimism, resilience and hard work have intensified. While effort has 'always been part of the meritocratic equation', they argue, it 'now occupies the prime position as *the* way that success must be achieved, evidenced and legitimised. Hard work is endowed with moral status. If you are not striving for social mobility you are failing in society's expectations and yourself' (original emphasis).[86] Equally within this austere meritocracy, success must be achieved via not only hard work but also authenticity, which is similarly a 'moral imperative that we know and express who we really are'.[87] Both hard work and authenticity offer the promise that this is all that is required to overcome insurmountable disadvantages.[88] These discourses of aspiration that characterize the 'austere meritocracy' circulate throughout the film and its extra-textual materials. The film's production notes provide tips on how to be a successful street dancer, including 'work hard' and 'be yourself' in line with this heightened importance of effort and authenticity.[89] The importance of authenticity to discourses of youth aspiration is also tied to the idea that adolescence is characterized by the search for the authentic self.[90] Nichola Burley draws on this as she describes the film as being 'all about [Carly] finding that inner strength and finding out who she is'.[91] Carly's authenticity is largely situated within her working-class roots, as signified by her northern accent. Burley uses her own Leeds accent in the film, which marks Carly as distinctive from (and more authentic than) her south London crew members and the middle-class ballet dancers. As Su Holmes suggests in regard to British reality television talent shows, class roots are 'used as a guarantor of authenticity' that reinforces the traditional discourses of stardom and celebrity where a star is both special and ordinary.[92] Northern accents in particular are often indicative of working-class roots, and their claims to authenticity are reinforced through their association with British social realist films and television that have traditionally been set in the north of England. The film's production and critical reception discourses, however, suggest that it is the film's explicit *rejection* of British cinema's realist tradition that serves as a marker of authenticity. Moreover, the suggestion that Carly had to leave her northern roots behind and move to London to fulfil her dream reinforces the film's depiction of London as a meritocratic site of aspiration that eludes the social and economic exigencies of those living under austerity, particularly outside of London and the home counties.

StreetDance's aspirational discourses suggest that Carly is able to achieve her dream despite her working-class background because she is represented as being in possession of the intense degree of effort, optimism, resilience and authenticity needed to be successful. As Burley explains: 'She's not had the luckiest of upbringings but, nevertheless, she has always carried on doing it and it's always driven her. She's challenged a lot throughout the film and the exciting and inspiring thing about it is how she overcomes those challenges.'[93] As Mendick et al. argue, within the austere meritocracy, aspiration is seen to emerge from within and is driven by self-knowledge as young people are encouraged to 'follow their dreams' no matter what, which is indicated by Burley's emphasis on Carly's drive and dedication.[94] The importance of psychological characteristics to discourses of aspiration is also indicative of what Rosalind Gill identifies as the intensification of postfeminism as a form of gendered neoliberalism, which is becoming increasingly dependent on a psychological register based on 'cultivating the "right" kinds of dispositions for surviving in neoliberal society', such as aspiration, confidence and resilience.[95]. This emphasis on individual attitude further enables concerns about structural inequality to be swept aside. The idea that a working-class girl like Carly could be held back by economic inequality is only fleetingly explored when the crew cannot afford to rent a rehearsal space. However, her talent is spotted when Helena, the owner of the ballet school, notices her choreography scrawled on the back of a sandwich bag delivered by Carly and offers her the rehearsal space. The film's depiction of Carly's path to success draws on Richard Dyer's 'success myth',[96] where ordinariness is the mark of the star; that lucky breaks may happen to anyone; and hard work and professionalism are necessary for stardom. As Holmes argues, discourses of fame and stardom that are organized through the 'success myth' are also knowingly evoked by television talent shows such as *The X Factor* (ITV 2004–) and *Britain's Got Talent*,[97] and *StreetDance* reinforces the relationship between the teen dance film and television talent shows through the presence of *Britain's Got Talent* contestants Flawless and Diversity. The film also draws on the lexicon of television talent shows, in which taking part is presented as the self-realization of a long-held dream. Such discourses are evident in Carly's opening voice-over:

> Ever since I was a young girl, you'd find me up in my room, dancing in front of the mirror. Carly and her street dance crew smashing it on some stage, the crowd going wild. It kept me going when I left home and came to London, and street dance led me to my new family: my crew. I'm still dancing and dreaming in front of that mirror. It's just, now, I share my dream.

Although she shares her dream with her crew, Carly is still granted heightened individual visibility, as she is singled out at various points in the film. As Colling argues, fun is one of the key pleasures of girl teen films, achieved via 'moments of visibility' and the 'spectacle of the self', which is in keeping with postfeminist girlhood's requirements for visibility and recognition.[98] *StreetDance* utilizes the music video style that is ubiquitous within the contemporary dance film genre that relies on fast editing and a dance performance that is synchronized with an R&B soundtrack to capture Carly rehearsing alone in the dance studio intercut with scenes of her writing choreography at various London locations. The scene is soundtracked by Swiss feat. Music Kidz's 'One in a Million', a song about aspiring, not being 'an average Joe' and working to achieve fame. Carly, too, is one in a million, her star quality is evident through the contradictory qualities of specialness and ordinariness, along with talent and hard work. This scene also draws attention to the contrast between the mediation of young women's ambition in *StreetDance* and *Fish Tank*. Both Mia and Carly are coded as working-class girls with dance ambitions, but Carly's are far more aligned in accordance with can-do girlhood. Mia watches other girls dancing in the car park pretending that they are in a music video and then dances alone and in secret in an empty room, confined in and by her estate that she eventually but ambiguously escapes. Scenes of Carly dancing alone function to highlight her individuality and star quality and Burley is filmed in such a way that she looks as if she is in one of the music videos that the girls in *Fish Tank* are so keen to emulate. The physical effort of dance is similarly glossed over in *StreetDance*, whereas Mia's corporeality is foregrounded through the sound of her heavy breathing. *StreetDance* presents an aspirational meritocracy where a British working-class girl like Carly can escape to the metropolitan city – a site of freedom and visibility – and achieve her dreams as long as she works hard, but the same cannot be said for Mia.

As Jade Boyd has highlighted, 'in these times of global recession, [dance media] perpetuate the myth that failure is an individual problem and success is based on the neoliberal principles of self-discipline, enterprise and productivity' with dance presented as the means for overcoming structural barriers.[99] In *StreetDance*, class is the primary structural barrier faced by Carly and her crew in line with contemporary British cinema's preoccupation with class as a central component of national identity, meaning that racial inequalities and binaries are less evident compared with the Hollywood teen dance film. As Lindner argues, US films such as *Step Up* and *Centre Stage* (Hytner 2000) adhere to binary structures whereby black dancers are depicted pursuing 'sexually suggestive, sensual and assertive' types of dance like hip-hop that 'foreground their exotic temperament and creative intuition' while white female characters pursue ballet, which is associated with upper-class, demure femininity.[100] However, racial binaries are not as evident in *StreetDance*, where a hip-hop crew is led by a white, working-class young woman, and the ballet company is racially diverse. Race is also not remarked upon, unlike class, where to be called 'posh' is an insult and a sign of incompatibility. This class tension is explored in the final dance number, which reflects the overall narrative of the film where the two initially hostile groups learn to work together and Carly is rewarded with a competition win and a heterosexual romance with Tomas. The routine begins with 'Dance of Knights' from Prokofiev's ballet of *Romeo and Juliet*, with Carly lying on a bed until she is lifted by Tomas. The soundtrack merges into dubstep and the rivalry between the two groups is re-enacted through a blending of ballet and street dance, along with Carly and Tomas' Romeo and Juliet–style love story forming from opposing positions. Lindner notes that in the final dance number, the female body 'whose physicality is variously foregrounded in early numbers, is gradually, and literally, converted from "active principle" to "form"'.[101] Although Carly starts the routine in a passive position, her active power is emphasized as she leads the street dance elements of the routine and ends the routine raised on the podium that also functions as the bed at the beginning, positioned above the other dancers. There is a further nod towards gender (and racial) self-reflexivity when Isabel, who is deemed too tall to be a successful ballet dancer, lifts one of the black male street dancers, with a knowing wink to the audience. The final dance number is a 'utopian' celebration of heterosexual romance and the 'overcoming' of differences,[102] and *StreetDance*'s final routine similarly glosses over these differences as the dancers wear matching androgynous white suits that subsume class and gender differences. Indeed, in this aspirational British film, structural barriers are not just glossed over or overcome, but dissolved as if they never existed, through the combination of talent, hard work and young female ambition.

'Top girls', posh girls and *Chalet Girl*(s) (2011)[103]

Tensions between aspiration and the British class system are also explored in Phil Traill's *Chalet Girl* (2011). Nineteen-year-old Kim (Felicity Jones) is a former skateboarding champion who gave up competing after the death of her mother. With her hapless father, William (Bill Bailey), as an unemployed single parent, she takes a job as a chalet girl in an Austrian ski resort where she rediscovers her competitive spirit through snowboarding and falls in love with the chalet owner's son, Jonny (Ed Westwick). The film was produced by the UKFC in association with the Ageis Film Fund. *Chalet Girl* opens with a fictional T4 segment that establishes Kim's backstory. T4 was Channel Four's weekend youth programming strand, which addressed the sixteen to thirty-four demographic and ran from 1998 to 2012.[104] T4 presenters Miquita Oliver and Rick Edwards discuss Kim's former career, where it is revealed that she was a skateboarding prodigy who won a major competition at just eleven years. Kim is positioned as a can-do girl who works hard and achieves her (sporting) goals and who is expected to have a bright future. The tone of the report then changes as they note sadly that Kim has not been seen in skateboarding competitions since the car crash that killed her mother. The scene ends with Oliver addressing Kim directly, with the line: 'Wherever you are, whatever you're doing we hope you're riding high and living the dream.' But Kim is not living the dream; she is working in a fast-food restaurant, lamenting how her 'summer job' became a 'rest-of-my-life job'. This juxtaposition is deliberately comedic, drawing on postfeminist discourses of successful femininity where young women have, as Kim Allen argues, 'become the central figures in propagating the neoliberal dream of upward social mobility'.[105] Young women are encouraged to avoid low-paid, gendered roles and be 'top girls', which, in the UK, was closely tied with New Labour's education policies and a drive to get the majority of young people into higher education.[106] Kim's acknowledgement that her low-paid service work has continued for longer than she had anticipated exposes the limits of the 'top girl' discourse, particularly with the intensification of neoliberalism under austerity that has fuelled precarious working conditions for young people in particular. As Allen argues, the proliferation of insecure and low-paid work like that which Kim is depicted doing during this period has extended to include middle-class graduates and 'points to social and economic conditions that are increasingly shared by working- *and* middle-class youth'.[107]

The 'top girl' discourse circulates prominently around Felicity Jones. The 'top girl' is an 'active and aspirational subject of the education system', the holder of qualifications who embodies the 'meritocratic values that New Labour sought to implement in schools',[108] and Jones is similarly presented as ambitious and aspirational. Jones' 'top girl' status is remarked upon throughout her publicity interviews, which highlight her studious demeanour. *Time Out*'s Cath Clarke notably describes her as processing a 'top-set-in-all-subjects charm'.[109] Others draw attention to the fact that Jones managed to successfully combine studying for a degree at Oxford University while continuing her role as Emma Grundy in BBC Radio 4's *The Archers*, a role she acquired aged fifteen.[110] Jones is positioned as a 'bearer of qualifications', with a degree from a renowned university no less, and an active contributor to the labour market.[111] She also has the aligned ambitions of the can-do girl as she has been crafting her acting career from a young age. Reviewers also praise Jones' successful performance, attributing her with the ability to single-handedly 'save' the film.[112] She is marked as an actress 'heading for the top',[113] and a 'rising star' comparable to fellow young British actor Carey Mulligan,[114] who is also noted for her 'top girl' characteristics, particularly in relation to her role as Jenny in

An Education, as discussed in Chapter 1. Indeed, Jones' star persona in this period is defined by these 'top girl' characteristics, including her roles in *Albatross* (2011), which is discussed in Chapter 3, and as Jane Hawking in *The Theory of Everything* (2015).

While Jones' star persona is firmly located within an ideal white, middle-class British femininity, Kim is depicted as less privileged, described by reviewers as an 'ordinary girl from an ordinary background'.[115] As with *StreetDance*, the culture clash that arises from opposing class positions provides much of the narrative tension. Unlike *StreetDance*, however, the existence and effects of the economic recession are acknowledged, at least initially, via William's unemployment. In both *StreetDance* and *Chalet Girl*, the 'posh' (upper-)middle class characters are open to mockery. When Kim's friend suggests that she takes a job as a chalet girl, the idea is described in a faintly ridiculous tone as 'serving champagne and tiny food to toffs for £12.50 an hour' – and far removed from Kim's experiences. The contrast between Kim's world and the one she is about to inhabit is comedically emphasized when Kim attends the interview for the role of chalet girl. The camera pans down the line of immaculately dressed girls who variously introduce themselves as Arabella, Henrietta, Isabella and Petronella before settling on a casually dressed Kim, who hesitates before saying her name, aware that it sounds out of place. The visual and aural dissonance is played for laughs but Kim is not the butt of the joke; rather, it is the posh girls who we are encouraged to laugh at. When Bella (Jessica Hynes) the interviewer attempts to dismiss Kim, she correctly surmises that her inability to afford a certain type of acceptable middle-class femininity and her appearance have cost her the job: 'I don't have 100 quid highlights, perfect nails or . . . expensively trimmed pubes. So even though I have *actual* experience of an *actual* job in the *actual* real world . . . I'm just not the right kind of girl.' The valuing of appearance over skills and experience is indicative of how, as Brenda R. Weber argues, under the contemporary intensification of neoliberalism, appearance 'functions as an indicator of professional competence' and this 'appearance-based citizenship is crucial for business success' in an increasingly globalized neoliberal economy.[116] Of course, when the desired candidate injures herself at the last minute, Kim is begrudgingly given the job.

Georgie (Tamsin Egerton), however, is the 'right kind' of (chalet) girl but, like her fellow chalet girls, she is initially a comical character, who, unlike Kim, is unaware of her privilege and does not understand the concept of earning and saving money. Egerton is closely associated with playing a particular type of posh, blonde girl who is comically not very intelligent. Reviewers refer to Georgie/Egerton as 'posh totty', which serves as both a character description and a reference to Egerton's earlier role in the *St Trinian's* films discussed in Chapter 1. Georgie and the chalet girls are reminiscent of the upper-middle-class girls who feature in E4's structured reality programme *Made in Chelsea* (2011–), which revolves around the tangled relationships of a group of wealthy and attractive young people in the London borough of Chelsea. As Faye Woods argues, 'the *Made in Chelsea* cast is born into privilege and influence, which the programme luxuriates in while simultaneously undercutting' by displaying the kind of aspirational glamour and wealth that is found in US structured reality programmes like *The Hills* (MTV 2006–2010), but it combines this with comedy and an 'edge of amused mockery' which is 'derived from the cast's lack of intelligence and awkward self-consciousness'.[117] These elements are also evident in *Chalet Girl*, which has a similarly ambivalent relationship to class that is in keeping with contemporary British cinema's girl-centred films through its simultaneous desire to be aspirational while also comedically mocking its privileged upper-class characters, who are treated like outsiders, even though it is Kim who is the outsider in their world.

As with *StreetDance*, *Chalet Girl* seeks to be aspirational in the same manner as Hollywood teen films, and once again, this is considered to be antithetical to British cinema's typical output. As Tamsin Egerton remarks in an interview, the film has 'quite a glossy script for something so British', echoing the tone of surprise found in the critical reception of *StreetDance*, which reinforces the notion that glossy filmmaking and British cinema are mutually exclusive.[118] *Chalet Girl* was filmed on location in Austria, with majestic mountains providing a beautiful glossy backdrop that belies the film's modest £8 million budget. The chalet is owned by Jonny's parents, Richard (Bill Nighy) and Caroline (Brooke Shields) and is far removed from what Kim knows. On seeing the chalet for the first time, Kim asks whether the owner is an 'evil criminal mastermind?' When Georgie replies that he is a banker, Kim sardonically says, 'That's a yes then', perpetuating the film's amused mockery of the wealthy and privileged while also acknowledging the recessionary context through reference to the banking sector's role in the global financial crash. This privilege is also presented as inherently patriarchal and sexist. The wealthy male guests objectify the chalet girls by trying to guess their bra sizes. Georgie shrugs this off as part of the job but Kim gets revenge by pouring hot tea into a man's lap. Kim's refusal to accept sexism points to a broader shift, which Rosalind Gill refers to as 'feminism's new luminosity in popular culture', where online feminist campaigns are part of a reigniting of feminist activism that refuses to accept sexism and harassment in the playful and ironic manner that earlier postfeminist 'lad' culture dictated.[119] By showing that class is no barrier to sexism, this scene also helps to bridge the divide between the two classes by providing renewed sympathy for Georgie and the other chalet girls.

British cinema has an ambivalent relationship with glamour, aspiration and wealth, as *Chalet Girl* demonstrates through its simultaneous desire to create an aesthetically aspirational film in line with the Hollywood sports film, while also expressing suspicion at wealth and privilege. However, aspirational aesthetics and glamour are difficult to achieve without Hollywood levels of funding. Costume designer Leonie Harthard revealed that Brooke Shields had to bring some Hollywood glamour to the film by wearing her own engagement ring because it was bigger and better than anything they could afford to provide, which suggests that there is tension between the British film industry's aspirations and what is actually possible as it will never be able to match Hollywood in terms of funding.[120] The aspirational wealth on display is attributed to economic neoliberalism and is seemingly out of step with, as Kim says, 'the actual real world'. As one of the clients remarks, 'it's as if the global recession is just something that happened to other people'. In this neoliberal postfeminist landscape, investment in consumer culture is mandatory and essential to crafting and maintaining an authentic personal identity.[121] The postfeminist makeover is paramount to enabling and maintaining normative femininity, which is inherently middle class. Initially, working-class Kim is presented as a 'tomboy': she does not wear dresses or make-up, she had previously pursued active sports like skateboarding and even her name is traditionally masculine. This, as Melanie Kennedy suggests, emphasizes not only a 'lack of femininity' on Kim's part but also that she belongs to a 'context after feminism where gender-neutral names are accepted'.[122] Kim's 'tomboy' status is linked to her class status, as Georgie, by comparison, displays typical middle-class femininity through her expensive blonde highlights and branded clothes. Kim's appearance also crucially 'functions as an indicator of professional competence',[123] and, as such, Kim is made to change her appearance and become more feminine under Georgie's direction. Trainers are swapped for high heels and she removes her leggings so that her long top is transformed into a short dress under a soft pink cardigan. Georgie provides Kim with make-up (Figures 2.3 and 2.4). Despite the

Figure 2.3 *Chalet Girl* (2011) Georgie (Tamsin Egerton) gives Kim (Felicity Jones) her make-up.

Figure 2.4 *Chalet Girl* (2011) Kim's makeover.

film's attempts to be aspirational, it is significant that Kim's makeover involves merely adapting the clothes she already owns. The lack of effort required to make Kim 'appropriately feminine' is in keeping with the postfeminist makeover trope, in which as Diane Negra and Brenda R. Weber argue, the makeover simply reveals the authentic feminine self that was inside all along.[124] This simplicity could arguably be attributed to her lack of disposable income as a working-class teenage character. More significantly, it is in keeping with the broader trend identified throughout this book for British cinema's young women to eschew overt consumption, which is seen as gauche and more commonly associated with Hollywood, compared to British cinema's emphasis on 'natural' beauty. As Jackie Stacey argues in her study of female stardom, British actresses are repeatedly attributed with natural beauty and charm in opposition with painted Hollywood glamour.[125] Kim's makeover emphasizes her authentic, natural beauty, which is reinforced by the star discourse surrounding Felicity Jones, which emphasizes her middle-class, 'top girl' charm.

However, *Chalet Girl*'s status as an aspirational sports romantic comedy means that branding and consumption are still integral to the film and its extra-textual materials. First, the casting of Ed Westwick as Jonny brings intertextual connotations of glamour and wealth.

Westwick is arguably most well known for his role in the US teen series *Gossip Girl* (Warner Bros. 2007–2012), which centred around a group of highly affluent teenagers who live in Manhattan's Upper East Side. As Helen Warner argues, *Gossip Girl* was noted for its focus on 'education about, and consumption of, contemporary fashions'.[126] Branding and consumption are also central to the film's marketing and promotional discourses. *Chalet Girl* was the first film to integrate Facebook's 'like' button into an interactive trailer to drive social media engagement, which was hosted on the UKFC site. Clicking on the 'like' button gives audiences access to cast and location information, and highlights brands featured in the film. Jamie Schwarz, vice president of theatrical marketing at Momentum Pictures, explained the reasoning behind the campaign: 'We don't want people to just watch the film's trailer; we want them to get involved, share it with their mates, and to identify themselves with the cool brands it features.'[127] The marketing campaign facilitates and encourages audiences to 'buy into the lifestyle' that is portrayed in the film, reinforcing the idea that consumption is essential to the formulation of a person's self-identity. Similarly, the display of a consumer lifestyle is key to postfeminist can-do girlhood and when Kim decides to enter the snowboarding competition, which has a prize of $25,000, it becomes clear that she must buy the right equipment in order to succeed.[128] This includes buying snowboarding equipment from women's sportswear brand Roxy, which features throughout the film. As Leslie Heywood argues, Roxy embodies the can-do girl ideal because sports associated with Roxy, such as snowboarding, require a 'body that can adapt to any situation', just as the global economy requires young women in particular to adapt to changing parameters.[129] The athletic female body is 'representative of the success a young woman will have in her life, and part of that success is as a member of the consumer culture who consumes [Roxy]'.[130] Participation in consumer culture is, therefore, both necessary for, and a reflection of, successful femininity. In many ways, Kim's success is dependent on her ability to purchase the right equipment that will improve her chances in the competition. She can then use her prize money to maintain this investment in consumer culture. Similarly, the film's interactive marketing campaign encourages the can-do girl in the audience to aspire and participate in consumer culture to ensure her own success.

Kim's success is (temporarily) uncertain, however, as every time she attempts a high jump she is haunted by flashbacks of the car crash that killed her mother. As Melanie Kennedy argues, the biological mother is often absent in teen and tween girl films, and 'the task of becoming the appropriate feminine subject of neoliberalism is all the more difficult without the presence of a biological mother to teach this process ... perpetuat[ing] this requirement to work hard to successfully achieve a neoliberal feminine identity'.[131] This also works to break the mother–daughter bond, preventing the passing down of feminism from mother to daughter.[132] In *Chalet Girl*, however, Kim's mother leads Kim to the success that enables her to discover her 'true' self, as she recalls her mother quoting Dr Seuss: 'You have brains in your head, you have feet in your shoes, you can steer yourself any way you choose.'[133] She also imagines her mum in the crowd waving a 'Go Kim' banner, which enables her to complete the highest jump and win the competition. Samantha Colling argues that in the twenty-first-century teen girl film, the protagonist's transformation is brought about 'through self-governance and product consumption; crafted by the magic of the commercial sphere' rather than the power of maternal love, as was previously the case in Cinderella narratives.[134] In *Chalet Girl*, however, the power of maternal love, even after death, still holds transformative potential.[135] This also means that the mother–daughter bond is not entirely broken, which allows for the passing down of feminism that is arguably in keeping with the increased visibility of feminism within British culture more broadly. The Dr Seuss reference is appropriated here to convey the myth of the neoliberal can-do girl through the suggestion that all a girl needs to succeed is determination because she is autonomous and responsible for her own life through the choices she makes.

Kim's status as a 'can-do' girl is cemented when she wins the competition – along with the $25,000 prize money – and enters into a romantic relationship with Jonny. Within contemporary girl films, the acquisition of a heterosexual romance is the 'prize' for successfully performing femininity and *Chalet Girl* is no exception.[136] Kim also wins the approval of Jonny's parents and gains acceptance and entry into their affluent upper-middle-class world. The narrative resolution emphasizes that through her determination, good choices and consumption, Kim has (re)discovered her 'true self'. Diane Negra observes how 'the postfeminist subject is represented as having lost herself but then (re)achieving stability' and in the final scene of *Chalet Girl*, Kim is interviewed by Miquita Oliver in the T4 studio, who congratulates her for winning the competition and for having a 'hot boyfriend', thus for achieving ideal postfeminist femininity and proving her worth.[137] This scene completes the circular nature of the film by recalling the opening scene in which Oliver and Edwards lamented Kim's absence from the competition. Now, Kim has meaningful visibility; she has been 'found' and she is present in the studio, complete with wealth and a boyfriend. In entering this new middle-class world, therefore, it is not that Kim has abandoned her previous life, but that she has simply, and inevitably, rediscovered her status as a successful girl.

'This is my time now': *Fast Girls* (2012)

British cinema turned to women's athletics in June 2012 with *Fast Girls*, designed to capitalize on the forthcoming London 2012 Olympic Games. *Fast Girls* follows the classic underdog sports film narrative. Shania Andrews (Lenora Crichlow) is a 22-year-old, unfunded, working-class, mixed-race athlete, who lives on a council estate in east London and trains with local shopkeeper Brian (Phill Davis). Shania gets spotted by the World Athletics team coach, Tommy (Noel Clarke), and is asked to join Britain's relay team when she subsequently narrowly beats golden girl Lisa Temple (Lily James). By contrast, Lisa is highly privileged; her father is a former gold medal–winning athlete who now runs British athletics. The girls develop an immediate rivalry before overcoming their differences and learning to work together for the good of the team. *Fast Girls* presents a feel-good narrative where sport acts as a panacea for social issues, and class inequalities can be eradicated through sporting success. In doing so, the film perpetuates the discourse surrounding the mediation of the London 2012 Olympic Games. As John Vincent et al. argue, the London 2012 Olympic Games were largely viewed as an opportunity to '(re)imagine and update British identity' that combined the internationalization of the Olympics with a 'new vision of Britishness that emphasized inclusion, openness tolerance and creativity' that could be viewed as an extension of New Labour's 'Cool Britannia' campaign discussed earlier.[138] At the centre of this attempt to re-energize the 'British brand' was a bid to transform a multicultural and socially deprived area of east London – the same area that Shania lives and trains in – with state-of-the-art sport facilities in the hope of encouraging participation in grassroots sport during a period of increasing depravation in such areas, which has been prolonged by the effects of austerity.[139]

Recognizing the timely potential of their idea in 2010, the production team worked quickly to bring the film to audiences by June 2012 to coincide with the Olympics, with shooting completed within six weeks in winter 2011. The film was backed by the BFI Film Fund, StudioCanal and Aegis and developed by the UKFC, and was a deliberate attempt to attract British youth audiences on the back of films such as *Kidulthood* and *Adulthood* and the highly successful *StreetDance*.[140] The production team was well placed for this, with Noel Clarke, who directed *Adulthood* (and later, the girl-centred crime thriller *4.3.2.1* [2012]), co-scripting and starring in the film, along with producer Damian Jones, whose producer credits include a number of female-led films such as *Very Annie Mary* (Sugarman 2001), *The Iron Lady* (Lloyd 2011), *Powder Room* (Delaney 2013) and *Belle* (Asante 2013). Like the producers of *StreetDance*, Jones also acknowledges the desire to create an aspirational and inspirational feel-good film. Director Regan Hall was chosen at the suggestion of the UKFC for this purpose due to his background in fashion commercials for luxury fashion brands such as Dolce & Gabbana and Swarovski. The film's production notes construct a remarkably similar production discourse to *StreetDance*, in which the film is positioned as the antithesis of 'typical' dark and gritty British films, particularly those that depict young people. As Jones asserts, 'It was never going to be a grimy version of Britain with Regan at the helm – it was always going to be heightened and celebratory.'[141] This discourse is also taken up within the film's critical reception. Writing in the *Sunday Mercury*, Graham Young enthuses about how *Fast Girls* is a 'hugely pleasant change from watching just another London estate drama about gangs wanting to kill each other', furthering this idea that *Fast Girls* represents a move away from 'typical' realist representations of young people in contemporary British films which focus on social issues such as crime and gang culture, for example Clarke's *Kidulthood*.[142]

As well as positioning *Fast Girls* as a move away from British cinema's usual output, the critical reception discourse also frames the film as a sporty girl power film in the manner of *Bend It Like Beckham*. This comparison is somewhat inevitable given that both films focus on young women who have to overcome various social barriers to achieve sporting success. As discussed in the introduction, Justine Ashby has notably argued that *Bend It Like Beckham* reflected the 'snug' fit between postfeminism and the New Labour government, as both were couched in a language of modernization, self-confidence and equality, with New Labour rhetoric dovetailing with and being reflected by postfeminist notions of girl power.[143] *Bend It Like Beckham*, Ashby argues, 'frames questions of racial and sexual identity in an upbeat postfeminist idiom' while assuaging a number of the more fraught social issues.[144] For the middle-class protagonists of *Bend It Like Beckham*, it is their 'laughably *prefeminist*' mothers who are the biggest threat to their sporting ambitions.[145] *Fast Girls* contains a similarly upbeat, postfeminist message, but it is class, rather than gender or race, that is the most significant structural barrier. Throughout the film, it is Shania's status as a working-class athlete that poses the biggest threat to her sporting ambitions, even if this is eventually overcome in accordance with the film's feel-good narrative. Like *Chalet Girl*, *Fast Girls* is situated within a post-crash Britain, where economic inequalities are more apparent.

Fast Girls engages with class from the outset, immediately establishing Shania and Lisa's opposing class positions. Shania is coded as an 'at-risk' girl (Harris 2004): she lives on a council estate with her aunt following the death of her mother, and trains on a derelict racetrack in battered trainers (spikes) because she cannot afford new ones. *Fast Girls* initially evokes a similar British realist mode to *Fish Tank*. Like Mia, Shania is energetic and unpolished in her east London dialect, seeking an escape through running. When we are introduced to Lisa, the mise en scène becomes brighter as she is in her bedroom in her parents' suburban home, surrounded by trophies and medals. She is evidently a can-do girl who plans her goals and achieves them, and is able to take advantage of family resources and buy the latest equipment. The contrast between the two characters is also established throughout the critical reception. Shania is referred to as 'feisty' or 'talented', whereas Lisa is referred to as 'ambitious', which is often included alongside 'middle class' and 'posh'.[146] Ambition, therefore, is presented as a specifically middle-class trait in keeping with aspirational discourses which construct the aspirational subject within the 'image of the middle class'.[147] Lisa's middle-class status is further emphasized through references to her 'blonde ponytail', as blonde hair is a typical marker of ideal postfeminist femininity.[148] The fact that Lily James was asked to dye her hair for the role suggests that blondness is a deliberate character trait. Although a natural brunette, James is perhaps most recognizable as a blonde in roles such as Lady Rose in the period drama *Downton Abbey* between 2012 and 2015, and as the blonde icon of contemporary girlhood Cinderella in Kenneth Branagh's (2015) film. James is, as Melanie Williams argues, part of the 'reiterative middle-class whiteness' that is characteristic of contemporary British female stardom, along with other actors such as Felicity Jones and Keira Knightley.[149]

Moreover, middle-class femininity is always coded as respectable, whereas working-class femininity is typically associated with vulgarity.[150] Shania's lack of respectability and 'vulgar' femininity are evident when she gets drunk at a networking event with potential sponsors. Lenora Crichlow's performance indicates Shania's insecurity and self-consciousness through excessive drinking and constantly tugging at her dress to try and make it seem longer than it is. Shania's working-class identity hampers her ability to be an aspirational subject because this relies on the ability not only to access resources but also to know 'how to display one's subjectivity properly', which is knowledge that Shania lacks.[151] Much like Mia, Shania's feelings boil over into aggression, particularly when Lisa criticizes her for getting drunk the night before a race. Shania's behaviour is indicative of a lack of self-responsibility that is crucial to successful girlhood and a sign of 'failed' femininity. The film also explores the intersections between class, gender and race, where Shania's working-class identity is viewed as a more significant barrier to her career than race. As Shania is getting ready for the networking event, her sister Tara (Tiana Benjamin) warns her not to get her hopes up. Shania assumes that this is a warning about racial inequality in sport and attempts to reassure Tara that 'lots of black athletes get funding' to which Tara replies: 'Yeah but they don't look like you. This event will be full of rich white men and you've got Primark written all over you.' While racial inequality in sport is acknowledged, class and access to resources are seen as a bigger barrier to success. The acknowledgement that Shania's future career is dependent on 'rich white men' exposes the limits of the individualistic neoliberal 'choice biography' in a capitalist society that denies structural barriers, so that the working-class subject can only display 'lack'.[152] Furthermore, associating Shania with the low-budget clothing store Primark reinforces her lack of middle-class respectability. Louise Wilks argues that stores like Primark have helped cultivate a 'Primarni culture' in the UK by enabling girls to participate in fashion and consumer culture on a limited budget.[153] (Primarni is a portmanteau of Primark and Armani.) This is in keeping with British articulations of postfeminism that for the most part eschew conspicuous consumption and designer branding. Here, however, Primark is evoked negatively as an indicator of low economic status and an inappropriate and insufficient route to respectable femininity.

While race is less of a barrier to achievement than class within the film's narrative, the production discourse highlights the wider issue of the lack of diversity within the British film industry. In the production notes, Damian Jones discusses the challenges involved in the production, including having to 'sell the idea of a mixed race lead actress'. Jones also claims that 'I think we're quite possibly the first major feature film in the UK to have a mixed race female lead', suggesting that the UK film industry, like the athletics body in the film, is led by 'rich white men'.[154] Out of the six lead actresses who play members of the relay team, only Lily James is white and the film's racial diversity was welcomed by reviewers. Cath Clarke sums this up in her review for *Time Out*: 'While this isn't a film about race, the leads do happen to be black or mixed race. Nice to see black women centre screen for a change . . . how depressing to even notice.'[155]

Although *Fast Girls* engages with class inequality, and race to a lesser extent, the producers' primary motivation was to create a celebratory inspirational film. Discourses of aspiration and inspiration circulate around the film in its promotional materials, contributing to the film's mediation of the ambitious girl. In an interview for the *Birmingham Evening Mail*, Lorraine Burroughs, who plays Trix Warren, discussed the gruelling regime the cast were forced to adopt. This included a 'six-week training camp, led by real-life sprinters Jeanette Kwakye and Shani Anderson . . . thousands of sit-ups', painful injuries and a rigid diet.[156] This emphasis on physical effort and transformation suggests that the film's depiction of female athleticism is authentic, while also demonstrating ambition and determination. Director Regan Hall notes, for example, that 'Lily [James] worked incredibly hard to bring her body into sprinter form . . . she was in the corner doing sit-ups just before going on camera and her hard work really shows on screen'.[157] Comments on James' dedication to achieving the ideal athletic female body demonstrate the intertwining of her character's ambition and her own can-do persona as an example of how girls' ambitions are mediated as part of a flow of discourses within and around the film.[158] Moreover, in a similar manner to *StreetDance*, the *Fast Girls* production notes also address the potential can-do girls in the audience, encouraging them to 'get as fit as the Fast Girls'. This feature includes advice from aforementioned professional athletes Kwakye and Anderson, like the exercise tips that call – rather ambitiously – for 600–800 sit-ups a day.[159]

In the current neoliberal context, women athletes are required to be glamorous as well as physically fit. Samantha Colling and Katharina Lindner highlight the glamorization of female athlete characters in contemporary sports films, and the media more broadly, where 'representations of women in sport also compulsively re-frame the female athletic body by focusing on the athletes' sex appeal rather than their performance'.[160] This is also apparent within a British context. The beauty industry utilized endorsements with British athletes in the lead up to, during and after London 2012, such as Jessica Ennis-Hill's work as a brand ambassador for cosmetics brand Olay. As part of her role, Ennis-Hill claimed she always wears make-up for a race in order to feel more confident and complete, suggesting there is a link between looking good (and appropriately feminine) and professional success.[161] This is also depicted in the film when Belle (Lashana Lynch) defends her decision to apply make-up before a race by asserting 'I look good and I run fast'. The inextricable relationship between physical power and glamour is shored up by the choice of Regan Hall as director due to his background in fashion commercials. Hall used various techniques to attempt to create a bright and glamorous aesthetic on a relatively small budget, such as using long lenses and high-key lighting, ensuring that outdoor scenes were shot towards the sunlight despite the fact that filming took place during a typical British winter.[162] As Lorraine Burroughs revealed, 'He has all these tricks like telling you to put your chin in a direction which suddenly makes you look like Cleopatra but you'd have never thought to do that yourself. It's amazing!'[163] This evocation of Cleopatra, an icon of glamorous femininity, reiterates the importance of glamour to representations of female athleticism, and this glamour is seemingly easy to achieve – as simple as moving one's chin. This emphasis on glamour exists in tension with earlier discourses of authenticity and displaying a 'realistic' athletic body. As Katharina

Lindner argues, this is part of the 'careful monitoring of the female body' in sports films, which serves to allay fears over 'masculinization'.[164] It is also, Lindner suggests, linked to the wider postfeminist culture that constructs 'femininity as a bodily property that needs to be continually "worked on", monitored and controlled' in order to be successful.[165]

In her analysis of contemporary female sports films, Lindner argues that the protagonists tend to be 'cut off' from other female characters, and often there is no hint of the bonding or shared achievement that sports can provide, which is in keeping with the depoliticized and individualistic postfeminist cultural context.[166] In teen girl films, however, as Samantha Colling notes, collective sports performances offer 'an experience of muscular bonding among girls: moments of felt partnership, affiliation and alliance'.[167] In *Fast Girls*, much of the narrative hinges on these two tropes. Initially, Shania and Lisa are rivals, and their ambition is presented as an individual endeavour as Lisa 'doesn't come to make friends' and Shania is 'not good in teams'. The film also implies that this individualism is built into the athletics world as the relay team is underfunded because team sports are not funded as much as individual pursuits. However, in a critique of individualistic ambition, the girls are unsuccessful until they learn how to work as a team and incorporate each other's strengths. Bonding mostly takes place off the track, such as during a girls' night out. Here, there is a similar but much more emphatic critique of misogynistic behaviour that was present in *Chalet Girl*, which suggests that girls should not have to accept this behaviour as if they are ironically 'in on the joke' and always present themselves as 'up for it', as earlier incarnations of postfeminism dictated.[168] When Lisa is subjected to unwanted male attention, the girls fight back and the gang of boys chase them down the street. Of course, the girls outrun them. They take off their high heels and hold them like a baton as they sprint down the street in a celebratory slow-motion sequence that allows the film to offer a critique while still maintaining its feel-good essence. In this scene, they are truly united for the first time. The scene was singled out in reviews as a 'memorable sequence' and the highlight of the film.[169] A review in the *Daily Telegraph* ruminates on how 'In another British urban drama, those yobs might be snarling anti-heroes, but here they're rightly relegated to a punchline', reinforcing British cinematic discourses that continuously frame British cinema as primarily concerned with stories about working-class men, and positioning *Fast Girls* as a welcome move away from this through its celebratory girl power narrative.[170]

Shania and Lisa continue to bond off the track when Shania takes Lisa to an underground car park to rehearse. This is a far cry from the corporate stadiums that Lisa is used to and it provides a more neutral space where class divisions and rivalries are dissolved in favour of teamwork and friendship.[171] The scene includes a training montage – a staple of the sports film – where Lisa and Shania practise passing the baton repeatedly and Lisa concedes that she must give up her prominent position as anchor in order to play to Shania's strengths and ensure the team's success.[172] Through its mediation of girls' ambitions, *Fast Girls* is ultimately critical of individualism, which is presented as inherently patriarchal. This is exemplified by Lisa's father (Rupert Greaves), who is determined that his daughter should replicate his success. Anything less than a gold medal is not good enough and he tells Lisa that 'this is our last chance'. However, her new friendship with Shania enables Lisa to ignore his advice and do what is best for the whole team, telling him, 'This is my time now.' Lisa's main source of support is actually her mother Ellie (Emma Fielding), who tells her that as long as she tries her best then it does not matter if she is not *the* best. As mentioned, mothers are typically absent in the teen girl film and those who are present are often a hindrance to their daughters' 'becoming'. However, *Fast Girls*, like *Chalet Girl*, marks a move away from this in its evocation of the supportive mother who is key to the protagonist's 'becoming' and success. In *Fast Girls*, this also shores up the distinction between patriarchal individualism and female (feminist) collectively. It is also, significantly, her mother whom Lisa runs to when the relay team win the final race at the end of the film. After hugging her mother, Lisa joins her euphoric teammates and they stand together with the Union Jack draped across their shoulders (Figure 2.5). This image, like the

Figure 2.5 *Fast Girls* (2012) The final relay.

film as a whole, is a celebration of Britishness, with Britain represented as a multicultural utopia where issues of class and race are rendered invisible thanks to hard work and team spirit.

Sporting success

The contemporary girl-centred British sports film functions as a key site for the mediation of discourses of girls' ambitions. The films themselves are varied, from commercially orientated films targeted at youth audiences to films more closely associated with realist modes of filmmaking. While it is important not to overlook the nuances, a number of similarities can be identified in relation to the mediation of girlhood ambition. Class is a prominent component that is explored via the working-class protagonist, and is presented – more so than race – as a significant barrier to success that is eventually overcome through displaying neoliberal can-do girl qualities such as hard work and resilience. The protagonist is rewarded with entry into a middle-class world, which is cemented by the acquisition of a middle-class male partner, as is the case in *StreetDance*, *Chalet Girl* and *Fast Girls*. Even where this is not possible, as in *Fish Tank*, there is nevertheless a sense of optimism that is furthered by the critical reception discourses that position the film as elevated beyond typical depictions of 'broken

Britain' through poetic realist aesthetics. This is reinforced by the narrative surrounding Katie Jarvis, in which she is transformed from an at-risk educational failure to a can-do girl determined to make the most of the opportunity she has been given. Similarly, although *Chalet Girl* and *Fast Girls* display unease about overt consumption via their acknowledgement of the socio-cultural and economic context of British austerity, and economic inequality and its impact upon working-class girls' ambitions, this is ultimately glossed over. Aspiration is central to the production, marketing and reception discourses of films such as *StreetDance*, *Chalet Girl* and *Fast Girls*, where glossy and aspirational aesthetics are discussed as a deliberate and welcome move away from the unambitious and also masculine-coded 'grittiness' that is viewed as a defining component of British cinema, enabling the films not only to mediate discourses of girls' ambitions but also to demonstrate the ambition of the British film industry itself.

Girl friendship and the formation
of feminine identity

Despite the dominance of the individualistic, hypervisible can-do girl figure, female friendship is key to postfeminist culture. As Alison Winch argues, in postfeminist 'girlfriend culture', same-sex friendship is essential in enabling normative femininity.[1] Girlfriend culture in adult women's media, Winch argues, presents girl friendship as strategic, offering the possibility of 'representability' (Negra 2009) and hypervisibility through mutual bodily surveillance via the 'girlfriend gaze', which is configured as entrepreneurial and empowering in keeping with the neoliberal postfeminist discourse of the self as a project that must be constantly worked upon.[2] Girlfriend media are also contradictory; offering the pleasure of belonging while also 'enacting surveillance and cruelty', which is reconfigured as solidarity.[3] Female friendship is not just central to adult women's media, however, as Mary Celeste Kearney argues that, since the 1990s, films centred around teen girls have foregrounded the development of self-identity and same-sex friendship rather than heterosexual relationships.[4] Looking beyond media culture, feminist sociologist Valerie Hey also emphasizes the importance of friendship to the development of girls' identities. Hey's ethnographic study of girls' friendships draws attention to how the 'pleasures and pain' of girl friendship contribute significantly to girls' constructions of themselves as girls on a daily basis.[5]

Contemporary British cinema's depictions of girl friendship similarly highlight the importance of same-sex friendship to the formation of feminine identity as the girl protagonists frequently undergo transformations through their friendship that, it is suggested, will have a fundamental impact upon their sense of self. Significantly, however, they often trouble the idea that female friendships yield the 'representability' and 'hypervisibility' that Winch argues are offered by girlfriend culture. This ambiguity, I argue, is in part grounded in British cinema's pervasive consciousness of, and concern about, class as a prominent and insurmountable barrier. Rather than friendships between groups of girls, the films discussed in this chapter – *Me Without You* (Goldbacher 2001), *Kicks* (Heymann 2008), *Albatross* (MacCormick 2011) and *My Summer of Love* (Pawlikowski 2004) – explore friendship between pairs of girls – typically one working-class girl and one middle-class girl – embarking on intense friendships that are exclusionary and closed off from outside influences. This emphasis on the construction of close, emotionally intense and passionate friendships between pairs of girls that are a rite of passage is reminiscent of the sentimental female friendship film that Karen Holinger outlines in her taxonomy of the genre, although British cinema's girl friendships lack sentimentality because they are highly ambivalent and ambiguous.[6] While in girlfriend culture, conflict is resolved through the 'childhood fantasy of "just being good friends"',[7] where power hierarchies are subsumed into a sentimental version of girlhood and idealized feminine relationships, in contemporary British girl friendship films, conflicts between girlfriends often relate to class and thus are not so easily resolved, and the films typically dwell on the shifting power dynamics of the pairs of friends. As such, the friendships themselves are often depicted in ambiguous ways. These ambivalent depictions of girl friendship locate the films within the broader context of the British woman's film, which, Melanie Bell and Melanie Williams argue, is often concerned with the 'pleasures and perils of female friendship'.[8]

The girl friendships depicted in these films are furthermore situated within what I call a retrospective girlhood framework that dominates the production discourse. As Timothy Shary argues, all films featuring young protagonists can, to an extent, be considered to be looking back into the past as they are made by adults who are potentially reflecting on their own experiences.[9] This backward glance is particularly overt in

British cinema's depiction of girl friendships. *Me Without You* evokes this notion of retrospective girlhood via an emphasis on autobiography and authorship, which are seen to enhance the authenticity of its depiction of girl friendship in a way that is intrinsic to the film's Britishness, while *My Summer of Love* evokes this retrospective girlhood trope via its timeless setting that suggests it is representing an essential 'truth' about girl friendship. Even *Kicks*, which is firmly situated within millennial celebrity culture, evokes this trope to support its feminist critique of celebrity culture. This looking back, however, does not necessarily equate with sentimentality. Indeed, British cinema's depictions of girl friendship are largely unsentimental. This is particularly true of *Me Without You*, to which I now turn.

'I don't know who I am when I'm not us': *Me Without You* (2001)

Me Without You tells the story of two girl friends – bookish and thoughtful Holly (Michelle Williams) and extrovert Marina (Anna Friel). The film follows the girls' friendship from their childhoods in the 1970s, through university and into adulthood. Holly and Marina's lives are intertwined but their friendship becomes increasingly claustrophobic. The film ends in 2001, when Marina and Holly are both married with children. *Me Without You* is directed by Sandra Goldbacher, who had previously directed the BAFTA award-winning *The Governess* starring Minnie Driver (1998). Goldbacher co-wrote the film with Laurence Coriat, who wrote the original story of *Kicks* (2008), which is discussed later in this chapter. The film was produced by Momentum Pictures, with the participation of BskyB.

As I have argued, the notion of retrospective girlhood is key to contemporary British cinema's depictions of girl friendship, and this is particularly apparent throughout *Me Without You* and its production and critical reception discourses. In an article written for the *Guardian*, director Sandra Goldbacher claims that the film is semi-autobiographical; an 'unsentimental film about the complications of women's friendship' that was inspired by her being 'haunted' by an 'early passionate friendship with a girl I haven't seen for over 20 years but who I have dreamt about constantly'.[10] In positioning the film as semi-autobiographical, Goldbacher also draws on and reinforces dominant ideas about the intensity of girls' friendship and its enormous significance on identity. Goldbacher's admission that she was 'haunted' by her girlhood friendship is reminiscent of Hey's assertion that adult women are ideologically encouraged to supress their memories of these intense girlhood friendships as 'merely a phase'. However, these formative memories cannot always be supressed, returning the woman to the difficult 'terrain of loss and recollection'.[11] That Goldbacher's early friendship was highly influential is evident through the connotations of authorship and autobiography that are threaded throughout the film, particularly within the film's aesthetics, where each decade is split into chapters, with the year appearing in a handwritten-style font, drawing on the iconography of a teenage diary. Later on, it is revealed that the adult Holly is writing a book about her experiences, which establishes her as the 'me' of the film's title and further develops the autobiographical link with Goldbacher as the writer-director. For the reviewers, the fact that Goldbacher is writing from experience imbues the film with authenticity that 'seeps from the pore of each set, costume and piece of dialogue'[12] with 'wincingly funny precision'.[13] Goldbacher is credited with creating a 'truth-ringing account'[14] of female friendship that is 'original'[15] and realistic. This authenticity is also seen as inextricably British. A review in the *Birmingham Evening Post* notes how 'Goldbacher sensibly keeps the film grounded in British reality without ever letting it become too fanciful or depressing' and does not try to be 'anything but itself'.[16] At the same time as being received as authentically British, *Me Without You* is also seen as a welcome surprise. Writing in the *Mail on Sunday*, Jason Solomon describes the film as 'bold' and 'refreshingly confident',[17] while *Time Out*'s Tom Charity notes how the film 'exudes an intelligence and emotional maturity all too rare

in British cinema'.[18] There are echoes here of the critical reception of
StreetDance in Chapter 2, where British cinema is synonymous with
gritty, dour and unambitious filmmaking, and attempts to move away
from this are received enthusiastically. Furthermore, *Me Without You*'s
highly praised authenticity is reinforced through its position as an
atypical 'chick flick'. Drawing on implicitly derogatory perceptions of
the chick flick as a low-brow woman's genre dependent on emotional
excess, the *Sunday Times*' critic Cosmo Landesman praises the film for
avoiding 'soppy female solidarity',[19] and in doing so, further highlights
the lack of sentimentality within British cinema's depictions of female
friendship, while another reviewer credits the film with 'giving the chick
flick a good name'.[20] The film is also linked to another key British chick
flick – *Bridget Jones' Diary* (Maguire 2001) – which was released around
the same time. Writing in the *Derby Evening Telegraph*, Ashley Franklin
suggests that *Me Without You* might appeal to those women who did
not like *Bridget Jones' Dairy* because *Me Without You* is 'vibrant', the
'grittier "diary"' of the two, reinforcing the idea that *Me Without You*
offers a more realistic and bold depiction of female friendship that
makes it a superior chick flick.[21]

   Me Without You opens in 1975 when Holly and Marina are children.
Scenes of the girls playing together in the garden dissolve into one
another, creating a sense of the never-ending idyllic summers that seem
to exist only in childhood. The dichotomies between Holly and Marina
are established from the beginning, as Marina instructs a blindfolded
Holly to step over a glass tumbler without smashing it. When Holly
hesitates, Marina asks, 'What's the matter? Don't you trust me?' Marina
is established as the confident leader who expects Holly to blindly
follow her. The construction of Marina and Holly as opposites also
features heavily within the critical reception. Anna Friel, as Marina, is
described as 'flighty' and 'flirty',[22] 'adventurous' and 'selfish';[23] the 'sexier
best mate'.[24] Friel's 'sexy' persona is reinforced through references
to her career-making role in the Channel Four soap opera *Brookside*
(1982–2003), where she played Beth Jordache from 1993 to 1995. In
1993, Friel caused controversy when her character was involved in the

first pre-watershed lesbian kiss on British television.[25] This is teasingly referred to in Jason Solomons' review, where he says, 'Oh, that Anna Friel, she is one for same-sex kisses'.[26] By contrast, Michelle Williams' Holly is referred to as 'thoughtful, bookish and romantic',[27] 'dowdy'[28] and 'mousy and submissive'.[29] Like Friel's role in *Brookside*, references are made to Williams' well-known role in US teen drama *Dawson's Creek* (1998–2003). *Dawson's Creek* was known for its serious and brooding tone, characteristics which are seen to feed into the character of Holly.[30] Williams is deemed 'impressive'[31] and 'simply extraordinary'[32] for her ability to adopt a credible British accent, which also furthers the authenticity discourse that runs throughout the critical reception.

As the film moves on to 1978, Holly and Marina are depicted during their teenage years, trying to alleviate the suffocating boredom of suburbia and negotiating their emergent sexualities. Looking (but not necessarily being) sexually experienced is presented as a key concern, and looking sexually inexperienced is the ultimate insult, such as when Marina tells Holly, 'You should dye your hair, Holly, you look like a virgin.' This line is evocative of the 'normative cruelties' that Emma Renold and Jessica Ringrose argue are key to performing normative subject positions for girls, and girls are socially sanctioned to express this meanness primarily through 'subtle and direct regulation of other girls' sexuality'.[33] In performing this 'normative cruelty', Marina is asserting her power and attempting to position herself as hypervisible through the inference that, unlike Holly, she does not look like a virgin, even though she is. Being referred to as a 'slut' is also part of this socially sanctioned meanness, which emphasizes the contradictions inherent in constructing idealized young femininity: appearing to be overtly and excessively sexually experienced is not appropriate but neither is looking completely inexperienced. While Marina employs normative cruelties in an attempt to become hypervisible, Holly strives for 'representability' through emulating Marina, such as wearing identical goth outfits made out of black bin liners to a party. As Hey argues, this mirroring is indicative of the intensity of girls' friendships and their 'vested interest in reproducing themselves as mirroring their friends'.[34]

As they get older, Marina and Holly continue to mirror each other – or rather, they try to assimilate aspects of the other's identity. When they both fall for their university lecturer, Daniel (Kyle MacLachlan), they each attempt to become hypervisible to him. Marina tries to impress Daniel by naming Ingmar Bergman films she knows through Holly, but the limits of her knowledge are exposed, making her look stupid. Holly, meanwhile, tries on one of Marina's dresses in an attempt to look more like her but quickly decides not to wear it, suggesting that, unlike Marina, Holly's identity is stable and authentic. Holly and Marina do not overtly compete with each other for Daniel's attention; instead, they rely on more subtle attempts to regulate each other's behaviour in accordance with postfeminist girlfriend culture, such as when Marina convinces Holly not to go to a party she knows Daniel will attend.

As Rosalind Gill argues, in postfeminist culture, a woman's body is the 'key (if not sole) source of her identity', and for the girl in particular, (hyper-)visibility is achieved via the body.[35] Marina's appearance changes throughout the film as part of her continuous attempt to become hypervisible (Figure 3.1). During the middle third

Figure 3.1 *Me Without You* (2001) Marina's (Anna Friel) changing appearance.

of the film, which is set during Holly and Marina's university years in 1982, Marina wears a large leopard-print coat, with long, bleached hair with dark roots, which are often signifiers of working-class femininity, along with promiscuity, even though she is constructed as middle class through her accent and education. Her costumes also reference Madonna's pop persona in the 1980s and draws comparisons with the film *Desperately Seeking Susan* (Seidelman 1985), which, like *Me Without You*, presents the friendship between two women within a good girl/bad girl pairing. *Desperately Seeking Susan* pairs two young women who are presented as opposites when dissatisfied housewife Roberta (Rosanna Arquette) meets free-spirited Susan (Madonna), who is characterized by her bleached hair, vintage clothes, black lingerie and costume jewellery. The film similarly plays on elements of mirroring and emulating after Roberta gets mistaken for Susan when she is wearing Susan's jacket.

The emphasis placed on Marina's appearance is indicative of conceptualizations of the reflexive self in which the self is constructed from a variety of available options and primarily signified through appearance. In making these choices, however, one must be authentic and work to construct a meaningful narrative of the self.[36] Mariana's changing appearance, however, is presented as inauthentic, particularly when positioned in relation to Holly, whose appearance does not change significantly. This consistency is an indicator of Holly's authenticity as she remains 'true to herself'.

Marina's ability to 'make' herself is rewarded in adulthood when – now styled as a femme fatale of film noir – she gets a seemingly glamorous job in the then-burgeoning area of music video production, which is indicative of her presentation as the ideal self-regulating and calculating neoliberal subject, which is deemed essential for success.[37] Holly, meanwhile, is a writer who feels trapped in her tiny apartment and is 'waiting to transmute into a successful adult'. This line articulates a common postfeminist anxiety, where, as Tasker and Negra note, 'female adulthood is defined as a chronic state of temporal neurosis',[38] which involves making the 'right' choices, at the right time, out of a supposed wealth of options available to women today – something which Holly feels she has been unable to do. In prioritizing Holly's subjectivity as the writer of the text, however, the film suggests that she is more successful because she has remained authentically 'true to herself'. In adulthood, Holly and Marina's friendship is presented as increasingly claustrophobic, an 'assemblage of "ugly feelings"' (Ngai 2005) such as shame, jealousy and inferiority that Ringrose and Walkerdine argue circulate in relations between women.[39] Holly confronts Marina with these 'ugly feelings', telling her: 'I don't want to be us anymore. I feel ugly, and suffocated, and not good enough.' Marina also admits to feeling 'disgusting' but, unlike Holly, she is unwilling to end their friendship, continuing to regulate Holly by threatening to kill herself if Holly leaves her. Marina tells her: 'There's no me without you' and 'I don't know who I am when I'm not us.' Marina's sense of identity is inextricably linked to her friendship with Holly and she needs Holly to remain the thoughtful and quiet one in order to achieve hypervisibility. Holly, however, responds with, 'I don't know who I am ever.' Despite this declaration, the film makes it clear that Holly does have a strong sense of her own identity because she rarely attempts to change: she is true to herself. Holly is thus rewarded for being 'authentic' as by the film's denouement she is happily married to Nat and they have a family in adherence with postfeminist femininity, which reinstates marriage and motherhood as the ideal. Marina, however, is shown stressed and hungover, the implication being that she is not happy within herself. The final image is of Holly and Marina's daughters playing together, with Marina's daughter wearing one of Marina's old prom dresses as a dressing-up costume. This image of the smiling girls is held in freeze-frame, echoing earlier images of Holly and Marina as children. It is a cyclical image suggesting a continuation of the intense, ambivalent friendship depicted throughout the film for the next generation of girls. These friendships might be difficult to navigate, but they are a rite of passage for girls that cannot be avoided, and the effects of which can be felt long into adulthood.

Class and identity in *My Summer of Love* (2004)

Pawel Pawlikowski's *My Summer of Love* also constructs a highly ambivalent girl friendship, although, unlike *Me Without You*, class plays a central role in the regulation of the friendship between Mona (Natalie Press) and Tamsin (Emily Blunt). Working-class Mona and middle-class Tamsin are two bored fifteen-year-old girls living in the Yorkshire Dales who meet one summer and develop an intense relationship. The film is freely adapted from the novel of the same name by Helen Cross (2001). *My Summer of Love* was produced by BBC Films and the Film Consortium with support from the UKFC. It is Pawlikowski's second feature film following *Last Resort* (2000), a film about a young Russian mother and her son who seek political asylum in the UK and end up confined in the seaside town of Stonehaven.

Pawlikowski is frequently positioned within contemporary British cinema's 'poetic realism' mode – as discussed in relation to *Fish Tank* in Chapter 2 – alongside filmmakers such as Andrea Arnold, Shane Meadows and Lynne Ramsay. These films continue contemporary British social realist cinema's focus on deprived youth but do so in a poetic realist mode where sociopolitical concerns provide a backdrop to a more aesthetically bold style of filmmaking. In these films, traditional realist locations, such as council estates, are rendered beautifully abstract, providing homes for the lost and lonely protagonists.[40] Pawlikowski's position within what David Forrest terms 'new British realism' plays a significant role in *My Summer of Love*'s critical reception. The *Guardian*'s Peter Bradshaw highlights the film's depiction of a 'swooning love story' within the 'Yorkshire Dales' sunlit expanses',[41] while the *Independent*'s Jonathan Romney describes how 'heat ripples off roofs [and] golden light shimmers off leafy canopies'.[42] In positioning the film as part of this new British realism, reviewers also draw attention to Pawlikowski's 'outsider' status as a Polish director working within British cinema. Pawlikowski's ability to respond to British, specifically English, traits of region and class is attributed to his status as an 'outsider'.[43]

The significance of class and Mona and Tamsin's classed identities are established from the opening scenes of the film. When Mona and Tamsin meet, Mona is lying on the ground next to her engineless scooter when Tamsin enters her vision on horseback and upside down. Metaphorically and literally above Mona, Tamsin is presented as Mona's potential knight in shining armour who can rescue her and provide her with the means to escape the confines of her class – a notion that is reinforced later in the film when Tamsin buys Mona an engine for her scooter. Mona's engineless scooter is a symbol of her lack of mobility and indicates her status as a 'lost girl' figure, which So Mayer argues, characterizes new British realist cinema.[44] The 'lost girl' is a social and cultural outsider, a 'runaway' girl, 'on the run from abuse, poverty of opportunity, domesticity and despair'.[45] Other 'lost girls' of contemporary British cinema include *Fish Tank*'s Mia, Leigh-Ann (Stephanie James) in *A Way of Life* (Asante 2004) and Morvern (Samantha Morton) in *Morvern Callar* (Ramsay 2002). Furthermore, Mayer notes, British cinema's 'lost girls' often come in non-biological pairs in relationships that are 'often fraught with tension but freighted with potential'.[46] I argue, however, that these ambivalent relationships between pairs of girls are not specific to the 'lost girls' of contemporary British cinema, but are instead – along with contrasting class backgrounds – a key characteristic of contemporary British cinema's depictions of girl friendship more broadly. The intensity of Mona and Tamsin's friendship is remarked upon throughout the film's critical reception, which is discursively similar to *Me Without You* in that this intensity is seen as unique to female friendships.[47] Natalie Press also draws on the idea of the unique intensity of female friendships in a promotional interview for the film, where she 'remembered the intimacy you have with girlfriends at a certain point in your life – when your bed becomes like an island with clothes and mess all over the floor – and you talk about everything'.[48] Press' evocation of an island is pertinent as it is suggestive of the intimacy and exclusion that characterizes the depictions of girl friendship within this chapter, where the girl pairs exist in isolated and exclusionary worlds. The friendship between Mona and Tamsin is situated in a world that is not only isolated but also timeless. This is created through the poetic aesthetics of new British realism discussed earlier and also through the lack of historical context, as Pawlikowski has removed the precise historical and political references within the source novel, which was set during the miners' strike in Yorkshire during the 1980s. This creation of a more timeless girlhood was a deliberate choice by Pawlikowski, who claims that a more contemporary film about British teenagers 'wouldn't interest me . . . . They'd be listening to music I hate, watching TV all the time and talking about [reality TV show] *Big Brother*.'[49] Pawlikowski exhibits a 'moral panic' view of British teenagers, as celebrity obsessed that is also evident in *Kicks*, which is discussed later on.[50] Pawlikowski's derogatory view of modern teenagers also influenced the casting process and his decision to hire Blunt and Press, who were twenty-one and twenty-three at the time of production: 'Most teenagers nowadays are totally sucked into this virtual world created by television, so it's very difficult to find an actress, or non-professional actress, who could carry that off.'[51] This approach is in stark contrast to Andrea Arnold's casting of seventeen-year-old Katie Jarvis for *Fish Tank* (discussed in Chapter 2) because she wanted a 'real' girl who could cause 'trouble for real'.[52] Meanwhile, *My Summer of Love* – this production discourse suggests – creates a timeless, essentialist construction of girlhood and girl friendship that is unburdened by historical context.

As with *Me Without You*, the critical reception for *My Summer of Love* presents Tamsin and Mona as binaries, which here denote their opposing class positions – 'working-class Mona and middle-class Tamsin'.[53] Both Tamsin and Mona are presented as being acutely aware of their class positions. Tamsin frequently demonstrates her class by using her superior education to impress Mona. Mona's acute awareness of her classed identity is most apparent when discussion turns towards the future:

> Mona: I'm gonna be a lawyer. [Pause]. I'm gonna work in an abattoir . . .
> get a boyfriend who's like, a bastard, and churn out all these kids
> with mental problems. And then I'm gonna wait for t'menopause.
> Or cancer.

The exploration in Chapter 2 of the girl-centred British sports film's mediation of aspirational discourses noted how contemporary discourses of aspiration are highly gendered, with young women constructed as the ideal aspirational subjects under neoliberalism, and the ideal aspirational subject is 'made in the image of the middle class'.[54] Mona's assertion that she is going to be a lawyer demonstrates an acute awareness of gendered and classed discourses of aspiration, where the ambitious middle-class can-do girl figure is held up as the dominant ideal, and the working class is viewed as a subject position from which one must want to – and should – escape.[55] At the same time, Mona's tragi-comic vision of a less successful future acknowledges the positioning of working-class girls as at-risk 'failure[s] in the making' who are unable to escape their circumstances.[56]

This acute awareness of their respective classed identities enables Mona and Tamsin to temporarily transcend these classed identities at various points in the film through elements of 'mimicry, exchange and masquerade'.[57] Once again, makeover is the key means through which the characters attempt to become visible and gain 'representability'. During the film's makeover scene, Mona tries on Tamsin's expensive, brightly coloured dresses and the girls dance around to Gilberto Gil's 'Três Caravelas', creating a carnival atmosphere that celebrates Mona's new 'girly' image, their close friendship and this temporary transcendence of class. During the scene, Mona stares at herself in the mirror with a wondrous expression, seemingly visible to herself for the first time thanks to the clothes given to her by Tamsin. Tamsin watches Mona, declaring her to be 'quite beautiful', but she subtly regulates Mona's visibility via the 'girlfriend gaze' by informing her that the dress that Mona is wearing belonged to her dead sister, Sadie, instantly altering the mood and breaking the spell. Despite this, classed identities and power relations remain fluid and ambiguous throughout the film. While Mona uses Tamsin's dresses to transcend the visible signs of her working-class identity, Tamsin is also able to perform a different classed identity through changing her image. When the girls visit the home of Mona's ex-boyfriend, Ricky, with the aim of getting revenge on him for the way he treated her, Tamsin mimics Mona's working-class identity through wearing a hooded top and large gold hoop earrings, typically associated with 'chav' culture, as discussed in Chapter 2. As Imogen Tyler argues, the figure of the 'chav' emerged in the 2000s to highlight deepening inequalities and class antagonisms, becoming a 'ubiquitous term of abuse for the white poor'.[58] The fluidity and ease with which Mona and Tamsin can enter into each other's worlds and exchange class identities in this way suggests that the makeover may not be the key to Mona becoming the hypervisible postfeminist girl subject after all because it is only temporary and inauthentic. Furthermore, while Tamsin's wealth does give her credibility that makes her seem superior and her false stories sound more plausible, Mona also has knowledge that Tamsin lacks. This knowledge takes the form of sexual knowingness, a valuable currency in girl culture, but here it is not used to regulate behaviour. When Tamsin asks Mona to show her what it is like to be 'shagged by Ricky', Mona gives a comically quick and unfulfilling demonstration of heterosexual sex, to which Tamsin replies, 'Is that it?' While providing a humorous critique of (hetero)sexual power relations, where pleasure is the privilege of the male, Tamsin's question highlights her sexual naivety as she looks to Mona to educate her. The shifting power dynamics at play within Mona and Tamsin's friendship show how their different class positions enable them to provide each other with something they currently lack, as part of the 'mutual development of hypervisibility'.[59] They become hypervisible to each other but only briefly, as this hypervisibility is not sustainable.

Mona and Tamsin's friendship comes to an end when Mona arrives at Tamsin's house to find Tamsin getting ready to go back to boarding school with her mother and her sister Sadie, whom Mona believed had died. In the film's final sequence, Tamsin catches up with Mona and tells her: 'I couldn't be myself in front of my mother; I was just playing a part. You *know* me' (original emphasis). Tamsin's assertion that Mona knows her is interesting considering she has lied to Mona on numerous occasions, but this line suggests that she believes that the version of herself that she exhibits when she is with Mona is the 'real' her when really it is just a fantasy identity. Tamsin's friendship with Mona enabled her to create an identity that provided her with greater visibility. For a short time, Tamsin used her cultural capital to create an almost idealized version of herself because Mona lacked the knowledge that would have enabled her to question the validity of Tamsin's statements.

On discovering Tamsin's lies, Mona coaxes Tamsin into the lake where she tries to drown Tamsin but lets her go at the last minute. The film's ambiguous final image is of Mona walking away from the lake, staring directly into the camera. For Joanna Rydzewska, the film's ending suggests that Mona will fulfil the passive version of herself that she so accurately described. She claims that 'far from portraying the experiences of one idle summer which changes the girls' lives forever by giving it a new and better direction', *My Summer of Love* is actually a 'perceptive portrait of people who cannot change their spots, trapped in a class system they will always endure'.[60] Claire Monk, meanwhile, argues that Mona's relationship with Tamsin has provided her with the mobility to move between class positions, albeit temporarily, which connects to 'Mona's ability to leave the valley – upwards and out – at the end of the film'.[61] While Monk's reading is more optimistic than Rydzewska's, what is clear is that Mona and Tamsin's friendship cannot be saved. Their friendship is depicted as intense and foreclosed in line with depictions of teenage girl friendship, particularly those British films discussed here. Like Holly and Marina's friendship in *Me Without You*, the constantly shifting power dynamics cannot be subsumed under a sentimental and idealized version of girl friendship. However, while Holly and Marina appear to still be friends by the end of the film, the same is not possible for Tamsin and Mona and this conflict cannot be resolved as postfeminist girlfriend culture suggests.[62] While their friendship provided Tamsin and Mona with temporary visibility, this visibility – and their friendship – was based on a fantasy that was not sustainable.

Somebodies, wannabes and nobodies: *Kicks* (2008)

While *My Summer of Love* was notable for its deliberate lack of historical context, Lindy Heymann's *Kicks* is firmly temporally and spatially located in the city of Liverpool in the mid-2000s as part of the filmmakers' desire to capture a specific moment in time in relation to girls and celebrity culture.[63] *Kicks* tells the story of the friendship between two fifteen-year-old girls: shy Nicole (Kerrie Hayes) and fame-hungry Jasmine (Nichola Burley) who wants to marry a footballer. The girls meet at Anfield football ground and bond over their obsession with fictional Liverpool footballer Lee Cassidy (Jamie Doyle). When it is announced that Cassidy is to transfer to Real Madrid, Jasmine and Nicole decide to kidnap him in order to convince their hero to stay. *Kicks* was created as part of the Digital Departures micro-budget film scheme run by the regional film agency Northwest Vision and Media in partnership with the UKFC and the Liverpool Culture Company, and was intended to celebrate Liverpool's status as the 2008 Capital of Culture, although it did not go on general release until 2010. Terence Davies' *Of Time and City* (2008) and Lawrence Gough's horror *Salvage* (2008) were also created through Digital Departures.[64]

The city of Liverpool is central to the film through its association with celebrity WAG culture. WAG is an acronym for 'wives and girlfriends' that is mostly associated with footballers. Liverpudlian Colleen Rooney is a prominent British WAG who is constructed as a Cinderella figure through a media narrative in which she made the seemingly effortless transition from high school student to magazine columnist and fashion designer through her relationship and then marriage to premier league footballer Wayne Rooney. Alison Winch highlights Colleen as an example of 'those working class women who have succeeded in celebrity culture. Consequently they signify fame and aspiration in an apparently meritocratic society.'[65] As Anthony Mullen argues, the figure of the WAG signifies the convergence of celebrity and working-class identity during the New Labour period.[66] The WAG also functions as a contemporary princess figure through promoting a fairy tale 'rags-to-riches' narrative through marriage, which is a reward for successfully working on the self in accordance with neoliberal postfeminist femininity.

Liverpool's association with WAG culture means that the city of Liverpool has, as Hannah Andrews describes, 'a reputation as a glamorous evening playground for the rich and famous'.[67] On screen, however, Liverpool is, as Andrews suggests, viewed as an 'aesthetically "televisual" space' due to its association with iconic British television programmes in the social realist mode such as *Boys from the Blackstuff* (BBC 1982) and *Brookside* (Channel Four 1982–2003).[68] *Kicks'* director Lindy Heymann was acutely aware of this televisual heritage. In an echo of the production discourse surrounding the British sports films in Chapter 2 – in which filmmakers sought to position the films in opposition to British cinema's 'typical' output, which is perceived as gritty, dull and aesthetically unambitious social realism – Heymann was also keen to avoid presenting Liverpool as part of 'gritty, squalid, grim-up-North Britain'.[69] Instead, Heymann created a more stylized and heightened aesthetic, where extreme close-ups of eyes and hands were favoured over wide shots of the surroundings. When the camera angle does widen, the city is rendered abstract, which, when combined with Liverpudlian group Ladytron's electro-pop soundtrack, creates an intense and unsettling effect (Figure 3.2). Like Pawlikowski, it is Spanish director of photography Eduard Grau's 'outsider's view' that Heymann credits with being key to the creation of a vision of Liverpool

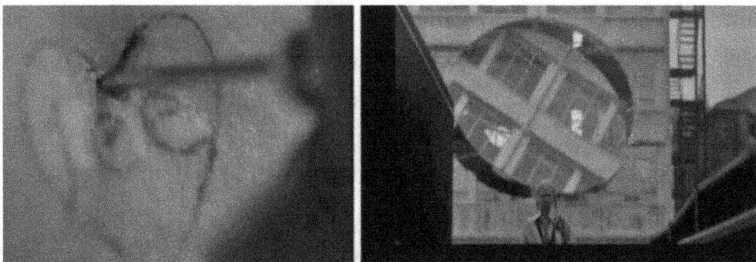

Figure 3.2 *Kicks* (2008) Minute details and Nicole (Kerrie Hayes) within Liverpool's circular landscape.

that is both recognizable and fresh. We see this version of Liverpool through Nicole's eyes. Nicole embodies Liverpool through her close proximity to the cityscape and her dedication to the football club; she is, according to Heymann, a 'metaphor for Liverpool'.[70] We go with her as she walks the city, gazing through circular shapes in the docks and running her hands along metal railings so that they make a clanging sound that echoes. Nicole's Liverpool is filled with circular shapes, and the way she looks through them is suggestive of voyeurism and establishes Nicole as someone who is watchful rather than watched, and her continuous need to touch things and create sound indicates that she is a girl who is trying to assert her existence – to be seen and heard – but lonely Nicole is ignored by those around her. Her mother is absent, her existence indicated only by the nurse's uniform hanging on the back of the door, and her father's attention is diverted towards his new family. If, as Samantha Colling argues, for teen girls in film 'the spectacle of the self is the singular way of taking up space and accessing power' then Nicole is powerless.[71]

As well as being a story of girl friendship, *Kicks* is firmly situated within the context of UK celebrity culture during the 2000s. As Sarah Projansky argues, discourses of contemporary girlhood and celebrity are mutually dependent on each other, with individualism, identity and self-realization at the heart of both girlhood and celebrity.[72] Discourses of girlhood and celebrity perpetuate what Projansky terms a 'spectacularization' of identity, with both girls and celebrities expected to be consistently visible and available.[73] Contemporary celebrity culture encapsulates both neoliberal and postfeminist discourses, as Melanie Kennedy argues, because celebrity culture speaks directly to 'the expectation of social mobility and the requirement for flexibility and self-realisation' within both postfeminism and neoliberalism.[74] The figure of the WAG exemplifies the kind of social mobility offered by celebrity, as working-class women are able to achieve fame and success while reinforcing the notion that the UK is a meritocratic society.[75] Jasmine's desire to be a WAG is presented as the logical conclusion to the social mobility she has already benefitted from, as reviewers describe her character as 'nouveau riche' – a somewhat derogatory term used to describe previously working-class people who have acquired wealth but lack taste.[76] This is also suggested within the film as Jasmine's parents are shown to be wealthy but lacking taste, such as when Jasmine's mum happily shows off her breast enlargement surgery to Nicole. It also highlights postfeminism's continuous requirement for girls and women to work on themselves and maintain a 'sexy' body in line with ideal heterosexual femininity.

Jasmine articulates the postfeminist neoliberal requirement for a self-reflexive identity that displays a coherent narrative of the self. As Giddens argues, this self-reflexive narrative can be made explicit through keeping a journal, which Jasmine does by making notes in her 'autobiography book'.[77] As well as constructing a self-narrative, Jasmine's autobiography book also functions as an object that can have future value through being marketed as a celebrity memoir should Jasmine achieve her dream of becoming famous. Jasmine also engages in the required self-surveillance as she examines her body in the mirror, while telling Nicole about her plans for the future.

> Jasmine: I'll get my boobs done, get my portfolio, little go of modelling – glamour and that – and maybe a part in a soap or something. It's better if you're famous yourself because then you go to the same parties and premiers and whatever, you're on the same circuit. Plus, if you're a bit of a celebrity then people won't think you're a gold-digger.
> Nicole: You're scary.

Jasmine's clear plan acknowledges that the route to success is via her body. As Alison Winch suggests, 'In the hypervisible landscape of popular culture the body is recognised as the object of a woman's labour: it is her asset, her product, her brand and her gateway to freedom and empowerment in a neoliberal market economy'.[78] While Jasmine is aware of the criticisms levelled at WAGs, she appears oblivious to the fact that the plans she outlines, such as glamour modelling, are viewed as 'illegitimate' routes to success for young women because they rely on their bodies rather than recognizable talent or skill. The film's implicit criticism of girls' supposed desire for fame and celebrity is conveyed through the slightly humorous tone of the dialogue and Nicole's incredulous reaction.

The film's depiction of Jasmine's ambitions to become a celebrity is located within the context of increasing concern in the UK's media, educational and political spheres over young people's aspirations and apparently 'inappropriate' desire to become celebrities.[79] These concerns are particularly gendered, as encapsulated by comments made in 2008 by Culture Minister Barbara Follett: 'Kids nowadays just want to be famous. If you ask little girls, they either want to be footballers' wives or win *The X Factor*. Our society is in danger of being Barbie-dolled.'[80] Follett's criticism places this seemingly ubiquitous desire for celebrity squarely upon young girls, even going so far as to suggest that this poses a 'danger' to British society. This anxiety also underpins the filmmakers' discussions of the film. Screenwriter Leigh Campbell explains how she was especially interested in 'looking at girls today and how they increasingly get their validation from what they look like and who they're with, rather than their own sense of self-worth'.[81] Similarly, Lindy Heymann believes it is crucial – and inevitable – for films centred around teenage girls to question this: 'If you're an intelligent woman and you're a film-maker you are going to be questioning the prevailing attitude among teenage girls that what you think is secondary to how you look.'[82] Campbell and Heymann's concerns echo wider media discourse at this time that perpetuated this moral panic around celebrity culture and the sexualization of teenage girls. In 2008, a headline in the *Telegraph* reported that 'teenage girls would rather be WAGs than politicians' based on a survey by teen website mybliss.co.uk. The article suggests that being a WAG was the most popular choice for the girls surveyed when in actual fact the majority (21.8 per cent) said they aspired to be like J. K. Rowling, author of *Harry Potter*, with only 2.4 per cent wanting to be a WAG.[83] However, as Heather Mendick et al. argue in their ethnographic research with young people, celebrity performs an important social function as a sense-making practice through which young people can think and talk about their futures. They demonstrate how, through this celebrity talk, young people place value on hard work and authenticity, where fame is valued as a by-product of hard work and talent, rather than in and of itself.[84] The anxiety inherent within Campbell and Heymann's depiction of girls' relationship to celebrity culture is also alluded to within the film's critical reception, with the film described as a 'cautionary tale about idol worship and the allure of WAG culture'.[85] Sukhdev Sandhu's review in the *Telegraph* presents *Kicks* as a 'parable about Britain's love-hate relationship with fame'.[86] This alludes not only to the film's moralistic approach to celebrity culture but also to British cinema's persistent ambivalence to glamour, consumption and celebrity that characterizes contemporary British cinema's depictions of young femininity.

While *Kicks* does present a particularly British examination of contemporary celebrity culture, the film's critical reception highlights how the film is really about the friendship between Jasmine and Nicole. Indeed, most critics felt that the depiction of girl friendship was the strongest aspect of the film, which was subsequently let down by the melodramatic kidnap plot at the end. For *Time Out*'s Dave Calhoun, this prevented the film from being a 'more credible exploration of teenage sexual infatuation and celebrity obsession'.[87] Peter Bradshaw, writing in the *Guardian*, similarly notes how 'The initial stages of the film – just hanging out with Nicole and Jasmine – are considerably more interesting than the rather strained denouement'.[88] Heymann also views the relationship between Nicole and Jasmine as 'crucial' because it 'underpins the whole movie'.[89] Casting the girls was hugely important and Heymann, like Pawlikowski, deliberately did not choose 'real' fifteen-year-olds because she wanted older actors who could 'draw on the insight and experience of being fifteen',[90] reinforcing British cinema's girl friendship films' reliance on the retrospective girlhood framework. The focus on the relationship between the two girls extends beyond the film text and its characters, with behind-the-scenes interviews emphasizing the relationship between Burley and Hayes and how this informed their performances. Burley talks about how she and Hayes worked together from the very first audition, and Hayes reveals that she lived with Burley for the duration of the shoot, spending a lot of time together on and off set, which enabled them to form a strong bond. This clearly paid off, as critics praise Hayes and Burley's portrayal of friendship between their characters, noting how 'Hayes and Burley play splendidly off each other'.[91] A review in the *Glaswegian* newspaper remarks how 'Hayes and Burley gel nicely' and the film 'builds the sisterly solidarity', which is key to girlfriend culture.[92] The film's critical discourse emphasizes a mutual supportiveness within *Kicks'* portrayal of girl friendship that contrasts with the depiction and discussion of Holly and Marina's friendship in *Me Without You*, which was more regulatory as Marina attempted to control Holly. The focus on Hayes and Burley's chemistry, along with the depiction of the relationship between their characters, demonstrates how – for the most part – *Kicks'* portrayal of girl friendship does not emphasize the cruel peer control that characterizes the girlfriend gaze within the postfeminist sisterhood, although that is not to say that power relations between the two do not shift throughout the film.

Jasmine and Nicole's friendship seems unique within the world of the film, where Liverpool is depicted as an individualistic place where there is a lack of solidarity among girls who are desperate for hypervisibility and fame. As Jasmine's acquaintance Jade (Laura Wallace) says, 'It's every girl for herself.' Jade is dismissive of Nicole and her child-like appearance, and refuses to stay behind when Nicole is refused entry into the nightclub. Jade's attitude and behaviour are indicative of 'girlfriend culture' where it is other women who are looking at, controlling and judging women's bodies as they strive for the 'perfect' feminine self.[93] Jasmine is torn between wanting to go into the club where she knows the footballers will be and wanting to be with Nicole. Although she does go in, she returns shortly after falling out with Jade who calls Jasmine a 'tease' for being unwilling to perform sexual acts in order to gain access to the VIP area. Jasmine and Nicole need each other to achieve the 'mutual hypervisibility' that is essential to girlfriend culture.[94] Together, they use Nicole's detailed knowledge of the city to find Lee Cassidy's apartment. This is also an example of the continuously shifting power relations between Jasmine and Nicole, as although Jasmine has more knowledge of WAG culture and how to make herself visible, it is Nicole's knowledge of Liverpool that actually brings them closer to Lee.

While Jasmine and Nicole do not enact the 'loving meanness' that is present within the previous case studies, their friendship is subtly regulated through the ubiquitous makeover. Once again, the makeover in *Kicks* is characteristic of contemporary British cinema's girl films in that it avoids conspicuous consumption, instead fashioning postfeminist femininity from hand-me-down clothes. Jasmine gives Nicole a red halterneck dress and lacy tights that are markedly different to Nicole's usual pink hoodies and trainers, so that their clothes mirror one another. Hannah Andrews likens Jasmine's appearance to the film noir femme fatale due to her long dark hair, smoky make-up and silky dresses, which, she argues, represents the 'generic conventions the film wants to emulate and a wider culture of young women who exploit their sexuality for material gain'.[95] In giving Nicole her clothes, Jasmine is aiding Nicole's quest for representability by enacting a form of peer surveillance through the 'girlfriend gaze' and providing her with a more 'normatively distinctive' feminine body that enables them to access the key nightclub and potentially be 'seen'.[96] This feminine normativity is also middle class by default. The initial contrast in their appearance points to the class differences between Jasmine and Nicole, where Jasmine's luxurious dresses reinforce her middle-class 'nouveau riche' background, whereas Nicole's costume is indicative of her working-class status, along with the fact that she lives on a council estate. While, as Colling argues, the right clothes typically have the power to dissolve class boundaries,[97] in British girl films, this is not so easily achieved. A close-up of Nicole's feet in a pair of Jasmine's shoes alludes to the Cinderella motif that is so prevalent in postfeminist girl culture, and the idea of the glass slipper. However, unlike Cinderella, Nicole's shoes do not fit properly, reinforcing her inability to transcend class boundaries and become the ideal postfeminist girl subject.

Although wearing the right clothes allows Jasmine and Nicole to enter the promised land of Liverpool's nightlife, the film suggests this glamour is just a veneer under which lies seediness and potential danger. While the city is typically constructed as a site of glamour that offers teenage girls the potential for visibility,[98] in *Kicks* the city is dark and hostile towards Nicole and Jasmine, failing to provide them with the visibility they crave. They must find their own space, away from the city: a disused caravan that initially offered Nicole and Jasmine freedom, but becomes increasingly claustrophobic when they kidnap Lee Cassidy and hold him hostage there in the thriller-esque final act. The girls blindfold Lee and tie him up, indulging in innuendo, with Lee ordering Nicole and Jasmine kiss each other, which Nicole does reticently. Ariel Levy has identified this performative female sexuality as part of postfeminist 'raunch culture', where women are offered a hollow form of empowerment through choosing to make sex objects of themselves to show that they are liberated by adhering to the male fantasy of femininity found in pornography. This includes performing lesbianism for male enjoyment.[99] Nicole is disgusted by this and starts to play loud music to distract Jasmine. Nicole's ability to hold Jasmine's attention suggests that Jasmine's friendship with Nicole is more important than she realizes. The sight of Jasmine dancing around in a carefree way also suggests that she is caught between wanting to seem sexually mature but not entirely comfortable with what this entails. In an interview, Lindy Heymann discusses the 'devastating' pressure British teenage girls are under to be sexual before they are ready.[100] Heymann's concerns echo the 'sexualization panic' discourse that has abounded in popular media in the UK over the past fifteen years that offers a simplistic and moralistic view of teenage sexuality, as discussed in Chapter 1, which constructs girls as being at risk of being sexualized at too young an age within a highly sexualized celebrity consumer culture.[101]

Kicks critiques this raunch culture through a critical feminist voice that emphasizes how contemporary culture encourages the derogatory (self-) objectification of young women. When Nicole and Jasmine get hold of Lee's phone, they discover that he lists girls under derogatorily sexual pseudonyms such as 'sexy arse' and 'fit tits'. They also discover a video of Jade performing oral sex on a footballer while his teammates jeer and laugh. Realizing that Lee does not know who she is, a horrified Jasmine says, 'We call her Jade', reinstating Jade's personhood in naming her and elevating her above the nameless girl whose purpose is merely to provide sexual gratification. This critique is also more specifically located within British football culture, where stories about how women are supposedly attracted to footballers' money and status only to find themselves swiftly disposed of have been a staple of the British tabloids over the past decade. The scene reaches a crescendo as Jasmine angrily starts to undress to give Lee 'what he came for' until Nicole fires a gun to make her stop. Unlike Jasmine, Nicole is unwilling to degrade herself and wants to protect her friend. While Jasmine initially seems like the driving force within their friendship – literally and metaphorically – as she facilitates Nicole's makeover and drives them to the caravan, Nicole has more power than is immediately obvious. She is able to stop Jasmine from doing things she might regret and uses her detailed knowledge of Liverpool to get access to Lee. Nicole also has a greater sense of her own identity. Whereas Jasmine is always trying to become 'somebody', Nicole – like Mona – is acutely aware that she is, and probably always will be, a 'nobody'. Pointing the gun at Lee's feet, she tells him: 'The only way I can have my dream is if you're a nobody like me.' Here, Jasmine and Nicole realize the futility of their dreams and let Lee go.

As with the other films in this chapter, Nicole and Jasmine's intense friendship is presented as a rite of passage that irrevocably transforms them. This rite of passage is depicted in the final scene when Jasmine and Nicole burn items related to Lee Cassidy. They walk together, looking out over Liverpool as the sun rises. Now that the hollowness of their dream has been exposed, they must start again as nobodies having achieved only temporary representability without managing to become hypervisible. *Kicks'* construction of girl friendship is situated within a heavy-handed critique of British celebrity culture – in which girls are pushed to their limits by their ubiquitous desire for fame –

Figure 3.3 *Kicks* (2008) Starting again.

that problematically represents and perpetuates simplistic moral panic discourses concerning celebrity and 'sexualization' that circulate around girls and girlhood in contemporary culture. However, the film also highlights the importance of sisterly solidarity and the strength of girl friendship as key to identity formation, even though dreams are shattered in the process.

Albatross (2011)

While *Kicks* explored teenage girl friendship through the murky world of celebrity, *Albatross* poses questions of identity and what it means to be 'somebody' via a gentle British comedy. Seventeen-year-old Emelia (Jessica Brown Findlay) bursts into the lives of Beth (Felicity Jones) and her family when she takes a job at the Clifftop Hotel owned by Beth's father, Jonathan Fischer (Sebastian Koch), who bought the hotel after it was the setting for his bestselling novel. Once again, girl friendship is depicted through the pairing of two teenage girls who are the opposite of one another. Beth is quiet and studious and destined for Oxford University, while working-class wild girl Emelia lives with her grandparents and believes she is related to Arthur Conan Doyle, author of Sherlock Holmes, a belief that fuels her ambition to be a writer. Despite their obvious differences, both girls are desperate to escape their sleepy seaside town, and their friendship offers them both the chance to experience a different life. That is, until it is damaged by Emelia's affair with Beth's father.

Albatross – like *Me Without You* – was produced by Isle of Man Film and shot on location in the Isle of Man over six weeks in 2009. It was directed by Niall MacCormick, making his feature film debut after directing *Margaret Thatcher: The Long Road to Finchley* (2008) for the BBC. The screenplay was written by first-time writer Tamzin Rafn. While the decision to shoot the film in the Isle of Man was no doubt influenced by New Labour film industry tax breaks and other financial incentives, director Niall MacCormick attributes this decision to wanting to create a sunny seaside setting because he 'didn't want to make it feel like a kitchen sink drama, or . . . Brit grit, where everyone is depressed because it's raining all the time and they're in England. . . . I wanted to make it more universal and as sunny and as bright as possible.'[102] Once again, the production discourse evokes a stereotypical and disparaging view of British cinema that equates it with 'gritty' small-scale social realist films in order to position *Albatross* as doing something different and with wider appeal. Reviewers, however, saw the film as having typically British characteristics, not as a social realist film but as a bittersweet coming-of-age comedy drama. It is described as 'one of those sweet, slightly sad comic dramas that only Britain can produce'[103] and 'a very British comedy, for good and ill', suggesting the film is not as universal as the filmmakers intended.[104]

Perhaps the biggest influence on the film's production and reception is David Leyand's *Wish You Were Here* (1987). Both films feature rebellious teenage girl protagonists who are out of place and confined within the small seaside towns they dream of escaping. The allusions to *Wish You Were Here* are prominent – not least when Emelia cycles around town on a bicycle with a basket attached to the front. Screenwriter Tamzin Rafn acknowledges the debt she owes Leyland's film, saying she was 'obsessed' with the film, which was set in Worthing where she grew up.[105] The relationship between the two films features heavily within reviews of the film, with *Albatross* branded '*Wish You Were Here* for the noughties'.[106] However, *Albatross* is seen to be unable to live up to these comparisons, with critics claiming that the film is too predictable and lacks originality.[107] Rafn also talks about how she likes 'Sherlock Holmes and naughty young girls', all of which feature heavily in *Albatross*. Rafn's highly personalized account of the writing process – her motivation being to simply write about things she likes – provides another example of girl friendship constructed through retrospective girlhood. In drawing so heavily on her own teenage years, Rafn has created a version of contemporary girlhood that looks nostalgic and anachronistic, particularly through the film's relationship to technology. Frequent scenes depict Emelia writing with a notepad and pen. Significantly, Jonathan writes – or, at least, attempts to write – on a MacBook, which Marie-Alix Thouaille argues, is a key symbol of contemporary authorship.[108] While Emelia's lack of access to a computer is explained away by the fact that she comes from a 'no parent family' and lacks the necessary resources, it constructs a romanticized depiction of authorship that removes the film from its contemporary setting and makes it seem oddly out of time. This is also a key criticism levelled at the film in its critical reception. As Cosmo Landesman writes in the *Sunday Times*, 'As if a girl of [Emelia's] generation, growing up in a seaside town, would give a toss about Conan Doyle.'[109]

Like *Wish You Were Here*'s Lynda before her, Emelia is a rebellious girl who is struggling against the confinements of her small town. The film's critical reception constructs Emelia (and, by extension, Jessica Brown Findlay) as rebellious through a gendered and classed discourse. This is furthered through comparisons to Brown Findlay's role as Lady Sybil in the ITV period drama *Downton Abbey* (2010–2015). As one reviewer states, 'Brown Findlay, known to millions as Lady Sybil from *Downton Abbey*, roughs up nicely as a wild child'.[110] Similarly, *Metro*'s Sharon Laugher notes how '*Downton*'s Jessica Brown Findlay swaps posh frocks and enunciated vowels for tarty skirts and dropped aitches'.[111] Emelia is constructed as a 'wild child' from the film's opening scene. Here, Emelia stares defiantly into the camera, which pans around to reveal that she is standing opposite a boy (Harry Treadaway). She kisses him passionately and then abruptly breaks away to light a firework, which she throws into a bin. Emelia's confrontational stare recalls British social realist films, such as *Kes* (Loach 1969) and *This is England* (Meadows 2006), where the young (usually male) protagonist looks directly into the camera, but the panning camera, the kissing teenagers, along with setting off the explosive, creates a sense of fun, 'exploding' these conventions, establishing Emelia as a wild child and demonstrating MacCormick's desire to move away from the kind of 'kitchen sink' drama with which British cinema is typically associated.

Although the film's critical reception presents Brown Findlay as the star of the film, for MacCormick, *Albatross* is 'kind of like a co-star movie, it's about the two of them'.[112] The friendship between Emelia and Beth is central to the film, and, as with all the films in this chapter, their friendship is constructed through the girls as binary opposites. While Emelia is rebellious and free-spirited, Beth is conformist. When we are introduced to Beth, she is studying in her bedroom as she works towards gaining a place at Oxford University. Her room is filled with 'first' trophies and the walls are adorned with rosettes. Studious Beth is positioned as a 'top girl' and an extension of Felicity Jones' 'top girl' star persona that was discussed in relation to *Chalet Girl* in Chapter 2. Prior to meeting Emelia, Beth appears to lack the girl friendship that postfeminist girlfriend culture deems necessary to enabling a normative feminine identity.[113] The girl friendship between Beth and Emelia is central to the film. As Winch argues, in girlfriend culture, women are hypervisible to each other, with men cast as hapless bystanders and accessories that prove a girl's worth to her girlfriends.[114] In *Albatross*, however, men have even less value. Emelia's relationships with men are unfulfilling, with both Jonathan and the boy presented as weak and immature. Beth also has a one-night stand with no further expectations of a romantic relationship.

The friendship between Beth and Emelia also helps them to gain a greater a sense of their individual identities and is, in some ways, reminiscent of Karen Hollinger's definition of the 'sentimental' female friendship film, which is psychologically enriching and 'stimulates personal and psychological growth' but this is inherently ambivalent.[115] Emelia also provides Beth with 'representability', again through a hand-me-down makeover. Beth's clothes are typically colourless and practical but when the girls go to a party in Oxford, Emelia lends Beth her leather jacket to wear over a revealing dress. Beth is initially hesitant, claiming that she looks 'ridiculous' but Emelia encourages her by saying: 'Look at you, hot patootie. You should wear what you want, you look amazing.' With Emelia's affirmation that she looks hot, Beth submits herself to the homosocial 'girlfriend gaze', which confirms the value of the female body. The male attention that Beth receives at the party is the welcome by-product of her new image and ability to perform postfeminist femininity. However, the girlfriend gaze here is not acting as a subtle form of control but encouraging Beth to be less restrained.

Beth and Emelia are confined by the identities bestowed upon them. Beth is the daughter of a famous novelist and lives in the Clifftop, a hotel that both features in and recreates the world of her father's novel, while Emelia believes she is the great-granddaughter of Arthur Conan Doyle. While Beth tries to make Emelia see that the Conan Doyle name is an albatross – and false at that – Emelia believes the name makes her special and her whole sense of identity is built upon it. Emelia's belief that her name makes her special and legitimizes her writing ability echoes Jasmine's idea that being famous would make her 'somebody' rather than just a 'nobody'. Now that she knows the truth, Emelia has the self-understanding that Giddens deems necessary to 'build a coherent and rewarding sense of identity'.[116] She tears up her writing and starts again; this time using the laptop Jonathan has given her because he thinks she can make better use of it. By the end of the film, it is clear that the characters have undergone a rite of passage that has led them to discover their 'true selves'. In the final sequence, Emelia prints her novel and we see that the cover page reads: 'Albatross by Emelia Doyle', asserting her newly discovered identity through her authorship. She also sees Beth, who is on her way to Oxford, wearing Emelia's

'I put out' t-shirt. The combination of Emelia's t-shirt with Beth's own clothes acknowledges the impact of their friendship, which enabled Beth to become less colourless and confined and more visible. Emelia's clothes, in contrast, have become more muted and comfortable. Beth looks down at the t-shirt and smiles as Emelia watches her drive away. The final image is of Emelia cycling away with her printed manuscript in her basket, which echoes Lynda defiantly pushing her pram at the end of *Wish You Were Here* (Leland 1987). Justine Ashby has noted how Lynda's escape from the confines of her father figure is somewhat muted by her move into motherhood.[117] In *Albatross*, Emelia's escape from the Conan Doyle name has provided her with a more 'authentic' sense of identity and new possibilities. In this way, *Albatross* is more in keeping with the feminist British women's films that Ashby identifies from the 1980s than the more recent 'desperate girl' films from the 1990s and 2000s where the young female protagonist remains stuck.[118] While Beth and Emelia's friendship could not survive the events of the film, *Albatross* depicts girl friendship as having a considerable impact on the characters' identities that, far from being destructive, leads to freedom and a more authentic sense of self.

British cinema's girl friendship: Ambiguous and ambivalent

British cinema's girl friendship films present girl friendship in all of its complicated ambivalence and ambiguity. While postfeminist 'girlfriend culture' presents friendship between women as an essential route to representability, these films trouble this in a number of ways. The fact that the protagonists exist in pairs and are largely closed off from others makes being visible difficult. Even in *Kicks*, where the city of Liverpool provides a glamorous, yet seedy, site of celebrity culture, this is not really accessible to Nicole and Jasmine. The dominance of the retrospective girlhood trope further complicates the films' relationship to postfeminist girlfriend culture, particularly through the depiction of a timeless girlhood and girl friendship, such as *My Summer of Love*, or a somewhat anachronistic or dated construction of girlhood as in *Albatross*. Throughout the films, the characters struggle to gain and maintain representability and hypervisibility. Makeover plays an important role in the characters' attempts to gain representability, but this is not always successful. Both Nicole in *Kicks* and Mona in *My Summer of Love* attempt image makeovers through clothes provided by their friend, but there is a sense that these new images do not fit or cannot be maintained. This is also tied to the fact that both Mona and Nicole are coded as working class, and they are unable to overcome their working-class status and become the postfeminist (middle class) ideal. Moreover, both Mona and Nicole are aware of their 'lack' of ideal, postfeminist femininity and the fact that they are likely to remain 'nobodies'. Class plays an important role within this chapter. With the exception of *Me Without You*, all of the friendships are presented in terms of working-class/middle-class binaries, but it is not simply a case of the middle-class girl providing the working-class girl with representability via the regulatory 'girlfriend gaze', as each character is able to provide something that contributes to the development of their friend's identity.

Although all of the films portray girl friendship unsentimentally, the narrative resolutions differ greatly. In *Me Without You* and *My Summer of Love*, the girl friendships are more regulatory and potentially more damaging. The ending of *Me Without You* suggests that Marina and Holly's fragile friendship will tentatively continue and history will repeat itself, while *My Summer of Love* presents a finite friendship that is totally destroyed. More recent films, *Kicks* and *Albatross*, however, are more optimistic. The ending of *Kicks* suggests that Nicole and Jasmine's friendship can survive the events of the film, while even though Beth and Emelia are no longer together, their friendship has enabled them to escape the confines of their respective identities, and allowed Emelia to author her own identity. Regardless, British girl friendship films all present friendship as hugely significant to the girl protagonist's sense of identity and their 'becoming' woman. This idea of 'becoming' is taken up in Chapter 4, which examines constructions of young femininity in British historical films.

4

Young femininity and the
British historical film

Introduction

No book on young women in contemporary British cinema would be complete without consideration of historical films. Historical films have always been central to the commercial success of British cinema – both at home and abroad – and are often synonymous with British cinema itself.[1] Chapter 1 discussed films set in the recent past – the 1960s – via *An Education* (Scherfig 2009) and *The Falling* (Morley 2014). This chapter focuses specifically on films set before 1900, and centres around real-life historical royal and aristocratic young women. That is, Anne Boleyn, Queen Victoria, Georgiana, Duchess of Devonshire, and Dido Elizabeth Belle in *The Other Boleyn Girl* (Chadwick 2008), *The Young Victoria* (Vallée 2009), *The Duchess* (Dibb 2008) and *Belle* (Asante 2013), respectively. These films mediate contemporary postfeminist discourses, producing what Jessica Taylor theorizes as a 'postfeminist historical sensibility'. This is achieved via protagonists who are depicted as 'forbearers of the "empowered" postfeminist woman – strong, intelligent young women who draw attention to the structural inequalities they face – while furthering postfeminist discourses relating to the "pastness" of feminism by confining it safely to the distant past'.[2] A simple glance at the films' titles reveals the assimilation of postfeminist discourses of girlishness though the frequent use 'girl' or 'young', as well as postfeminist individualism through the use of the singular 'the' (*The Other Boleyn Girl*, *The Young Victoria*, *The Duchess*). As such, this chapter explores how these films use figures from the past to mediate the discourses of postfeminist girlhood that emerge consistently throughout this book, such as the can-do girls and ambitious young women; anxieties surrounding girls' sexualities and the transition into womanhood; ideas around consumption, identity and image and the relationship between girlhood and celebrity culture. As well as mediating key postfeminist discourses of 'empowerment' and choice, these films also emphasize the 'postfeminist enthusiasm for femininity', exemplified by the figure of the princess, through highlighting the sparkling objects that signify royalty, such as crowns, gowns and jewels, in accordance with sparkle as a key signifier of postfeminist girlhood.[3] However, in the British historical films discussed here, rather than being 'empowering', the sparkly signifiers of royalty bring very little pleasure to the protagonist, functioning instead as sources of confinement and unhappiness. This is in keeping with contemporary British cinema's ambivalence towards glamour and consumption, which, I argue, is a significant recurring characteristic of contemporary British cinema's mediation of young femininity.

As Belén Vidal argues, within this postfeminist context, the 'woman-centred monarchy film [has] become part of a profitable generic cycle' since the millennium.[4] This cycle extends beyond British cinema to include films such as Sofia Coppola's *Marie Antoinette* (2006) and the Danish film, *A Royal Affair* (Arcel 2012), which, like *The Duchess*, features a love triangle and an unhappy marriage. The films in this chapter can be viewed as British cinema's eager response to this cycle and the increased cultural interest in girls and young women more broadly. As Sukhdev Sanhu writes in his review of *The Duchess*, 'Every time you look there's another movie about a nervy, underprepared young girl taking tentative steps towards a life of pomp, ceremony and unsatisfying sex.'[5] Whereas Vidal identifies the millennium as the starting point for this particular cycle of films, I argue that British cinema's current interest in the royal historical film began in the late 1990s with Shekhar Kapur's *Elizabeth* (1998), which marked a turning point in the British historical film genre. *Elizabeth* is a historical thriller that explores the early years of the reign of Elizabeth I (Cate Blanchett), focusing in particular on the young Elizabeth's (sexual) relationship with Robert Dudley (Joseph Fiennes). As Kara Mckechnie argues, the release of *Elizabeth* signalled a 'revival' of the British monarchy film that marked a move away from the heritage films of the 1980s, such as Merchant Ivory's *Howard's End* (Ivory 1992) and *A Room With a View* (Ivory 1985), which were tasteful adaptations of classic literature that were ideologically located within the context of Thatcher's Britain.[6] As such, *Elizabeth* is often referred to as a 'post-heritage' film, as it emerged alongside films such as *Carrington* (Hampton 1995) and *Orlando* (Potter 1992), which were notable for their explicit concern with 'non-dominant gender and sexual identities'[7] and an emphasis on visual spectacle. This prioritizing of spectacle over authenticity remains a key feature of the British historical film, as expressions of filmmakers' desire to move away from the 'typical' British heritage film's associations with Merchant Ivory dominate the production discourses that circulate around the films discussed in this chapter. *Belle* is the exception, however, as the inclusion of a bi-racial protagonist within this overwhelmingly white genre is seen as radical enough to necessitate a strictly conservative aesthetic. As this discussion suggests, the heritage film debate is ongoing within British cinema studies. Therefore, I have chosen to use the less critically loaded, more neutral term 'historical film' in line with James Chapman's assertion that historical films are 'based, however loosely, on actual historical events or real historical persons'.[8]

Kara McKechnie attributes the revival of the monarchy film to interest in scandal and instability within the royal family, such as the tensions within the marriage of Prince Charles and Princess Diana.[9] *Elizabeth* was seen to respond to this through the film's exploration of the conflict between private desire and public duty inherent within the depiction of Elizabeth's relationship with Robert Dudley. In doing so, the film was also seen to respond to, and further, the sense of 'Diana hysteria' that was apparent within the media at the time. The 'Diana narrative' continued to influence British historical films into the millennium, becoming most overt in *The Duchess*, as the marketing and reception discourses drew heavily on the ancestral links between Diana and Georgiana, as I discuss later on. *Elizabeth* is most notable, however, for its mediation of the postfeminist girl power discourse. As Andrew Higson argues, this was achieved through the film's portrayal of a youthful and sexy Elizabeth I that was in stark contrast to the popular image of the Virgin Queen, and the conflict between individualized love and public duty that highlights the postfeminist notion of 'having it all' and the impossibility of this.[10] The incorporation of postfeminist discourses signals the filmmakers' intent to attract a more youthful and 'politically aware feminist audience' that was not the usual target audience for British historical films.[11] Central to the film's take up of postfeminist discourses was its engagement with women's pleasure and choice, exemplified when Elizabeth decides to prioritize duty over love and 'become' the Virgin Queen at the end of the film by cutting her hair and whitening her face – the image of Elizabeth I that is most recognizable to audiences.

The films in this chapter represent the intensification of British cinema's interest in historical royal and aristocratic women, which can be attributed in part to the pervasive spread of postfeminism, and, more importantly, to what Diane Negra and Yvonne Tasker refer to as 'a renewed fascination with aristocratic elites' in a recessionary media culture that has emerged since 2008. Negra and Tasker highlight media events such as the royal wedding in 2011 between Prince William and Kate Middleton as emblematic of this contemporary fascination with the aristocracy, in line with wealth and inequality becoming 'key themes across numerous media genres and modes' during a period of deepening inequality in the UK.[12] More recently, Britain's current monarch has been mobilized as part of a mediation of austerity discourses which draw on the Second World War as part of incitements to 'keep calm and carry on' as a way to survive the recession.[13] The British film *A Royal Night Out* (Jarrold 2015) follows teenage princesses Elizabeth (Sarah Gadon) and Margaret (Bel Powley) as they escape from the confines of Buckingham Palace for one night only on V.E. Day in 1945, while the Netflix series *The Crown* begins with the young Queen Elizabeth II

(Claire Foy) navigating becoming queen during the difficult post-war period and has been a hit with critics and audiences. It is clear that this interest in royal young women shows no sign of waning.

'When did ambition stop being thought of as a sin and become a virtue?': *The Other Boleyn Girl* (2008)

Ten years after *Elizabeth* triggered a fundamental shift within British historical films, *The Other Boleyn Girl* explored the story of Anne Boleyn (Natalie Portman) and her sister Mary (Scarlett Johansson). The film was dubbed 'Elizabeth The Prequel', in acknowledgement of the influence of the earlier film on the genre.[14] Released during a period of Tudor revival in film and television in the mid-2000s that included *Elizabeth: The Golden Age* and the HBO series *The Tudors* (2007–2010), *The Other Boleyn Girl* benefitted from creative personnel with experience of British heritage productions. Director Justin Chadwick had previously directed *Bleak House* (2005) for the BBC and the screenplay was written by Peter Morgan whose credits also included *The Queen* (Frears 2006), which depicted Queen Elizabeth II (Helen Mirren) in the period following the death of Diana, Princess of Wales. *The Other Boleyn Girl* is an adaptation of Philippa Gregory's (2001) novel that covers Thomas Boleyn's attempts to gain status by having his daughters, Anne and Mary, earn prominent places within the court of Henry VIII (Eric Bana). Mary becomes the king's mistress but is soon replaced by Anne, who is believed to be more intelligent and fashionable. In order to be Queen of England, Anne must convince Henry to break with the church, get his marriage to Catherine of Aragon annulled and provide him with a male heir. The film follows her attempts to do so, culminating in her beheading.

Here, I explore how *The Other Boleyn Girl* mediates the figure of Anne Boleyn through postfeminist discourses of ambition and 'empowerment', constructing her as an ambitious young woman, while also offering a critique of postfeminist 'empowerment'. Although the film emphasizes Anne Boleyn's determination and ambition, it also suggests that she is at the mercy of her father and uncle, and thus a victim of patriarchy and the social conventions of her time. Anne's ambition is emphasized in the film through the positioning of Anne and Mary as binary opposites, in which Anne is clever and different, whereas Mary is fair, 'simple and uncomplicated'. This opposition extends to the film's critical reception, which further highlights Anne's ambitious character through a girl power lexicon of words such as 'feisty'.[15] However, Anne's ambition is also presented in gendered terms that suggest she is threatening and dangerous, as critics describe her character as 'bewitching'[16] and a 'scheming, cruel trollop'.[17] Initially, it is Anne who is referred to as 'the other Boleyn girl', while sweet and innocent Mary attracts the attention of the king when she uses her maternal qualities to care for Henry after his riding accident.

However, when it is clear that Henry's attention has turned to Anne, the girls' father and uncle plot how best to secure the family's position. It is suggested that Anne functions as a business transaction as when, in a sinister scene, her father and uncle sit around a large table in a darkened room discussing the situation without any regard for her thoughts or feelings. This also harks back to the opening scene of the film where the Boleyn children play together in an evocation of childhood freedom while their parents discuss their futures. Anne is singled out as a high achiever, with her father claiming that 'Anne can do much better than a merchant's son'. Scenes such as these serve to highlight the lack of choice for women during the period in comparison with today, as the film suggests marriage was a woman's only means of securing her future. This is reinforced through the character of Anne's mother (Kristin Scott-Thomas), who functions as the critical feminist voice within the film and angrily asserts that her daughters' education has been in vain as they continue to be 'traded like cattle for the advancement and amusement of men'. The feminist mother figure is common throughout these films, providing what Maggie Andrews refers to as 'fragments of feminism that although culturally familiar by the millennium had become marginalised'.[18]

The film's mediation of the postfeminist ambitious young woman discourse is partly achieved through the construction of Anne as a high achiever. When Anne is sent to the French court as punishment for her role in Henry's riding accident, her mother encourages a can-do attitude in Anne, telling her to make the most of the opportunities and chances she never had. While Anne may not be able to develop a career in a way that is recognizable to modern audiences, it is evident that her time at the French court was educational, helping to further her aim to 'catch the King and keep him', and she returns to England transformed. In his review of the film for *Time Out*, Dave Calhoun claims Anne is 'emboldened by her spell at the French court (it's a small mercy she doesn't return with a copy of *The Second Sex* under her arm)'.[19] Despite its mocking tone, Calhoun's evocation of Simone de Beauvoir's key second-wave feminist text highlights how these films work to rewrite feminist history, incorporating feminist ideas into a prefeminist setting in order to construct the characters as 'forebears of the "empowered" postfeminist'.[20] Anne returns to court with a ballsy, girl power attitude; she is able to hold the attention of the male court, joking that 'women now accept [men] as equal'. Her sexuality is also filtered through discourses of postfeminist 'empowerment', presenting Anne as the actively desiring sexual subject, who chooses to objectify herself in the name of sexual liberation and empowerment.[21] In postfeminist culture, women are expected to possess a certain level of sexual knowingness, and Anne is keen to demonstrate hers when she joins Henry and his men on a hunt. Anne declines Henry's offer to ride with him, explaining that she will use a new type of saddle that allows her to ride on her own. When Henry asks how she proposes to stay on the horse without a man to hold on to, Anne flirtatiously replies, 'As you do, my Lord, with my thighs', suggesting that Anne is a modern, 'empowered' woman who is ahead of her time, and whose identity is located within her (sexy) body.

The 'can-do' girl is the dominant figure of postfeminist discourses of ambition, and Anne displays the 'desire, determination and confidence' of a can-do girl to achieve her goal of becoming the Queen of England through encouraging Henry to divorce Catherine of

Aragon.[22] Although Anne achieves her goal, she becomes increasingly powerless as she struggles to produce a male heir. She confesses that she has to 'resort to evermore degrading means' and is raped by Henry, who is seemingly provoked by her inability to produce a male heir. As Jessica Taylor argues, within these 'historical chick flicks', marital rape is a key 'historical artefact' that serves to obscure continuing gender inequalities within postfeminist culture by confining them to the past since marital rape is now illegal in Western cultures.[23] The intensity of this scene is further heightened as it is followed by the scene of Anne's coronation. The colour palette is harsh, consisting of cold blues and greys as Anne stares blankly ahead, looking ostensibly regal but also passive and empty. The coronation scene draws attention to the glittering signifiers of royalty, which produce the sparkle that provides the kind of visibility that is essential to postfeminist femininity as part of the film's 'postfeminist historical sensibility'.[24] Anne is most visible at this point and yet the violence of the rape scene reminds us that, far from empowered, she is powerless (Figure 4.1).

This issue of power becomes intertwined with questions of blame as Anne begins to lose control. Mary blames Anne for being too ambitious, invoking the myth of Icarus who flew too close to the

Figure 4.1 *The Other Boleyn Girl* (2008) Anne's (Natalie Portman) coronation.

sun as she tells her, 'You reached too high.' Anne too blames herself for the situation, and attempts increasingly drastic solutions to the problem of conceiving a male heir, even considering committing incest. As she frantically cries to Mary, 'It's slipping away from me and its all my fault', we see the key problem inherent within neoliberal postfeminist discourses of choice: if a woman is entirely free to make her own life choices then she must also take full self-responsibility for those choices. Ulrich Beck refers to this blaming of oneself for perceived failures as 'guilt ascription', which is a particular burden associated with the choice of biography and the risk of the 'chosen' personal identity.[25] However, the film questions whether Anne is truly responsible as her ambition was initially cultivated by her father and uncle, who plotted to advance the family's position. For all it seems that Anne has been managing her own ambitions, her decisions – and their consequence – have been influenced and underpinned by patriarchal figures. Anne's mother is also critical of the emphasis placed on young women's ambition, asking 'When was it that ambition stopped being thought of as a sin and became a virtue?' As the critical feminist voice within the film, Anne's mother functions to highlight not only the constraints women faced historically but also the challenges young women face in the twenty-first century with the widespread dominance of the figure of the can-do girl and the ways in which young women are expected to be ambitious, 'fully self-actualised neoliberal subjects', and the burden this creates.[26] In questioning the emphasis placed upon young women's ambition, the film highlights the problematic postfeminist notion of 'having it all', which, as Charlotte Brunsdon argues, is recognized as a 'postfeminist fantasy of femininities'.[27] Anne and Mary represent both sides of this postfeminist fantasy, as Anne is ambitious and career-minded while Mary seeks love and a family. Once again, the fantasy remains just that, as it is Mary who finds personal happiness through her marriage to William Stafford (Eddie Redmayne), while Anne's struggle to maintain her status as Queen of England leads to her death. As Louise Wilks suggests, the ending of *The Other Boleyn Girl* – and also *The*

Duchess – subverts notions of postfeminist empowerment as things 'end darkly' for both Anne and Georgiana.[28]

Ultimately, in constructing Anne Boleyn as a postfeminist ambitious young woman, *The Other Boleyn Girl* offers a critique of postfeminist discourses of ambition. It questions the supposed empowerment on offer by drawing parallels between Anne's situation and the film's audience, and by highlighting the perils of wanting 'too much' and the default positioning of young women as aspirational subjects. However, the film also demonstrates that Anne was not entirely to blame – she was not acting freely but instead at the mercy of patriarchal forces. Indeed, Anne is celebrated in the final scene of the film when an image of a young girl playing with other children is accompanied by intertitles informing us that Anne 'gave Henry a strong red-headed girl' called Elizabeth, who would 'rule over England for forty-five years'. Anne is presented as ultimately successful because she gave birth to Elizabeth. The close-up freeze-frame image of a young Elizabeth that closes the film links *The Other Boleyn Girl* to Kapur's *Elizabeth* in a 'highly reflexive "knowing" mode of address' that characterizes recent heritage films.[29] This image also evokes comparisons with a moment at the beginning of the film when the Boleyn children are playing together while their parents discuss their futures. The repetition of this image creates a sense of cyclicality, suggesting that the issues of female power and autonomy that Anne faced will also be faced by her daughter, as explored in Kapur's film, and they persist for women today.

From 'ordinary' princess to extraordinary queen: *The Young Victoria* (Vallée 2009)

Questions about women's power and freedom are also raised in *The Young Victoria*. Unlike *The Other Boleyn Girl*, *The Young Victoria* is aimed at a younger, teenage audience, with a strict PG certificate rather than a 15 certificate like *The Other Boleyn Girl* and *The Duchess*. The desire to target a younger audience, Maggie Andrews suggests,

influenced the decision to abandon 'the trope of victimhood' present
in films such as *The Other Boleyn Girl* and *The Duchess* and replace it
with the postfeminist 'trope of girl power',[30] with Victoria portrayed as
'sassy, both an ordinary and extraordinary teenager'.[31] The film focuses
on the life of the teenage Queen Victoria (Emily Blunt), who lives at
Kensington Palace under the guard of her mother and uncle. As the
heir to the throne, Victoria must live by a strict set of rules, known as
the 'Kensington System', devised by her mother and uncle ostensibly
for her own protection but, more importantly, as a means of control.
They believe Victoria is too young to rule and try to force her to sign
a regency order to pass control to her uncle (Jim Broadbent). When
Victoria meets and falls in love with Prince Albert (Rupert Friend),
he encourages her to maintain control and marry someone who is her
equal who can work with her. As Victoria starts to doubt her abilities,
becoming too politically reliant on Prime Minister Lord Melbourne
(Paul Bettany), Albert convinces her to let him share her work and the
pair remain happily married until Albert's death.

   The Young Victoria was directed by French-Canadian director Jean-
Marc Vallée, who, like Kapur, was not known for making historical dramas,
having previously directed the French family drama C.R.A.Z.Y. (2005). The
film's historical credentials were bolstered by Julian Fellowes as screenwriter,
who won an Oscar for the period drama *Gosford Park* (Altman 2001),
but is more recently known as the creator of *Downton Abbey* (ITV 2010–
2015). The production team also boasted a real-life royal in the form of
Sarah Ferguson, Duchess of York as producer, alongside Graham King and
Martin Scorsese. According to King, it was the Duchess of York who first
pitched the idea of making a film about a young Queen Victoria, having
devised the premise after co-authoring two books on Queen Victoria and
Prince Albert. King notes how Ferguson wanted to portray Queen Victoria
'in a different way' to how the monarch has typically been portrayed on
screen.[32] Representations of Queen Victoria in British cinema have tended
to portray her as an older queen who is mourning the death of Prince
Albert in films such as *Victoria the Great* (Wilcox 1937) and *Sixty Years
Glorious* (Wilcox 1938), starring Anna Neagle, and more recently in *Mrs*

Brown (Madden 1997), starring Judi Dench. Emily Blunt's portrayal of a young Victoria who is, as Peter Bradshaw notes in his review of the film for the *Guardian*, 'very much amused',[33] marks a point of departure for British cinema. British television, by contrast, has favoured more youthful portrayals of the queen. This includes John Erman's 2001 television drama *Albert and Victoria*, which explored the royal couple's marriage, and *Victoria* (ITV 2016–), which stars former *Doctor Who* companion Jenna Coleman as the young queen.

In their desire to portray Victoria differently, the producers echo the production discourse surrounding *Elizabeth*, which emphasized Elizabeth's youthful sexuality over the more typical image of her as the Virgin Queen. Moreover, like *Elizabeth*, the ability to produce a revised portrayal of the queen is attributed to the director's outsider status. As Emily Blunt explains, 'It's good not to have an English . . . director, because he doesn't hold this period in too much reverence', which enables him to take a more 'modern' approach.[34] Vallée agrees that he had a helpful distance from British history, as he 'didn't want to make a classic British period film',[35] a sentiment also echoed by Shekhar Kapur when making *Elizabeth*. Graham King also highlights this desire for *The Young Victoria* to have a more contemporary visual style that is 'less restrained than . . . "your typical BBC-type movie"'.[36] This move away from restraint is encapsulated by pre-release promises of 'a new, more sexed-up portrayal of Britain's longest-reigning monarch'.[37] However, this pledge to create a sexier portrayal of Victoria exposes a point of tension between the producers' intentions and the film's target audience. As King explains, 'there will be a bedroom scene [but] there will not be a sex scene' because 'we're going to be tasteful in what we show'.[38] King's comment not only reinforces the idea that *The Young Victoria* is aimed at a younger audience (for whom explicit sex scenes would be inappropriate) but also undercuts previous claims about the film not being a 'classic British period film'. In vowing to be 'tasteful', King is also acknowledging a need to adhere to certain conventions and audience expectations about the genre, highlighting the tension between these two discourses.

As with *The Other Boleyn Girl*, part of this 'modernizing' process involves presenting the young would-be monarch as a twenty-first-century postfeminist woman in a prefeminist world. In the film's production notes, Emily Blunt reinforces the idea of the film's 'postfeminist historical sensibility' by noting how, having researched Queen Victoria, 'She seemed like a very modern character, a very twenty-first century sort of woman'.[39] Director Jean-Marc Vallée, meanwhile, evokes girl power discourses of ballsy femininity by emphasizing how Victoria overcame gender barriers in order to succeed: 'She was a woman in a man's world and despite being tiny, she had balls.'[40] Julian Fellowes further attempts to position Victoria in the twenty-first century by linking Victoria's story to the idea of 'instant celebrity' – an 'ordinary' person who is quickly catapulted to fame. According to Fellowes, 'One minute Victoria is living under virtual house arrest, the next she is the most famous woman in the world.'[41] While Fellowes is keen to stress the parallels between Victoria and the modern-day figure of the instant celebrity, this parallel has its limits as, although sheltered, Victoria was still a royal princess and thus far from being an ordinary girl. Although the film's production team aimed to present Victoria as a modern, sexy, twenty-first-century young woman, the film's critical reception suggests that this was not particularly successful. The film is described as 'a film of polished niceness',[42] and 'about as sexy as a cold fish and as imaginative as a kipper'.[43]

In suggesting that Victoria is both an ordinary girl and a princess, *The Young Victoria* is positioning itself alongside the 'significant increase in the mainstream output of tween princess films' in the twenty-first century, such as *The Princess Diaries* (Marshall 2001), in which sixteen-year-old schoolgirl Mia (Anne Hathaway) learns that she is heir to the throne of Genovia.[44] As Melanie Kennedy argues, these 'princess films' – films that centre on the figure of the princess narratives that are conscious reworkings of well-known fairy tales – often 'construct and address the figure of the tween – the pre-adolescent girl – [. . .] in a process of transformative becoming'.[45] In aligning itself with the 'princess film' through its emphasis on the teenage Victoria's 'becoming' (both woman and queen), *The Young Victoria* is also reinforcing its attempts to appeal to a younger audience than the other films discussed in this chapter. In doing so, the film also evokes the 'fairy tale motif of the princess in the golden cage'.[46] This is particularly apparent in the opening voice-over, in which Victoria explains: 'Some people are born more fortunate than others; such was the case with me. But as a child, I was convinced of quite the opposite. What little girl does not dream of growing up a princess? . . . [But] even a palace can be a prison.'

As well as establishing Victoria's subjectivity, the voice-over also serves to reinforce Victoria's supposed ordinariness by highlighting how she was unaware of her privilege and did not realize that she was next in line to throne until she was eleven years old. The film is also quick to establish that being a princess is not all it seems, as 'even a palace can feel like a prison', and Victoria will face the same issues of 'becoming-woman' as other girls. Victoria's confinement is conveyed repeatedly in the film's opening scenes. Victoria is also shown staring out of windows while her voice-over explains how she 'dream[s] of the day I might be free and pray for the strength to meet my destiny'. This scene then cuts to Victoria's coronation – a recurring image in the film. The mise en scène is regal, emphasizing the vast spectacle of Westminster Abbey, with Handel's 'Zadok the Priest' as the coronation anthem. As the crown is placed upon Victoria's head, the music stops and the camera zooms in to capture her stare directly into the lens, emphasizing the burden of her position in a manner that is reminiscent of Anne's coronation in *The Other Boleyn Girl* (Figure 4.2). As Melanie Kennedy argues, princess films take pleasure in emphasizing the sparkly markers of royalty – the crowns, gowns and jewels – as sparkle is a key signifier of contemporary girlhood; yet, this is at odds with the notions of authenticity that are integral to the princess films and neoliberal postfeminist culture more broadly.[47] However, in the British historical films discussed here, the sparkly signifiers of royalty are shown to be artificial and also symbols of the royal figure's confinement and unhappiness in accordance with the ambivalence towards consumption and glamour that is found across contemporary

Figure 4.2 *The Young Victoria* (2009) Victoria's (Emily Blunt) coronation.

British cinema's girl-centred films. The iconography of the coronation scene, moreover, marks the beginning of the film quoting royal portraiture, as the scene is inspired by John Martin's *The Coronation of Queen Victoria* (1839).[48] This trope is common in historical films, serving to reinforce historical authenticity while drawing attention to the monarch as 'a visual representation, a symbolic construct'.[49] In drawing on royal portraiture during the coronation scene, the film is presenting Victoria's transition from a young girl (who happened to be a princess) into the symbolic image of Queen Victoria.

However, the symbolism inherent in the film's presentation of Queen Victoria is largely depoliticized through the focus on Victoria's relationship with Albert. According to producer Graham King, the film is 'pure love story . . . it's a human story'.[50] Initially, Victoria and Albert's meeting is shown to be a political venture devised by their families, where Albert is coached in Victoria's likes and dislikes. As in *The Other Boleyn Girl*, this serves to highlight the lack of autonomy for women of the period. As their relationship develops, it becomes clear that it is a love match above all. Victoria also confides in Albert about her feelings of powerlessness as she is caught between her own desires and the will of her family, asking: 'Do you ever feel like a chess piece being played in a game against your will?' She tests Albert by asking if he thinks she should find a man to play the game for her, to which he replies, 'You find a husband to play it with you, not for you.' Albert's reply implies that their future marriage would be based on equality, thus presenting Victoria and Albert as a 'modern' couple familiar to contemporary audiences. However, as Vidal argues, 'By depicting their arranged marriage as a love union between two equals, this strangely quaint film isolates Victoria from her turbulent socio-political era.'[51] In doing so, the film reinforces the idea that recent historical films are 'filtered through the lens of the postfeminist movement'[52] through depoliticizing the issues they aim to address. In the case of *The Young Victoria*, the feminist issue of female autonomy is depoliticized and subsumed into the key narrative arc of the love story between the young couple.

The question of power and, by extension, Victoria's ability to fulfil such a role, is raised throughout the film. Victoria's youth and vulnerability are emphasized when she is awoken in the middle of the night to be informed of her uncle's death. She is guided down the stairs in her white nightdress into a dark room as men in mourning clothes kneel before her and announce, 'Long live the Queen'. The contrast is stark as this innocent young girl suddenly holds the most powerful position in England. As such, concern and doubt circulate around Victoria, who, like Anne Boleyn, experiences anxiety. She has anxiety dreams before her coronation, dreaming of chess pieces being moved along the board and voices whispering, 'She's too young'. Although this is only a brief sequence within the film, it furthers the representation of Victoria as a modern young woman through evoking the discourses circulating around contemporary girlhood in which girls are constructed simultaneously as more capable and socially powerful than ever before but also in psychological crisis as the 'never-good-enough girl who must perpetually observe and remake herself'.[53] Victoria's youth and inexperience make her an object of public concern due to her over-reliance on Lord Melbourne, bringing the country to the brink of a constitutional crisis. Just like Elizabeth, Victoria causes political instability when she prioritizes personal desire over duty, which leads to a 'media scandal' as she is mocked in cartoons that refer to her as 'Mrs Melbourne'. Concerns over public image and media representation are prominent in historical films featuring young female protagonists, with the political cartoons of the day equated with tabloids and gossip magazines that thrive on scandal.

Victoria's marriage to Albert is attributed with bringing much-needed stability to her reign while also working to further 'normalize' Victoria through her role as a wife. Historical records show that Victoria asked Albert to marry her, as he was of lower status than the queen.[54] However, the film's depiction of the proposal shows Victoria struggling to express her wishes, with Albert eventually proposing marriage to her. Here, Victoria's power and status are subsumed into traditional patriarchal cultural norms that dictate it is the man's responsibility to propose. Albert also addresses Victoria as 'wife', reinforcing her supposed ordinariness and reducing her status to that of wife rather than queen. This normalization of Victoria and Albert positions them as ancestors of, and draws parallels with, the current royal family, who in recent years have 'actively engaged . . . in the representation of themselves . . . as a "normal", modern [. . .] ideal middle-class family'.[55] As Kim Allen et al. argue, 'ordinariness' has always played a role in justifying the royal family's wealth and privilege, but this has taken on even greater significance since the recession when public spending has been under intense scrutiny.[56] The normalization of Victoria as an 'ordinary' wife and mother echoes contemporary discourses circulating around the Duchess of Cambridge, who is normalized through continued references to her as the more ordinary-sounding Kate Middleton, as well as to the fact that she was not born into the aristocracy. Since her marriage to Prince William in 2011, the duchess has been further rendered ordinary through a media discourse which presents her as a hard-working wife and mother, as part of attempts to 'defus[e] resentment at the growing inequalities' since the recession.[57]

The normalization of Victoria further allows for the film to explore the idea of conflict between love and duty, while diluting the film's feminist politics. The film's publicity materials hinge on this conflict between love and duty, as the trailer informs us that 'Her destiny belonged to an empire but her heart belonged to one man'. This tension is the main source of conflict in what is otherwise presented as an idyllic relationship. Matters of private and public concern clash when Victoria and Albert are arguing over government issues in their private bedchamber. Victoria attempts to assert her authority by reminding Albert of her position before linking this to the status of women more generally by angrily claiming, 'You thought I was a woman who is to be ignored.' Albert responds by criticizing her for becoming over-excited as it is harmful to the baby she is carrying and disobeys Victoria's orders by leaving the room before being dismissed. This normalizing of Victoria also works to depoliticize her in accordance with postfeminism, where young women are allowed to 'come forward' on the condition that feminist politics fades away.[58] In initially voicing reluctance to give up her newly acquired power by becoming trapped in a marriage, Victoria is presented as being aware of the need for feminism but the film suggests that the best way for her to manage her power is to give some of it to Albert. The film takes this further by implying Victoria *needs* Albert when he risks his life to save her from a bullet. The synopsis in the production notes details how at this point 'Victoria realizes what a selfish woman she has become,'[59] employing the language of postfeminist 'backlash' against feminism to portray Victoria as a selfish (feminist) woman who prioritizes her work over her husband. It is this dramatic event as well as Melbourne's suggestion that Victoria let Albert 'share [her] work' that leads to Victoria placing Albert's desk next to hers where the film's closing caption tells us they 'reigned together for twenty years' until Albert's death. This image of Victoria and Albert working side by side reinforces the film's commitment to presenting them as a couple who were ahead of their time with a marriage based on equality. However, this is undermined as Victoria has to relinquish some of her power in order for the film's love story narrative to have the required happy ending. Once again, we see the impossibility of the desire to 'have it all', as Victoria is forced to share her position, and in turn, lose some of her status, in order to sustain her marriage, which is presented as the true marker of her success.

Constructing *The Duchess* (2008)

The Young Victoria went to great lengths to highlight the fact that the marriage between Victoria and Albert was – unusually – based on love. This is not the case in *The Duchess*, where the much older Duke of Devonshire (Ralph Fiennes) marries seventeen-year-old Georgiana (Keira Knightley). For the duke, this is a marriage of convenience with the sole aim of producing a male heir. He has numerous affairs, including with Georgiana's best friend Bess (Hayley Atwell). However, it soon becomes clear that 'the Duke is the only man in England not in love with his wife' as Georgiana's popularity soars and she becomes an eighteenth-century celebrity and fashion icon. The film explores the idea of sexual 'double standards' when Georgiana falls in love with Lord Grey (Dominic Cooper) and is forced to give up their child. *The Duchess* is based on Amanda Foreman's biography of Georgiana Cavendish, *Georgiana: Duchess of Devonshire* (1998). Like Anne and Victoria, Georgiana is presented as a modern, intelligent young woman confined in a prefeminist world. She is politically active, lending her support to Grey's Whig Party, and critical about the way women are treated in society. Unlike *The Young Victoria*, questions of women's power and freedom in *The Duchess* cannot be easily subsumed into a love story and neatly resolved.

The casting of Keira Knightley in this £15.3 million historical drama came as no surprise to film reviewers given her previous roles in period dramas, such as Joe Wright's film adaptations of *Pride and Prejudice* (2005), *Atonement* (2007) and *Anna Karenina* (2012). As the *Daily Telegraph*'s Benjamin Secher remarks, '[Knightley] may be the British actress who best represents her generation but when film directors look at Keira Knightley they see a face that belongs to the past.[60] She is also, more disparagingly, referred to as 'an experienced wearer of corsets'.[61] While Knightley was seen as an obvious choice to play the Duchess of Devonshire, the choice of Saul Dibb as director came as a surprise. As the director of *Bullet Boy* (2004), a film that explored contemporary gang culture in east London, Dibb was an unusual choice. As with the films discussed earlier, Dibb's status as an outsider to the genre is seen as a way to enable him to move away from the 'Merchant Ivory' idea of British heritage films and create a film that has relevance for twenty-first-century audiences: 'It's a story with a modern sensibility. Here we are in the bedrooms and corridors of these aristocratic people dealing with messy relationships. That, to me, is not the stuff of Merchant Ivory . . . I tried to look at it with immediacy than with nostalgia.'[62]

Dibb's emphasis on the 'messy relationships' within the film works to depoliticize the film for a postfeminist audience, as structural inequalities between men and women are reframed as personal problems that the individual must solve. As part of attempts to make the film relevant to modern audiences, the filmmakers also employ discursive formations around Princess Diana, such as 'victimization, life story as empowerment and domestic life into the public sphere'.[63] While all of the films analysed so far in this chapter have employed, what Maggie Andrews terms, 'the Diana narrative', *The Duchess* does so most overtly, capitalizing on the fact that Georgiana is an ancestor of Diana. The links between Diana and Georgiana occur frequently within the film's press, with specific reference being made to the film's trailer, which explicitly links the two women.[64] The theatrical trailer intercuts images of Knightley as Georgiana and Diana, while the captions inform us that the two women were 'related by ancestry, united by destiny' as 'this summer, history repeats itself'.

Like the other films discussed in this chapter, *The Duchess* explores feminist history through its concern with women's freedom, or lack thereof. The opening scene of the film depicts the teenage Georgiana playing games in the garden with a group of friends, including Charles Grey, while the duke watches from a window and discusses his plans to marry Georgiana with her mother. Georgiana seems unaware of the discussions taking place, and the green expanse of the garden highlights the youthful freedom she currently has in contrast to the confinement of the marriage she is about to embark on. The scene has echoes of the opening scene of *The Other Boleyn Girl*, and it seems that Georgiana, like Anne and Mary before her, will be 'traded like cattle' in order to secure a man's position when it is made clear that she will be handsomely rewarded when she provides a male heir. This lack of freedom is further emphasized when Georgiana learns of the duke's intention to marry her and she excitedly assumes that he loves her, despite having only met twice. Georgiana's belief that it is a proposal borne out of love positions her within a contemporary (post-) feminist context in which it is accepted that (Western) women now marry for love above all else. Postfeminist audiences can relate to this, while feeling relieved that women today 'have it better' and the kind of situation that Georgiana finds herself in is confined to the past.

The film's 'postfeminist historical sensibility' is also produced through an emphasis on image and consumption, which in postfeminist culture is presented as key to attaining a personal identity, particularly as the body acts as a 'window onto one's interior life'.[65] Georgiana articulates the importance of clothing to women's personal identity as the duke attempts to undress her on their wedding night, prompting him to ask why women's clothes are so complicated. Georgiana explains that clothes are 'our way of expressing ourselves . . . we must make do with hats and dresses'. Georgiana's comment draws attention to the limited means available to women in the eighteenth century to express themselves and the idea that they had to 'make do' with forming their personal identities from their clothing as this was the only means available to them. The significance of clothing to women's identity is indicative of the film's 'postfeminist historical sensibility' in that it echoes postfeminist discourses of consumption while drawing attention to the lack of choice for women like Georgiana in comparison to women today who are supposedly free to choose from a range of consumer options available to them. Clothing is also both a literal and a symbolic source of confinement for Georgiana, as the frustrated duke resorts to cutting open her dress. It makes an audible tearing sound, undermining the idea of this consummation scene as a typical love scene through this aggressive moment that is inflicted upon Georgiana's body and, by extension, her personal identity, which foreshadows the violent rape that occurs later in the film, resulting in the birth of Georgiana's only son.

Georgiana's costumes are central to the film – Knightley reportedly wore twenty-seven individual costumes – as a means of mediating postfeminist discourses of fame and celebrity. As Sarah Projansky argues, postfeminist and celebrity discourses are inextricably linked, contributing to the 'specularization' of girls in contemporary media culture, and the film casts Georgiana as a celebrity in line with these discourses.[66] Georgiana is presented as a celebrity and fashion icon of her day whose outfits draw gasps from the crowds, rendering her highly visible and enabling her to use her status to campaign politically for the Whig Party (Figure 4.3).[67] The use of extravagant costumes is a prominent trope in recent historical films more broadly, exemplified by Sofia Coppola's *Marie Antoinette*. Coppola's film employs a self-reflexive and ironic style, where a candy-coloured mise en scène, use of designer fashion brands and a contemporary soundtrack all work to highlight the 'constructed nature of representation'.[68] As Fiona Handyside argues, '[*Marie Antoinette*] demonstrates fashion's ability to renegotiate identity', while also underscoring 'the vulnerability of an identity that can be so manipulated'. She notes how within this discourse of royalty and celebrity, the power of a fashionable body is 'precarious, shifting on the whims of the people'.[69] Writing in the *London Evening Standard*,

Figure 4.3 *The Duchess* (2008) Georgiana (Keira Knightley), 'the Empress of Fashion'.

Charlotte O'Sullivan highlights the relationship between *Marie Antoinette* and *The Duchess* as both being about 'poor little It girls' that foreground the protagonists' identities as young women who are constructed through fashion and consumption.[70] Within *The Duchess*, the discourse around clothes is similarly self-reflexive. Georgiana's costumes enable her to construct her persona of 'the Duchess' and become spectacular, but this undermines the idea of the makeover as revealing the 'authentic' self because her identity is so clearly artificially constructed. Like Marie Antoinette, Georgiana is also very vulnerable, and her outfits and her performance of femininity become more outlandish as her personal difficulties increase. Georgiana moves from being spectacular to scandalous as she is depicted suffering from seemingly modern, postfeminist disorders such as eating disorders and addiction.[71] Her addictions become public knowledge when she drunkenly stumbles at a ball, crashing into a chandelier, which causes her ostentatious wig to catch fire. She rips her wig off, falling literally and symbolically in front of an audience, hairnet exposed, revealing the artificiality of her image.

The constrictive nature of Georgiana's clothes is also highlighted by Knightley in interviews where she discusses the difficulties she experienced while wearing the lavish costumes. Talking about a particularly tall wig, Knightley says, 'I couldn't lift my head, it was so heavy. Halfway through a scene Saul said, "We can't see your eyes any more", and it was because my neck couldn't hold the weight of my own head'.[72] This resulted in crew members making a board for Knightley to lean against to protect her neck between takes. The costumes undoubtedly impacted upon Knightley's performance by restricting her movements. Knightley's comments suggest that the weight of her costume rendered her almost mannequin-like, with eyes demurely downcast, creating the sense of an artificial performance of femininity that was dictated by what she was wearing. By contrast, the film suggests that when Georgiana is with Charles Grey, she can be her authentic self, indicated through her simpler clothes and brighter mise en scène away from Devonshire House. While the film's use of restrictive eighteenth-century corsets suggests women's confinement has been relegated to the past, the film's critical reception frames discussions of Knightley's performance within a rhetoric of postfeminist bodily surveillance. Knightley's performance is reduced to her image, with critics referring to her as 'a stunning centrepiece', who is 'coiffed and primped to within an inch of her life',[73] and who 'gives great profile'.[74] Many of the comments are steeped in misogyny, with a particular focus on Knightley's supposed excessive pouting. The *Guardian's* Peter Bradshaw claims Knightley's 'lips are once again perennially shaped to express something between a pout and a moue',[75] while a reviewer for the *Nottingham Evening Post* questions whether being 'posh, pretty and pouting' is enough to enable Knightley to carry the film.[76] Other reviewers also claim that she is too thin,[77] a criticism that has plagued Knightley throughout her career, making her the target of vitriolic attacks, particularly online. The intense criticism levelled at Knightley is thus indicative of postfeminism's strict policing of women's bodies, where a woman must be slim but not skinny, and her value is bound up in her ability to conform to these arbitrary standards.[78]

Within the film, women's oppression is explored through the strict social conventions of the period, where men like the duke could have affairs without consequence while Georgiana had to give up the baby girl she has with Charles Grey and return to Devonshire House, leading Dibb to refer to the film as a 'feminist tragedy'.[79] The explicit reference to feminism here draws attention to what Jessica Taylor refers to as the film's 'radical potential' to push back against postfeminist logic through evoking feminist politics.[80] Similarly, Amanda Foreman draws attention to the postfeminist fantasy of having it all through her description of Georgiana as a 'modern woman who is struggling to have it all, like the rest of us' but 'you can't have it all. That's what her life shows us.'[81] Unlike, *The Young Victoria*, where the issue of women's autonomy is solved through the sharing of power within the love story narrative, *The Duchess*, like *The Other Boleyn Girl*, makes it clear that such problems cannot be overcome. The final shot of the film is an aerial shot of the children running around, echoing the earlier scene of playful freedom that indicates cyclical repetition from which it is impossible to escape. From Georgiana to Diana and beyond, women will remain trapped in a system that continually denies them true freedom and happiness.

'I don't know that I find myself anywhere': Race, representation and identity in *Belle* (2013)

The films discussed throughout this book have predominantly featured white, middle-class, able-bodied young female protagonists, highlighting both the privileging of a very narrow version of girlhood within twenty-first-century media culture and the lack of opportunities available to women of colour in the British film industry, both in front of and behind the camera. This emphasis on whiteness is particularly apparent within British heritage cinema, which has always been overwhelmingly white. Amma Asante's *Belle*, then, stands out as an anomaly within the genre as the first British heritage film to feature a bi-racial woman protagonist.[82] The film was chosen to represent the 'three ticks' diversity audit of the BFI when it was launched in 2014. The scheme aimed to encourage on- and off-screen diversity and promote social mobility, with films required to have at least one tick in a minimum of two areas. As So Mayer notes, the 'three ticks' scheme has particular implications for the British heritage genre, which is slow to diversify, despite this lack of diversity being historically inaccurate.[83] *Belle* is based on the true story of Dido Elizabeth Belle (Gugu Mbatha Raw), the illegitimate daughter of a Royal Navy admiral, who is sent to live with her great-uncle Lord Mansfield (Tom Wilkinson) and her cousin Elizabeth Murray (Sarah Gadon), who is fatherless and without independent wealth. Dido falls in love with John Davinier, a young lawyer who alerts her to the Zong ship trial, where hundreds of slaves were pushed overboard and the insurers refuse to compensate for 'loss of cargo', and over which Lord Mansfield is presiding as Lord Chief Justice. The film suggests that Lord Mansfield's relationship with Dido directly influenced his decision to hold the ship's owner responsible for the event in a ruling that the film attributes to leading to the abolition of slavery in Britain. *Belle* – a £7 million co-production between the BFI and Fox Searchlight Pictures – is Asante's second feature film following the BAFTA award–winning *A Way of Life* (2004). *A Way of Life* also explored the intersections of race, class and gender but from opposite ends of the class system. Set in the Welsh valleys, the film centres around teenage mother Leigh-Anne (Stephanie James), who carries out a racist attack on her neighbour.

This chapter has continuously demonstrated how portraiture is used to foreground the notion of identity construction while drawing attention to the self-reflexive nature of the genre.[84] In *Belle*, the use of portraiture serves to emphasize Dido's lack of identity while self-reflexively drawing attention to the overwhelming whiteness of the genre. This is most striking when a young Dido arrives at her new life in Kenwood House and she is depicted standing in the middle of a large room filled with paintings depicting the Mansfield lineage of white men. The wide-angle shot creates the impression of Dido being overwhelmed by her new surroundings, and noticeably the only person of colour. In order to confront this overwhelming whiteness, the film employs the conventional aesthetics of the period drama. The film's use of period drama conventions is repeatedly highlighted within its critical reception, usually through evoking comparisons with Jane Austen due to the film's marriage plot, exploration of social etiquette and 'lush' period detail.[85] The work of Jane Austen, and the figure of Austen herself, gained cultural prominence in the 1990s during a period of 'Austenmania', which included Andrew Davies' BBC adaptation of *Pride and Prejudice* (1995), and film adaptations of *Emma* (McGrath 1996), *Sense and Sensibility* (Thompson 1995) and *Mansfield Park* (Rozema 1999). This continued into the millennium with key films such as Joe Wright's adaptation of *Pride and Prejudice* (2005), starring Keira Knightley, along with a film about the young Jane Austen – *Becoming Jane* (Jarrold 2006) – starring Anne Hathaway. For Asante, the allusions to Jane Austen were deliberate, as she felt it was crucial to explore issues of race and gender through a conventional period aesthetic by creating a film that was 'as much Amma-esque as Austenesque'.[86] Asante explains how 'It was important to us to place this unexpected character in a very expected world . . . . It was important not to change the audience's perception of that world. So we went for classic all the way'.[87] This deliberate decision to adhere to generic conventions and expectations is in stark contrast to the production discourses of the previous films discussed in this chapter, which all emphasized a desire to move away from these conventions and to not be like a 'typical Merchant Ivory' film, regardless of whether this was actually achieved. For the producers of *Belle*, having a bi-racial young woman protagonist in a British heritage film was subversive enough.

Belle uses the Austen marriage plot to explore the intersections of attitudes towards class, gender and race in the Georgian period. Both Dido and Elizabeth are depicted as being constrained by the attitudes of the time. Elizabeth is due to 'come out' into society and is under pressure to find a suitable husband. She is struggling to do this as her biological father would not acknowledge her as his daughter, leaving her without any inheritance that would encourage men to marry her. Meanwhile, Dido's race prevents her from marrying above her current status but it would also be unacceptable for a woman of her class to marry for less. However, this issue is neatly sidestepped when Dido inherits £2,000 a year from Captain Lindsay, leaving her financially secure and free of the pressure to marry, unlike Elizabeth. As with the other films discussed in this chapter, *Belle* makes it clear that marriage has historically been the only route to security for women, and to marry for love rather than money would leave them 'poor and broken-hearted'. This stance is overtly articulated through the character of Elizabeth, who informs Dido (and the audience): 'We have no choice. We are but their property, forbidden from any activity that allows us to support ourselves.' In explicitly addressing the lack of freedom and autonomy for women in the eighteenth century, the film, once again, raises a feminist struggle while reassuring the viewer that it is safely confined to the past because they have the ability to choose to marry for love and be economically independent. Again, the film's 'historical postfeminist sensibility' works to construct Dido and Elizabeth as modern young women whose attitudes and beliefs are at odds with those around them, which is reinforced throughout the film's critical reception, as Mark Kermode writes in the *Observer* that Dido is a 'woman out of time'.[88] However, the supposed heavy-handedness of the film's dialogue attracted criticism from reviewers such as Henry Fitzherbert for sounding 'too much like the words of a 21st century screenwriter'.[89]

Belle's exploration of the intersections between gender, class and race is also apparent through a discourse of authorship, as in promotional interviews in which Asante draws parallels between Dido's situation and her experience as one of a small number of black women filmmakers working within the British film industry. Asante claims she feels 'privileged' to have achieved a certain degree of success within the film industry, 'but that doesn't negate the setbacks that gender and race can bring' and that she does not feel 'fully equal'.[90] Indeed, while Asante may be considered successful within the British film industry, there is still a ten-year gap between the BAFTA award–winning *A Way of Life* and *Belle*, indicating that she has faced a variety of struggles as a filmmaker, despite early success.[91] Within the film, Dido also has a degree of privilege as Lord Mansfield's niece but, like Asante, still isn't 'fully equal'. Attention is frequently drawn to classed, raced and gendered norms and how these intersect, and are continuously renegotiated within the film. When Lord Mansfield has guests for dinner, he informs Dido that, although she usually joins the family at the table, she cannot do so because 'we cannot impose on others our disregard for the rules'. Following her confrontation with Lord Mansfield, Dido is shown angrily striding down a dark narrow corridor as the previously spacious rooms of Kenwood House suddenly seem claustrophobic as Dido – like Georgiana – discovers that women, but especially women of colour, can be just as confined within the private realm of the home as they are in public.

Dido is presented as experiencing an 'identity crisis' due to the restrictions and contradictions she experiences through the intersection of gender, race and class. As the aforementioned discussion of the use of portraiture within the film demonstrates, Dido is unable to see herself due to the lack of representation of women of colour both within her home and outside in the wider society. In a striking scene, Dido beats her chest and claws at her face in frustration while staring into a mirror – the only place where she can see herself. The tactility and aggression inherent in these gestures suggest that Dido is upset and angry that the colour of her skin marks her out as different from those around her, and that she has to feel her skin in order to confirm that she exists. This is all the more resonant within the postfeminist context of the film's production and reception, as the body is the key site of a woman's identity. As Fiona Handyside argues, in order to perform girlhood successfully, non-white girls must perform the qualities associated with white identity, even though this will be more difficult, because these characteristics of whiteness are naturalized and perpetuated.[92] Dido demonstrates the difficulties of performing the qualities of white femininity when she gets frustrated because she is unable to brush her Afro-Caribbean hair without it getting tangled. Seeing Dido upset, the servant Mabel (Bethan Mary-James) – significantly the only other speaking character who is a woman of colour – takes the brush and brushes Dido's hair for her, explaining how she was taught to brush her hair by her mother. Dido's struggles convey how feminine beauty practices are inherently white; even the tools that are used – such as a hairbrush – are exclusionary when they are ineffective on Afro-Caribbean hair. The issue of class also intersects here as Dido is attempting to adhere to upper-class conventions of appearance but her hair makes it more difficult to conform. The fact that Dido has to be shown how to manage her hair by the working-class servant also reinforces her unusual and isolating position as an aristocratic woman of colour and compounds her sense of unbelonging.

Dido becomes more politically aware when she meets John Davinier, who teaches her about the Zong slavery trial, which leads her to further question the position of people of colour within British society, and her relationship to this. She also challenges Lord Mansfield's position, reminding him that she is evidence that he is willing to break the rules when it matters. Becoming more aware enables Dido to become 'empowered'. As Asante explains, Dido transforms from a girl who says, 'As *you* wish, sir', to a woman who says, 'As *I* wish – this is what I need, this is what is important to me'.[93] Asante is keen to convey that Dido does this not because 'she is a privileged young woman who wants more' but because she wants equality both within her household and the wider world. Despite Asante's claims, her comments echo contemporary discourses of individualism, particularly as the film's production notes reinforce this individualistic notion of empowerment through the idea that falling in love enables Dido to become more aware. As Asante explains: 'I saw her as a girl who grows into a woman by falling in love, and by falling in love, she learns the information that allows her to become a woman.'[94] Once again, the film's feminist and racial politics become subsumed and neutralized within a love story, as was apparent in the earlier discussion of *The Young Victoria*. In a further echoing of *The Young Victoria*, Davinier allays Dido's fears about being confined in a marriage by assuring her that this will not be the case if she marries someone who is 'her true equal' and who respects her, suggesting that equality is achieved at a personal level within a marriage, rather than in society more broadly.

While the film's politics largely become incorporated into its love story narrative, the filmmakers remain committed to issues of race and representation throughout. Dido's dialogue explicitly addresses this lack of representation when she sees a painting of a young black slave with a white master and says, 'just as in life, we are no better in paintings'. The inspiration for *Belle* came when screenwriter Missay Sagay saw a painting, thought to be by Zoffany (1779), of two girls – Dido and Elizabeth. In the painting, the girls are sitting next to each other and of equal status at a time when it was unusual for people of colour to feature in paintings as anything other than servants.[95] This painting is recreated at the end of the film when Lord Mansfield asks Dido to sit next to Elizabeth to be painted, eliciting a shocked response from Dido, who is unsure whether it would be acceptable for her to

Figure 4.4 *Belle*'s (2013) re-creation of Zoffany's (1779) painting next to the original.

do so. The unusualness of the situation is evident in Zoffany's original painting, where Dido appears to be pointing to herself, as if to draw attention to the fact that she is occupying a space from which society typically excludes her. In the film, the painting is revealed to Dido, who is stunned to see a representation of herself staring back at her from the canvas (Figure 4.4). Recreating the Zoffany painting, which is displayed over the closing credits, is a particularly self-reflexive moment. However, unlike the recreations of portraiture in *Elizabeth* and *The Duchess*, Dido is not 'becoming' an image so much as finally being able to see herself. In representing Dido, Asante has begun to explore the intersections of race, gender and class in the British historical film, reinforcing the need for women of colour's place in British history to be represented on screen.

Between the past and the (postfeminist) future

Films featuring young royal and aristocratic women have played a significant part in contemporary British cinema's output. Films such as *The Other Boleyn Girl* and *The Duchess* are positioned as part of the 'post-heritage' emphasis on spectacle and excitement, with filmmakers who are adamant in their desire not to produce a 'typical' staid heritage film in the style of Merchant Ivory, and this discourse was perpetuated by an emphasis on directors who were from either outside the UK or outside of the genre. *The Young Victoria*, meanwhile, adopts this stance while also being targeted more towards younger audiences familiar with Hollywood 'princess' films. Amma Asante's *Belle*, on the other hand, consciously evoked more traditional heritage aesthetics in acknowledgement that a bi-racial protagonist greatly subverts expectations of the genre.

These contemporary historical films all construct a 'postfeminist historical sensibility', at once drawing attention to the inequalities faced by the young woman protagonist while also safely confining these issues to the past.[96] In doing so, they also mediate key discourses of girlhood. *The Other Boleyn Girl* explored the figure of the ambitious can-do girl via the figure of Anne Boleyn and her attempts to become queen, while *The Young Victoria* and *The Duchess* evoked notions of celebrity where a young woman is seemingly catapulted to fame and the psychological crisis this creates through the employment of a 'Diana narrative' that is a key trope of this cycle of films. This is most overt in *The Duchess*, which explores the implications of the need to create an artificial persona and that sparkle – the key signifier of (royal) status and of girlhood – is a heavy burden. Typically, the issues of structural inequality that are raised throughout the films are subsumed into a love story and subsequently solved in keeping with this 'postfeminist historical sensibility'. However, this is not always neatly contained, as in *The Other Boleyn Girl* and *The Duchess*, which use the construction of these historical figures as modern women to express concern about contemporary postfeminist femininity. *The Other Boleyn Girl* questions how far Anne was to blame for her situation by depicting her as at the mercy of patriarchal forces while also employing a feminist critique of the postfeminist emphasis on ambition and can-do femininity through the construction of Anne as a forbearer of postfeminism. *The Duchess* similarly presents a 'feminist tragedy' where gender inequality and constraints cannot be solved by love. While *Belle* does temper its politics through the love story narrative, the very presence of Dido provides a much needed and welcome change within the British historical film.

Conclusion

Young femininity in contemporary British cinema

This book has sought to capture the state of contemporary British cinema's constructions of young femininity and, in doing so, showcase the dynamism of British film production during this period. What is clear is that British cinema's girl-centred films span a variety of genres and modes of production, and target audiences in a manner that is symptomatic of the industry's current organizational structures. Films such as *St Trinian's* (Parker and Thompson 2007, 2009), *Chalet Girl* (Traill 2011) and *StreetDance 3D* (Giwa and Pasquini 2010) are indicative of the industry's broader push towards commercialization while remaining culturally British, while women filmmakers such as Andrea Arnold, Lone Scherfig and Carol Morley continue to develop their critically acclaimed bodies of work. Also apparent within contemporary British cinema's output is a more concerted attempt to attract youth audiences via sports films such as *StreetDance, Chalet Girl* and *Fast Girls* (Clarke 2012); girls' school films such as the revived *St Trinian's* series and *Wild Child* (Moore 2008) – Working Title's first attempt at attracting the tween audience. The historical film, a cornerstone of British cinema, has also worked to attract young audiences familiar with contemporary 'princess' films via *The Young Victoria* (Vallée 2009).

Films about girls and young women play a significant role in the mainstreaming of British film culture in this period. Key to this was the positioning of the films by producers, filmmakers and critics alike as pushing back against social realist traditions of, as *Kicks* director Lindy Heymann puts it, 'gritty, squalid, grim-up-North Britain'.[1] British cinema is synonymous with 'grit' and this discourse is particularly prominent in the discussion of British sports films in Chapter 2, where glossy aesthetics are evoked as part of a mediation of girls' ambitions in sports films that reflect the aspirations of the British film industry itself. The filmmakers responsible for the historical films discussed in Chapter 4 were also keen to position their films as atypical for the genre, which is most closely associated with the Merchant Ivory heritage films of the 1980s and 1990s. At the same time, notions of authenticity remain key to how British cinema perceives itself, and wants to be perceived.

British cinema has always had a close relationship with Hollywood that is defined by a somewhat ambivalent relationship of influence and distinction, and British cinema's contemporary girl films are no exception. Chapter 1 demonstrated how films such as the revived *St Trinian's* series and *Wild Child* were positioned as a distinctly British take on the Hollywood high school teen film, drawing on contemporary Hollywood teen film conventions such as the high school clique and the prom within the culturally specific setting of the British girls' school. Similarly, the discussion of the contemporary British sports film in Chapter 2 included British cinema's attempt to emulate the Hollywood 3D dance film with the hugely successful and aspirational *StreetDance*. *StreetDance* was highly praised by critics for its unusually glossy representation of London – and, by extension, Britain – in arguably the most overt rejection of the 'Brit grit'[2] tradition of filmmaking. Interestingly, it was this explicit rejection of British realism that the producers and reviewers felt heightened the film's authenticity, as an example of a film that showcased the talent and aspirations of British youth and British cinema itself.

A key aim of this book was to examine how young femininity is mediated in contemporary British cinema within a postfeminist cultural climate. In doing so, I have argued for a nationally specific postfeminist framework and sought to offer new ways of understanding how postfeminism informs British cinematic culture, and the specific ways in which it is modified and articulated in a British context. A nationally specific understanding of postfeminism is more urgent than ever as, far from waning, postfeminism has merely tightened its hold and spread to all aspects of cultural life.[3] As the thematic focus of the chapters suggests, contemporary British cinema engages with cross-cultural themes that dominate depictions of postfeminist girlhood, such as the evocation of the figure of the can-do girl, and the significance of the sporting body as a key site in which this can-do girlhood is mediated, concerns about girls' sexuality and sexualization, and the prominence of girl friendship as key to feminine identity formation. However, two key themes have emerged across the corpus of films discussed here that contribute to our understanding of how postfeminism is articulated in a British context, regardless of genre, mode of production or target audience. First, the mediation of the postfeminist makeover trope works to construct a specifically British postfeminist femininity, as it is indicative of British cinema's long-held ambivalence to glamour and consumption in line with British femininity's association with 'naturalness' and 'respectability' in opposition to American glamour and artifice.[4] Where a makeover takes place, overt consumption is eschewed in favour of clothes swaps and second-hand items. Consumption is framed as a particularly American trait, demonstrated most effectively in *Wild Child*, where Poppy's excessive consumption is stripped back to reveal her authentic *British* femininity underneath. Even deliberately aspirational films such as *Chalet Girl* present a sardonic unease with the wealth and consumption on display, particularly within the context of austerity. British cinema's ambivalence to glamour is all the more significant given that sparkle is a key signifier of postfeminist girlhood.[5] While historical films centred on royal young women draw attention to the sparkling signifiers of royalty, such as crowns, gowns and jewels, these are presented as inauthentic and a burden. *The Duchess* is perhaps the most overt example of this, as Keira Knightley's account of the debilitating impact of Georgiana's costumes makes particularly apparent.

A similar ambivalence can also be found in the films' mediation of discourses of celebrity, as the films engage with discourses of celebrity as integral to contemporary girlhood but often uneasily. As discussed in Chapter 3, *Kicks* offers the most overt critique of millennial celebrity culture through its exploration of the UK's – and Liverpool's, more specifically – WAG culture. In doing so, the film reproduces and perpetuates the wider moral panic that circulates around girls and their ambitions, particularly the belief that girls want to be famous at all costs, and that looks are more important than talent. Celebrity culture plays a central role in *Kicks* but its presence is felt in a number of films. In *Fish Tank*, Mia and Tyler scornfully watch aspirational US reality television about exceptionally privileged young people, which provide a stark contrast with their lives. Meanwhile, the presence of American Mischa Barton as PR coach J. J. French in *St Trinian's* suggests that celebrity culture is something that Britain has uneasily learnt from America. The historical films that are the focus of Chapter 4 also mediate anxieties around celebrity. Royal women such as Victoria in *The Young Victoria* and Georgiana in *The Duchess* are presented as the celebrities of their day, but celebrity, and the fashion and consumption inherent within this, is presented simultaneously as a means of visibility and confinement.

Class remains a defining preoccupation of contemporary British cinema, and this focus on class is also indicative of the ways in which postfeminism is modified in a British context. Postfeminist femininity is notably white and 'middle class by default',[6] yet British girl-centred films often draw attention to class differences and classed identities rather than eliding them. This is frequently tied to the films' representation of the postfeminist makeover. In postfeminist culture, the makeover is 'the key ritual of the female coming into being',[7] that enables the revelation of the 'self that has been there all along'.[8] As Rachel Mosley argues, in teen girl texts in particular, the makeover acts as the 'mechanism through which appropriate feminine identities are constructed and reinforced'.[9] Such 'appropriate feminine identities' are typically white and middle class in keeping with the dominant ideals of postfeminist girlhood. In British cinema's constructions of young femininity, however, the makeover largely fails to facilitate this. It also, for the most part, fails to grant the girl character the (hyper-)visibility that is so essential to the validation of girlhood identity.[10] As discussed in Chapter 3, friendships – and the makeovers that often take place within them – are essential in enabling and maintaining feminine normativity, but British cinema's constructions of young femininity frequently trouble this, as the makeover provides, at best, temporary visibility. The makeover works, in part to demonstrate that 'the right clothes, worn properly, have the power to shatter class boundaries and allow characters to climb social ladders'.[11] British cinema's girl films are highly ambivalent about this, as class is a prominent concern and frequently presented as an insurmountable barrier. Aspirational, youth-orientated films such as *Fast Girls*, *Chalet Girl* and *StreetDance* tend to be more optimistic, as the girl protagonist is able to transgress class boundaries through performing successful can-do femininity, which allows her to assimilate middle-class norms and gain entry into the middle class via a heterosexual romantic partnership with a middle-class boy. However, despite their utopian endings, these films display an acute awareness of the British class system and they repeatedly draw attention to the socio-economic barriers faced by the working-class girl protagonist, reinforcing class as a continued prominent concern within British cinema, more so than race.

It cannot go unremarked that whiteness continues to characterize contemporary British cinema's representations of young women, as demonstrated by the films discussed throughout this book – *Fast Girls* and *Belle* (2013) being two significant exceptions. This under-representation is indicative of the barriers faced by women of colour in the British film industry, starkly conveyed by *Fast Girls* producer Damian Jones' comment about the challenge of having to 'sell the idea of a mixed race lead actress'.[12] Indeed, a comparative glance at the career trajectories of Lenora Crichlow and her *Fast Girls* co-star Lily James reinforces this, as James has gone on to achieve stardom through high-profile roles such as the young Donna in *Mamma Mia: Here We Go Again* (2018), while Crichlow mostly works in television, such as her role as Annie in the BBC's *Being Human* (2009–2012). British cinema is marked by a lack of diversity both on and off screen, as the crucial research by the Calling the Shots: Women and Contemporary UK Film Culture project has demonstrated. As of 2015, women made up only 20 per cent of key creative personnel in the UK film industry, and of those, only 7 per cent were from a black, Asian and ethnic minority (BAME) background, meaning that women from a BAME background made up only 1.5 per cent of all personnel working in those key roles.[13] However, initiatives such as the BFI's 'three ticks' approach to film production are working to diversify British cinema, and I can only hope that this continues.

The introduction highlighted feminism's 'new luminosity' in contemporary culture[14] during the period in which this book is situated, along with a period of austerity as a result of the global financial crisis. Where possible, I have attempted to draw attention to British cinema's shifting engagement with feminism and feminist discourses in line with broader cultural patterns. Unsurprisingly, this consists of both continuity and change – more so the former than the latter.[15] Films such as *Fast Girls* and *Chalet Girl* draw attention to the continued privilege afforded to rich, white men and the impact this has on working-class young women, such as Lisa's father's role as head of British athletics in *Fast Girls* or the bankers who populate the ski resort at which Kim works following the financial crash. There is also a sense in these films that there is less willingness to tolerate 'ironic' sexism and be 'in on the joke' as earlier incarnations of postfeminism suggested.[16] Feminism was particularly visible in 2015 when British cinema produced a historical film that explored the history of women's suffrage in the UK. *Suffragette* included an all-women creative team with Sarah Gavron as director, screenwriter Abi Morgan and producer Alison Owen. The film was notable for its focus on a young working-class woman, 24-year-old laundry worker Maud Watts (Carey Mulligan), rather than more well-known figures such as the middle-class Emmeline Pankhurst. While, as discussed in Chapter 4, films set in the past work to explore feminist issues while safely confining them to the past in accordance with postfeminist discourses that perpetuate the 'pastness' of feminism,[17] *Suffragette* works to keep feminism in the present. As the film's tagline tells us, 'The time is now'. Likewise, the film's closing titles provide a list of the years that women were granted the vote around the world, with the recentness of many of the dates showing that feminism is still very much needed as a global political movement.

This book has provided a study of young femininity in British cinema between 2000 and 2015, during which time there has been a noticeable increase in films centred around girls and young women, and this interest has shown little sign of waning. As this book draws to a close, I want to briefly draw attention to Lone Scherfig's recent comedy drama *Their Finest* (2017) for its construction of young femininity and self-reflexive mediation of British cinema history. The film is based on Lissa Evans' novel *Their Finest Hour and a Half* (2009) and set during the Second World War. Catrin Cole (Gemma Arterton) is a Welsh, working-class, young woman who is employed by the Ministry of Information to write the 'slop' (women's dialogue) for their latest propaganda film about the Dunkirk evacuation during the Battle of Britain, designed to entice America to join the war effort. (Catrin is loosely based on Ealing screenwriter Diane Morgan.) Scherfig employs a similar feminist stance to *An Education*, which emphasizes the limited opportunities for girls in the 1960s and the importance of an education; here she highlights the inequality women face(d) in the film industry – Catrin is paid significantly less than her male colleagues – and highlights the central, yet often overlooked, role women have played in British cinema throughout its history. The ministry's watchwords are 'optimism' and 'authenticity' and Catrin is tasked with researching and writing about twins Rose and Lily who reportedly took their father's boat in order to aid the evacuation (although it is later revealed that they never reached Dunkirk thanks to a broken propeller). The making of the film – eventually titled The Nancy Starling – explores British cinema's ambivalent relationship with the United States and Hollywood, as the team attempts to resist the demands for a more American-friendly – that is, dramatic – ending and reluctantly include all-American hero soldier Carl Lundbeck (Jake Lacy), complete with gleaming teeth. British cinema's relationship with social realism and a supposed lack of ambition is also explored, as Catrin's colleague, Buckley (Sam Claflin) dismissively refers to a director as not being interested in dialogue, only 'fishing nets and local children', a tone not dissimilar to the disparaging 'Brit grit' production discourse that recurs throughout this book. Catrin's authorship is attributed to creating a film that is optimistic yet authentic, as required, while enabling young women to be active at the centre of the story, as she rewrites the ending so that Rose frees the propeller that allows them to get to Dunkirk. However, this is only accepted as Carl Lundbeck has to return to the army, which would halt production.

Their Finest, then, offers a mediation of British cinema history that places young women front and centre, both on and off screen. The research in this book was largely motivated by a desire to elevate and pay attention to critically and culturally maligned texts, as films about, and particularly, for young women are continuously dismissed. This is evident throughout girl culture but perhaps more so within British cinema which has been so reliant on masculinity and masculine images.[18] The lack of cultural value attributed to British cinema's girl films is due, in part, to the fact that the male reviewers who dominate popular film criticism are not the intended audience for these films. The *Guardian*'s film critic, Peter Bradshaw, acknowledges this in his review for *Wild Child*, where he says: 'Here is another girly-tweeny movie on which I suspect I am about as qualified to pass judgment as on variant patterns of weather on the moons of Saturn.'[19] In reasonably acknowledging that the film is not 'for' him, Bradshaw simultaneously contributes to the cultural dismissal of the film through the infantilizing phrase 'girly-tweeny'. Nevertheless, analysing these reviews, along with the films themselves, their production and other paratextual materials, together with broader socio-cultural discourses of postfeminist girlhood, has enabled me to ascertain how British young femininity is discursively (re)produced and mediated by British cinema. Above all, this study has demonstrated that, in their multiplicity, British cinema's films for and about young women have made a significant contribution at the heart of its output in the twenty-first century. They deserve to be made visible and taken seriously.

Notes

Introduction

1 Sarah Projansky, *Spectacular Girls: Media Fascination & Celebrity Culture* (New York: New York University Press, 2014), p. 95.

2 Brooks Barnes, 'At the Box Office, It's No Longer a Man's World', *The New York Times*, 22 March 2015.

3 See Sarah Hill, 'Young Femininity in Contemporary British Cinema: 2000-2015', PhD Thesis, (University of East Anglia, 2015).
   I am referring to films with a young female protagonist, rather than films specifically targeted at girls, although these are included.

4 Henry Fitzherbert, 'Winning Belles', *Sunday Express*, 10 February 2009, p. 21.

5 Charles Gant, '*StreetDance 3D* Shimmies into First Place at UK Box Office', *The Guardian*, 25 May 2010.

6 Melanie Bell and Melanie Williams, 'The Hour of the Cuckoo: Reclaiming the British Woman's Film' in Melanie Bell and Melanie Williams (eds.) *British Women's Cinema* (Oxon: Routledge, 2010), pp. 1–18, p. 7.

7 Melanie Williams, *Female Stars of British Cinema* (Edinburgh: Edinburgh University Press, 2017), p. 3.

8 Lucy Bolton, 'A Phenomenology of Girlhood: Being Mia in *Fish Tank* (Arnold, 2009)' in Fiona Handyside and Kate Taylor-Jones (eds.) *International Cinema and the Girl: Local Issues, Transnational Contexts* (Hampshire: Palgrave Macmillan, 2016), pp. 75–84.

9 Louise Wilks, '"Boys Don't Like Girls for Funniness": Raunch Culture and the British Tween Film', *Networking Knowledge*, 5:1 (2012), pp. 100–24.

10 Sophie Mayer, *Political Animals: The New Feminist Cinema* (London: I.B. Tauris, 2016).

11 Yvonne Tasker and Diane Negra, 'Introduction: Feminist Politics and Postfeminist Culture' in Yvonne Tasker and Diane Negra (eds.)

Interrogating Postfeminism: Gender and the Politics of Popular Culture (Durham and London: Duke University Press 2007), pp. 1–25, p. 13.

12 Jessalynn Keller and Maureen Ryan, 'Call for Papers: Emergent Feminisms and the Challenge to Postfeminist Media Culture', Circulated 12 May 2015; Imelda Whelehan, 'Remaking Feminism: Or Why Is Postfeminism so Boring? *Nordic Journal of English Studies* 9:3 (2010), pp. 155–72.

13 Nicola Rivers, *Postfeminism(s) and the Arrival of the Fourth Wave* (London: Palgrave Macmillan, 2017), p. 20.

14 Angela McRobbie, *The Aftermath of Feminism: Gender, Culture and Social Change* (London: SAGE, 2009).

15 Rosalind Gill, 'Postfeminist Media Culture: Elements of a Sensibility', *European Journal of Cultural Studies*, 10:2 (2007), pp. 147–66.

16 Sarah Projansky, *Watching Rape: Film and Television in Popular Culture* (New York: New York University Press, 2001), p. 88.

17 Rosalind Gill, 'The Affective, Cultural and Psychic Life of Postfeminism: A Postfeminist Sensibility 10 Years On', *European Journal of Cultural Studies*, 20:6 (2017), pp. 606–26, p. 613.

18 Gill, 'Postfeminist Media Culture', pp. 147–66; McRobbie, *The Aftermath of Feminism*, p. 54.

19 Gill, 'Postfeminist Media Culture', p. 152.

20 Anthony Giddens, *Modernity and Society: Self and Society in the Late Modern Age* (Cambridge: Polity Press, 1991); Nikolas Rose, *Inventing Ourselves: Psychology, Power and Personhood* (Cambridge: Cambridge University Press, 1998).

21 Gill, The Affective, Cultural and Psychic Life of Postfeminism', p. 609.

22 Ibid.; Melanie Kennedy, *Tweenhood: Femininity and Celebrity in Tween Popular Culture* (London: I.B. Tauris, 2019), p. 12.

23 Justine Ashby, 'Postfeminism in the British Frame', *Society for Cinema and Media Studies*, 44:2 (Winter 2005), pp. 127–33, p. 128.

24 Gill, The Affective, Cultural and Psychic Life of Postfeminism', p. 610.

25 Tasker and Negra, 'Introduction', p. 2.

26 Diane Negra, *What a Girl Wants?: Fantasizing the Reclamation of the Self in Postfeminism* (Oxon: Routledge, 2009), pp. 123–4.

27 Samantha Colling, *The Aesthetic Pleasures of Girl Teen Film* (London: Bloomsbury Academic, 2016), p. 52.

28 Williams, *Female Stars of British Cinema*, p. 6.

29 Negra, *What a Girl Wants*, p. 124.

30 Jackie Stacey, *Star Gazing: Hollywood Cinema and Female Spectatorship* (Oxon: Routledge, 1994), p. 117. See also Christine Geraghty, 'Crossing over: Performing as Lady and a Dame', *Screen*, 43:1 (2002), pp. 41–56.

31 Colling, *The Aesthetic Pleasures of Girl Teen Film*, p. 36.

32 Anita Biressi and Heather Nunn, *Class and Contemporary British Culture* (Basingstoke: Palgrave Macmillan, 2013).

33 Colling, *The Aesthetic Pleasures of Girl Teen Film*, p. 3.

34 Phil Cohen, 'Mods and Shockers: Youth Cultural Studies in Britain', in Andy Bennett, Mark Cieslik and Steve Miles (eds.) *Researching Youth* (London: Palgrave Macmillan, 2003), pp. 29–54, p. 43.

35 Carol Dyhosue, *Girl Trouble: Panic and Progress in the History of Young Women* (London: Zed Books, 2013).

36 Projansky, *Spectacular Girls*, p. 11.

37 Anita Harris, *Future Girl: Young Women in the Twenty-First Century* (London: Routledge, 2004).

38 Ashby, 'Postfeminism in the British Frame', p. 129.

39 Gill, 'The Affective, Cultural and Psychic Life of Postfeminism', p. 611.

40 Projansky, *Spectacular Girls*, p. 5.

41 McRobbie, *The Aftermath of Feminism*, p. 15.

42 Ibid., p. 73.

43 Sean Coughlan, 'The Symbolic Target of 50% at University Reached', *BBC News*, 26 September 2019.

44 Projansky, *Spectacular Girls*, p. 6.

45 Jessica Ringrose, *Postfeminist Education? Girls and the Sexual Politics of Schooling* (Oxon: Routledge, 2013), p. 42.

46 McRobbie, *The Aftermath of Feminism*, p. 54.

47 Mary Celeste Kearney, 'Sparkle: Luminosity and Post-girl Power Media', *Continuum: Journal of Media & Cultural Studies*, 29:2 (2015), pp. 263–73, p. 271.

48 Projansky, *Spectacular Girls*.

49 McRobbie, *The Aftermath of Feminism*, p. 54; Projansky, *Spectacular Girls*.

50 Kearney, 'Sparkle', p. 263.

51 Ibid., p. 264.

52 Justine Ashby and Andrew Higson, 'Introduction' in Justine Ashby and Andrew Higson (eds.) *British Cinema, Past and Present* (Oxon: Routledge, 2000), pp. 1–19, p. 9.

53 Faye Woods, *British Youth Television: Transnational Teens, Industry, Genre* (London: Palgrave Macmillan, 2016), p. 118.

54 Ibid., p. 5.

55 Projansky, *Spectacular Girls*, p. 7.

56 Kim Allen, 'Girls Imagining Careers in the Limelight: Social Class, Gender and Fantasies of "Success"' in Su Holmes and Diane Negra (eds.) *In the Limelight and Under the Microscope: Forms and Functions of Female Celebrity* (London: Continuum, 2011), pp. 149–73, p. 151.

57 Ibid., p. 150.

58 Williams, *Female Stars of British Cinema*, p. 25.

59 Ibid., p. 197.

60 Heather Mendick et al., *Celebrity, Aspiration and Contemporary Youth* (London: Bloomsbury Academic, 2018), p. 157.

61 The Britishness of Watson's star persona is reinforced by her defining role in the *Harry Potter* film series and her role as an ambassador for the British high-end fashion brand, Burberry.

62 Williams, *Female Stars of British Cinema*, p. 5.

63 Mendick et al., *Celebrity, Aspiration and Contemporary Youth*, p. 2.

64 Ibid., p. 11.

65 Diane Negra and Yvonne Tasker (eds.), *Gendering the Recession: Media and Culture in an Age of Austerity* (London: Duke University Press, 2014), p. 14.

66 Ibid., p. 6.

67 Ibid., p. 5.

68 Nunn and Biressi, *Class and Contemporary British Culture*, p. 171.

69 Negra and Tasker, *Gendering the Recession*, p. 7.

70 Gill, 'The Affective, Cultural, and Psychic Life of Postfeminism', p. 611.

71 Ibid., p. 610.

72 Jess Butler, 'For White Girls Only? Postfeminism and the Politics of Inclusion', *Feminist Formations*, 25:1 (2013), pp. 35–58.

73 Tanya Ann Kennedy, *Historicizing Post-Discourses: Postfeminism and Postracialism in United States Culture* (New York: State University of New York Press, 2017), p. 19.

74 Negra and Tasker (eds.), *Gendering the Recession*; Nunn and Biressi, *Class and Contemporary British Culture*.

75 Alison Winch, *Girlfriends and the Postfeminist Sisterhood* (Hampshire: Palgrave Macmillan, 2013).

76 Laura Bates, *Everyday Sexism* (London: Simon & Schuster, 2014).

77 Rivers, *Postfeminism and the Arrival of the Fourth Wave*, p. 106.

78 Ibid., p. 127.

79 Angela McRobbie, 'Notes on the Perfect', *Australian Feminist Studies*, 30:83 (2015), pp. 3–20, p. 4.

80 Hannah Hamad and Anthea Taylor, 'Introduction: Feminism and Contemporary Celebrity Culture', *Celebrity Studies*, 6:1 (2015), pp. 124–7, p. 125.

81 Lorraine Candy, 'Emma Watson, The December 2014 ELLE Cover Interview', *Elle*, 6 March 2015.

82 Jessalynn Keller and Jessica Ringrose, '"But then feminism goes out the window!": Exploring Teenage Girls' Critical Response to Celebrity Feminism', *Celebrity Studies*, 6:1 (2015), pp. 132–5, p. 132.

83 Catherine Rottenberg, 'The Rise of Neoliberal Feminism', *Cultural Studies*, 28:3 (2013), pp. 418–37, p. 419.

84 Ibid., p. 420.

85 Rosalind Gill, 'Post-postfeminism?: New Feminist Visibilities in Postfeminist Times', *Feminist Media Studies*, 16:4 (2016), pp. 610–30, p. 612.

86 Sarah Street, *British National Cinema* (Oxon: Routledge, 2009), p. 126.

87 Ibid, p. 1.

88 Ashby, 'Postfeminism in the British Frame', p. 130.

89 Ibid.

90 Ibid.

91 James Leggott, *Contemporary British Cinema: From Heritage to Horror* (London: Wallflower Press, 2008), p. 3.

92 Gillian Doyle et al., *The Rise and Fall of the UK Film Council* (Edinburgh: Edinburgh University Press, 2015), p. 177.

93 Gurinder Chadha quoted in Vanessa Thorpe, 'Hollywood Wakes up to Girl Power: Teen Heroines Look Set to Reclaim Cinema Screens from Comic Book Superheroes', *The Observer*, 27 July 2008, p. 15.

94 Baz Bamigboye, 'Teenage Angst and a Hilarious Kiss and Tell', *Daily Mail*, 4 July 2008.

Bamigboye's reference to a 'perfect English pitch' is indicative of a common slippage that makes Englishness the 'hegemonic identity of Britishness' when the film is actually British in scope. (See Williams, *Female Stars of British Cinema*, p.14.)

95 Kevin Maher, 'Ewww, Like, This Is Totally Gross', *The Times (Times 2)*, 24 July 2008, p. 17.

Byker Grove was a British youth television show set in a youth club in Byker, an inner-city area of Newcastle in the north east of England and was known for tackling controversial topics such as drug abuse and homophobia (BBC 1989–2006).

96 Woods, *British Youth Television*, p. 5.

97 Peter Bradshaw, '*Angus, Thongs and Perfect Snogging*', *The Guardian*, 25 July 2008.

98 John Hill, 'UK Film Policy, Cultural Capital and Social Exclusion', *Cultural Trends*, 13:2 (no. 50, June 2004), pp. 29–39, p. 33.

99 Leggott, *Contemporary British Cinema*, p. 17.

100 Andrew Higson, *Film England: Culturally English Filmmaking since the 1990s* (London: I.B. Tauris, 2011), p. 9.

101 Leggott, *Contemporary British Cinema*, p. 9.

102 Hannah Andrews, *Television and British Cinema: Convergence and Divergence since 1990* (Hampshire: Palgrave Macmillan, 2014), p. 82.

103 Jason Deans, 'Jackson: I Got It Wrong with FilmFour', *The Guardian*, 22 September 2003.

104 Andrews, *Television and British Cinema*, p. 83.

105 Ibid., p. 106.

106 Ibid.

107 Ibid., p. 84.

108 Ibid., p. 126.

109 Ibid., p. 129.

110 Ibid., p. 127.

111 Doyle et al., *The Rise and Fall of the UK Film Council*, p. 183.

112 Ed Vaizey, 'The Future of the UK Film Industry', 29 November 2010.

113 David Cameron quoted in Xan Brooks, 'Make More Films like Harry Potter, David Cameron Tells UK Film Industry', *The Guardian*, 17 November 2010.

114 Andrews, *Television and British Cinema*, p. 187.

115 John Hill, 'British Cinema as National Cinema: Production, Audience and Representation' in Robert Murphy (ed.) *The British Cinema Book* (London: BFI, 2009), pp. 11–20, p. 18.

116 Williams, *Female Stars of British Cinema*, p. 196.

117 BFI, 'New BFI Filmography Reveals Complete Story of UK Film 1911-2017', 20 September 2017.

118 Williams, *Female Stars of British Cinema*, p. 203.

119 Julie Walters quoted in Simon Hattenstone, 'Julie Walters: "People like me wouldn't get a chance today"', *The Guardian*, 24 January 2015.

120 BFI, 'BFI Obligates and Supports Lottery Funding Recipients to Reflect Diversity in the UK', 30 November 2015.

121 Mayer, *Political Animals*, p. 98.

122 Stuart Hall, 'Introduction' in Stuart Hall, Jessica Evans and Sean Nixon (eds.) *Representation* (Milton Keynes: Open University Press, 1997), pp. xvii–xxvi, p. xxii.

123 David Buckingham, *Youth, Identity and Digital Media* (Cambridge, MA: MIT, 2008), p. 4.

124 Mendick et al., *Celebrity, Aspiration and Contemporary Youth*, p. 7.

125 Ibid.

126 Harris, *Future Girl*, p. 191.

127 Tasker and Negra, 'Introduction', p. 18.

128 Barbara Klinger, *Melodrama and Meaning: History, Culture, and the Films of Douglas Sirk* (Bloomington and Indianapolis: Indiana University Press, 1994), p. 69.

129 Biressi and Nunn, *Class and Contemporary British Culture*.

130 Negra, *What a Girl Wants*, p. 124.

131 Mendick et al., *Celebrity, Aspiration and Contemporary Youth*, p. 59.

132 Buckingham, *Youth, Identity and Digital Media*, p. 2.

133 Winch, *Girlfriends and the Postfeminist Sisterhood*.

134 Ibid., p. 2.

135 Bélen Vidal, *Heritage Film: Nation, Genre and Representation* (Chichester: Wallflower, 2012), p. 105.

Chapter 1

1 Stephen Glynn, *The British School Film: From Tom Brown to Harry Potter* (London: Palgrave Macmillan, 2016), p. 245.

2 Ibid., p. 8.

3 Andrew Roberts, 'Back to School', *Sight & Sound*, August 2007.

4 Glynn, *The British School Film*, pp. 7–8.

5 Roberts, 'Back to School'.

6 Shelley Anne Galpin, 'Harry Potter and the Hidden Heritage Films: Genre Hybridity and the Power of the Past in the Harry Potter Film Cycle', *Journal of British Cinema and Television*, 13:3 (2016), pp. 430–49, pp. 431–2.

7 'Pikey' is a variation of the word 'chav', a derogatory word for the white working-class poor, which I discuss in Chapter 2.

8 Glynn, *The British School Film*, p. 245.

9 Tasker and Negra, 'Introduction', p. 2.

10 Jane MacKichan, 'Meet the Tribes of St Trinian's', *Daily Mail*, 6 December 2007.

11 Glynn, *The British School Film*, p. 245.

12 Ringrose, *Postfeminist Education?*, p. 47.

13 McRobbie, *The Aftermath of Feminism*, p. 54.

14 Ibid., p. 73.
   The figure of the 'top girl' will be explored in more detail in Chapter 2.

15 Ibid., p. 15.

16 Ringrose, *Postfeminist Education?*, p. 20.

17 Rosa Prince, 'David Willets: Feminism has Held Back Working Men', *The Telegraph*, 1 April 2011.

18 Ibid., p. 47.

19 Linda Papadopoulos, 'Sexualization of Young People Review', *UK Home Office*, 25 February 2010.

20 Mumsnet, 'Let Girls be Girls Campaign', 2010.

21 Ariel Levy, *Female Chauvinist Pigs: Women and the Rise of Raunch Culture* (London: Zed Books, 2006).

22 Ringrose, *Postfeminist Education?*, p. 4.

23 Kennedy, *Tweenhood*, p. 167.

24 Ibid., p. 168.

25 Lynn Spigel, 'Postfeminist Nostalgia for a Prefeminist Future', *Screen*, 54:2 (2013), pp. 270–8, p. 271.

26 Emma Bell, 'The Belles of St Trinian's' in Emma Bell and Neil Mitchell (eds.) *Directory of World Cinema: Britain* (Bristol: Intellect, 2012), pp. 113–15, p. 100.

27 Ibid., p. 115.

28 Guy Adams, 'St Trinian's Belles to Ring Once More', *The Independent*, 10 October 2006.

29 Fitzherbert, 'Winning Belles', p. 21.

30 Diana Lodderhose, 'St Trinian's', *Screen International*, 27 March 2008.

31 Natalie Brenner, 'Once More with Ealing Interview', in *The Money Programme*. [TV] BBC 2. 27 July 2007, 1900 hrs.

32 Talulah Riley, quoted in Will Lawrence, 'The St Trinian's Girls Go to Pot', *The Daily Telegraph*, 14 December 2007.

33 Ashby, 'Postfeminism in the British Frame', p. 129.

34 Chris Tookey, 'Sorry Girls… Must Do Better', *Daily Mail*, 21 December 2007, p. 52.

35 Gemma Arterton, quoted in Liz Hoggard, 'Rising Starlet Is Top of the Class at St Trinian's', *Evening Standard*, 21 December 2007.

36 Damon Smith, 'Fearsome Minxes? Not this Lot', *Herald Express*, 22 December 2007, p. 25.

37 Ibid.

38 Tookey, 'Sorry Girls… Must Do Better', p. 52.

39 Ringrose, *Postfeminist Education?*

40 Harris, *Future Girl*, p. 14.

41 Cosmo Landesman, 'We're, Like, So over Jolly Hockey Sticks Now', *Sunday Times*, 23 December 2007.

42 Angela McRobbie, 'Top Girls', *Cultural Studies*, 21:4–5 (2007), pp. 718–37, p. 732.

43 Wilks, '"Boys Don't Like Girls for Funniness"', p. 117.

44 Jeff Sawtell, 'St Trinian's' *Morning Star*, 21 December 2007.

45 Henry Fitzherbert, 'Top of the Class for Jolly Japes', *Sunday Express*, 23 December 2007.

46 Landesman, 'We're, Like, So over, Jolly Hockey Sticks Now'.

47 Tookey, 'Sorry Girls… Must Do Better'.

48 Barnaby Thompson and Oliver Parker quoted in Jane MacKichan, 'The Tribes of St Trinian's', *Daily Mail*, 7 December 2007, p. 66.

49 Imogen Tyler, 'Chav Mum, Chav Scum: Class Disgust in Contemporary Britain', *Feminist Media Studies*, 8:1 (2008), pp. 17–34, p. 21.

50 Ibid., p. 31.

51 Samantha Colling, *The Aesthetic Pleasures of Teen Girl Film* (London: Bloomsbury Academic, 2017), p. 67.

52 Kennedy, *Tweenhood*, p. 40; Negra, *What a Girl Wants?*, p. 123.

53 Stacey, *Star Gazing*, p. 117.

54 Wilks, "'Boys Don't Like Girls for Funniness'", p. 100.

55 Ibid., p. 117.

56 Mark Adams, 'St Trin's… All Grins', *Sunday Mirror*, 16 December 2007, p. 52.

57 James Christopher, 'Carry on Rampaging', *The Times*, 20 December 2007, p. 14.

58 Steven Gerrard, *The Carry on Films* (London: Palgrave Macmillan, 2016), p. 3.

59 Allen, 'Girls Imagining Careers in the Limelight', p. 157.

60 Graham Young, 'A Headteacher's Headache', *Birmingham Evening Mail*, 18 December 2009, p. 43.

61 Sukhdev Sandhu, 'St Trinian's', *The Telegraph*, 18 December 2009, p. 33.

62 Oliver Parker quoted in Lisa Sewards, 'The Tribes of St Trinian's', *Daily Mail*, 11 December 2009.

63 Ibid.

64 McRobbie, 'Top Girls', p. 33.

65 Working Title Films, '*Wild Child* Production Notes', pp. 1–21, p. 5.

66 Mark Adams, 'School's Pout', *Sunday Mirror*, 10 August 2008; Richard Bacon, 'Wild and Childish', *The Sunday People*, 10 August 2008; Gary Beckwith, 'A Second-Class Comedy', *Newcastle Evening Chronicle*, 15 August 2008; Chris Tookey, 'Public School Gets a Makeover', *Daily Mail*, 15 August 2008, p. 53.

67 R. W. Connell, *Gender and Power: Society, the Person and Sexual Politics* (Cambridge: Polity, 1987); Kennedy, *Tweenhood*, p. 37.

68 Working Title, '*Wild Child* Production Notes', pp. 1–21, p. 6.

69 Ibid., p. 1.

70 Beverley Skeggs, *Formations of Class and Gender* (London: SAGE, 1997), p. 99; Stacey, *Star Gazing*, p. 117.

71 Colling, *The Aesthetic Pleasures of Girl Teen Film*, p. 28.

72 Kennedy, *Tweenhood*, pp. 39–40.

73 Working Title, '*Wild Child* Production Notes', p. 6.

74 Wilks, "'Boys Don't Like Girls for Funniness'", p. 111.

75 Damon Parkin, 'Are Schoolgirl Antics too Wild for Comfort', *Derby Evening Telegraph*, 15 August 2008, p. 28.

76 Tookey, 'Public School Gets a Makeover', p. 53.

77 Beckwith, 'A Second-Class Comedy'.

78 Wilks, "'Boys Don't Like Girls for Funniness'", p. 109.

79 Emma Renold and Jessica Ringrose, 'Normative Cruelties and Gender Deviants: The Performative Effects of Bully Discourses for Girls and Boys in School', *British Educational Research Journal*, 36:4 (2010), pp. 573–96, p. 586.

80 Dominic Sandbrook, *Never Had It So Good: A History of Britain from Suez to the Beatles* (London: Abacus, 2005), p. xvii.

81 Christine Geraghty, 'Women and 60s British Cinema: The Development of the "Darling" Girl' in Robert Murphy (ed.) *The British Cinema Book* (London: BFI, 2009), p. 313.

82 Ibid., p. 315.

83 Melanie Bell, 'Young, Single, Disillusioned: The Screen Heroine in 60s British Cinema', *The Yearbook of English Studies*, 42 (2012), pp. 79–96, p. 80.

84 Spigel, 'Postfeminist Nostalgia for a Prefeminist Future', p. 271.

85 Ibid., p. 277.

86 Lynn Barber, *An Education* (London: Penguin, 2009).

87 'An Education Press Kit', *Mongrel Media* (2009), pp. 1–28, p. 5.

88 Lynn Barber quoted in 'An Education Press Kit', p. 4.

89 Rachel Mosley, 'Trousers and Tiaras: Audrey Hepburn, a Woman's Star', *Feminist Review*, 71 (2002), pp. 37–51, p. 39.

90 Ibid., p. 44.

91 Ibid., p. 49.

92 Toby Young, 'Top of the Class in Biology and Humanity', *The Times*, 30 October 2009, p. 13.

93 Gill, 'Postfeminist Media Culture', pp. 147–66.

94 Lone Scherfig quoted in 'An Education Press Kit', p. 5.

95 Alison Rowat, 'Seduced by a Very Charming Man', *The Glasgow Herald*, 29 October 2009, p. 17.

96 Janet Fink and Penny Tinkler, 'Teetering on the Edge: Portraits of Innocence, Risk and Young Female Sexualities in 1950s' and 1960s' British Cinema', *Women's History Review*, 26:1 (2017), pp. 9–25, p. 14.

97 Peter Bradshaw, 'An Education', *The Guardian*, 29 October 2009.

98 Ringrose, *Postfeminist Education?*.

99 Lone Scherfig quoted in Hermione Hoby, 'Film: *An Education*: Director: Lone Scherfig', *Observer Review*, 4 October 2009, p. 5.

100 McRobbie, *The Aftermath of Feminism*, p. 15.

101 Carol Morley, 'Mass Hysteria Is a Powerful Group Activity', *The Observer*, 29 March 2016.

102 Ibid.

103 Ibid.

104 Mark Kermode, 'Swoon with a View', *The Observer*, 26 April 2015.

105 Morley, 'Mass Hysteria Is a Powerful Group Activity'.

106 Carol Morley quoted in Ben Beaumont-Thomas, '*Guardian* Live: The *Guardian* Film Show', 28 April 2015.

107 Kermode, 'Swoon with a View'.

108 Carrie Tarr, '"Sapphire", "Darling" and the Boundaries of Permitted Pleasure', *Screen*, 26:1 (1985), pp. 50–65, p. 64.

109 Catherine Driscoll, *Girls: Feminine Adolescence and Popular Culture and Cultural Theory* (New York: Columbia University Press, 2002), p. 25.

110 Elizabeth Marshall, 'Schooling Ophelia: Hysteria, Memory and Adolescent Femininity', *Gender and Education*, 19:6 (2007), pp. 707–28, p. 712.

111 Ibid., p. 724.

112 Kate Muir, 'Extra House Points All Round', *The Times*, 24 April 2015, p. 43.

Chapter 2

1 Katharina Lindner, 'Blood, Sweat and Tears: Women, Sport and Hollywood' in Joel Gwynne and Nadine Muller (eds.) *Postfeminism and Contemporary Hollywood Cinema* (London: Palgrave Macmillan, 2013), pp. 238–55, p. 238.

2 Ibid., Leslie Heywood, 'Producing Girls: Empire, Sport and the Neoliberal Body' in Jennifer Hargreaves and Patricia Vertinsky (eds.) *Physical Culture, Power and the Body* (London: Routledge, 2006), pp. 101–20, p. 107.

3 Ibid., p. 113.

4 Patrick Wintour, 'David Cameron Presents Himself as Leader of
   "aspiration nation"', *The Guardian*, 10 October 2012. Available from https
   ://www.theguardian.com/politics/2012/oct/10/david-cameron-leader-
   aspiration-nation (accessed 31 January 2020).

5 Kim Allen, '"Blair's Children": Young Women as "aspirational subjects"
   in the Psychic Landscape of Class', *The Sociological Review*, 62 (2014),
   pp. 760–79, p. 761.

6 Ibid., pp. 760–1.

7 Allen, '"Blair's Children"', p. 761.

8 BBC News, 'David Cameron's Plan to Fix "Broken Britain"', 31 March
   2010. Available at http://news.bbc.co.uk/1/hi/uk_politics/8596877.stm
   (accessed 24 January 2019).

9 Angela McRobbie, *Feminism and Youth Culture* (London: Macmillan,
   2000), pp. 200–1.

10 McRobbie, *The Aftermath of Feminism*, pp. 57–8.

11 Ibid., p. 15.

12 Mendick et al., *Celebrity, Aspiration and Contemporary Youth*, p. 5.

13 Ibid., p. 162.

14 Ellis Cashmore, *Sports Culture* (New York: Routledge, 2000), p. 132.

15 Glen Jones, 'In Praise of an "invisible genre"? An Ambivalent Look at the
   Fictional Sports Feature Film', *Sport in Society*, 11:3 (2008), pp. 117–29,
   p. 121.

16 Glen Jones, '"Down on the floor and give me ten sit-ups": British Sports
   Feature Film', *Film & History: An Interdisciplinary Journal of Film and
   Television Studies*, 35:2 (2005), pp. 29–40, p. 36.

17 Brogan Morris, '10 Great British Sports Films', *BFI*, 21 March 2018.

18 Jones, '"Down on the floor and give me ten sit-ups"', p. 34.

19 Ibid.

20 Samantha Colling, *The Aesthetic Pleasures of Teen Girl Film* (London:
   Bloomsbury, 2016), p. 71.

21 Ibid.

22 Lindner, 'Blood, Sweat and Tears', p. 245.

23 Katharina Lindner, 'Spectacular (Dis-) Embodiments: The Female
   Dancer on Film', *Scope*, 20 (June 2011), p. 1.

24 Jones, '"Down on the floor and give me ten sit-ups"', p. 34.

25 Peter Bradshaw, 'Fish Tank', *The Guardian*, 10 September 2009.

26 David Forrest, 'Better Things (Duane Hopkins, 2008) and new British Realism', *New Cinemas: Journal of Contemporary Film*, 8:1 (2010), pp. 31–43, p. 33.

27 Ibid., p. 32.

28 Claire Monk, '"If You Can't Make a Good Political Film, Don't": Pawel Pawlikowski's Resistant Poetic Realism', *Journal of British Cinema and Television*, 9:3 (2012), pp. 480–501.

29 Bolton, 'A Phenomenology of Girlhood', p. 76.

30 Harris, *Future Girl*, p. 14.

31 Barbara Schneider and David Stevenson, 'The Ambitious Generation', *Educational Leadership*, 57:4 (2000), pp. 22–5, p. 22.

32 Tyler, 'Chav Mum, Chav Scum', p. 21.

33 Ibid., p. 22.

34 Ibid., p. 21.

35 Charlotte Higgins, 'How Row Set in Train Life-Changing Offer for *Fish Tank* Star', *The Guardian*, 14 May 2009.

36 Katie Jarvis quoted in *Fish Tank Press Book*, Artificial Eye (2009), p. 7.

37 Allen '"Blair's Children"', p. 760.

38 Mendick et al., *Celebrity, Aspiration and Contemporary Youth*.

39 Richard Dyer, *Stars* (London: British Film Institute, 1979).

40 Higgins, 'How Row Set in Train Life-Changing Offer for *Fish Tank* Star'.

41 McRobbie, *The Aftermath of Feminism*, p. 54.

42 Tyler, 'Chav Mum, Chav Scum', p. 17.

43 Harris, *Future Girl*, p. 26.

44 Andrea Arnold quoted in Ben Hoyle, 'Instant Stardom for Girl from Tilbury Station', *The Times*, 15 May 2009, p. 27.

45 Allen, '"Blair's Children"', p. 761.

46 Barbara Ellen, 'Katie Jarvis: "Walking down the red carpet, people screaming… madness!"', *The Observer*, 20 December 2009.

47 Levy, *Female Chauvinist Pigs*.

48 Gill, 'Postfeminist Media Culture', p. 151.

49 Colling, *The Aesthetic Pleasures of Girl Teen Film*, p. 49.

50 Susan Douglas, *Enlightened Sexism: The Seductive Message that Feminism's Work Is Done* (New York: Times Books, 2010), p. 14.

51 Harris, *Future Girl*.

52 Laura Mulvey, 'Visual Pleasure and Narrative Cinema', *Screen*, 16:3 (Autumn 1975): pp. 6–18.

53 Kevin Maher, 'A Diamond in the Rough', *The Times*, 11 September 2009, p. 37.

54 Ryan Gilbey, 'Fish Tank', *New Statesman*, 14 September 2009, p. 47.

55 Bolton, 'A Phenomenology of Girlhood', p. 81.

56 Colling, *The Aesthetic Pleasures of Girl Teen Film*, p. 49.

57 Su Holmes, '"Reality Goes Pop!" Reality TV, Popular Music, and Narratives of Stardom in Pop Idol', *Television & New Media*, 5:2 (2004), pp. 147–72.

58 Gill, 'Postfeminist Media Culture', p. 152.

59 Bolton, 'A Phenomenology of Girlhood', p. 82.

60 Charles Gant, 'StreetDance 3D Shimmies into First Place at UK Box Office'.

61 In the less successful sequel, the humiliated leader of the rival crew, Ash (Falk Hentschel), looks for a rematch.

62 Anita Singh, 'StreetDance 3D tops UK Box Office with Record Takings', *The Telegraph*, 24 May 2010.

63 Ross, 'Spectacular Dimensions' 3D Dance Films', *Senses of Cinema*, 61 (December 2014), p. 1.

64 Mark Adams, 'Flawless Dancers', *Sunday Mirror*, 16 May 2010; Tim Robey, '*StreetDance 3D Review*', *The Telegraph*, 21 May 2010; Chris Tookey, 'Let the Dancers Do Their Stuff', *Daily Mail*, 21 May 2010; Lindsay Winship, 'Close Up: StreetDance 3D', *Time Out*, 20 May 2010, p. 69.

65 Richardson quoted in '*StreetDance* Film Production Notes', Vertigo Films, p. 2.

66 Richardson, quoted in Winship, 'Close Up: StreetDance 3D', p. 69.

67 Ashby and Higson, 'Introduction', p. 9.

68 Colling, *The Aesthetic Pleasures of Girl Teen Film*, p. 2.

69 Jade Boyd, 'Dance, Culture and Popular Film', *Feminist Media Studies*, 4:1 (2007), pp. 67–83, p. 74.

70 Alina Cojocaru, 'Revisiting "Cool Britannia": The Cinematic Construction of London as a Global City in Four British-Asian Films', *Altre Modernità*, 20 (2018), pp. 89–105.

71 Albert Moran, 'Global Franchising, Local Customizing: The Cultural Economy of TV Program Formats', *Continuum: Journal of Media & Cultural Studies*, 23:2 (2009), pp. 115–25, p. 116.

72 Colling, *Aesthetic Pleasures of Girl Teen Film*, pp. 60–1.

73 Kearney, 'Sparkle', pp. 263–73.

74 Ibid., p. 263.

75 Kennedy, *Tweenhood*, p. 75.

76 Robey, '*StreetDance 3D Review*'.

77 Adams, 'Flawless Dances', *Sunday Mirror*, 21 May 2010, p. 34.

78 Maria Duarte, 'A Hit in 3D for Teen Dancers', *Morning Star*, 21 May 2010, n.p.

79 Henry Fitzherbert, 'Yes, We have Serious British Dance Talent', *Sunday Express*, 23 May 2010, pp. 56–7.

80 Unattributed, 'Dancing in the Street', *Wales on Sunday*, 13 May 2010.

81 Gant, 'StreetDance 3D Shimmies into First Place at UK Box Office'.

82 Fitzherbert, 'Yes, We have Serious British Dance Talent'.

83 James Richardson quoted in Vertigo Films, 'StreetDance Production Notes', p. 4.

84 Woods, *British Youth Television*, p. 118.

85 Richard Winsor quoted in Unattributed, 'Dancing in the Street'.

86 Mendick et al., *Celebrity, Aspiration and Contemporary Youth*, p. 162.

87 Ibid., p. 59.

88 Ibid.

89 Vertigo Films, '*StreetDance* Production Notes', p. 22.

90 Woods, *British Youth Television*, p. 227.

91 Nichola Burley quoted in '*StreetDance* Production Notes', p. 7.

92 Holmes, 'Reality TV Goes Pop!', p. 157.

93 Nichola Burley quoted in '*StreetDance* Production Notes', p. 7.

94 Mendick et al., *Celebrity, Aspiration and Contemporary Youth*, p. 59.

95 Gill, 'The Affective, Cultural, and Psychic Life of Postfeminism', p. 610.

96 Dyer, *Stars*, p. 42.

97 Holmes, 'Reality TV Goes Pop!' p. 156.

98 Colling, *The Aesthetic Pleasures of Girl Teen Film*, p. 116.

99 Jade Boyd, '"Hey, We're from Canada but We're Diverse, Right?": Neoliberalism, Multiculturalism, and Identity on So You Think You Can Dance Canada', *Critical Studies in Media Communication*, 29: 4 (2012), pp. 259–74, p. 265.

100 Katharina Lindner, 'Bodies in Action: Female Athleticism on the Cinema Screen', *Feminist Media Studies*, 11:3 (2011), pp. 321–45, p. 335.

101 Lindner, 'Spectacular (Dis-) Embodiments', p. 11.

102 Ibid.

103 Parts of this analysis were originally published in Sarah Hill, 'The Ambitious Young Woman and the Contemporary British Sports Film', *Assuming Gender*, 5:1 (2015), pp. 37–58 and are included here with the kind permission of the editors.

104 Faye Woods, 'Teen TV Meets T4: Assimilating The O.C. into British Youth Television', *Critical Studies in Television*, 8:1 (2013), pp. 14–35, p. 15.

105 Kim Allen, 'Top Girls Navigating Austere Times: Interrogating Youth Transitions since the "crisis"', *Journal of Youth Studies*, 19:6 (2016), pp. 805–20, p. 807.

106 McRobbie, 'Top Girls', p. 722.

107 Allen, 'Top Girls Navigating Austere Times', p. 806.

108 Ibid.

109 Cath Clarke, 'British Film's New It-Girl?', *Time Out*, 17 February 2011.

110 Ibid. See also Carole Cadwalladr, 'Charmed, We're Sure', *The Observer*, 20 February 2011; Rob Driscoll, 'From Skiing Zero to Hero', *The Western Mail*, 11 March 2011.

111 McRobbie, 'Top Girls', p. 722.

112 Dave Calhoun, '*Chalet Girl*', *Time Out*, 17 March 2011; Robbie Collin, '*Chalet Girl*', *News of the World*, 13 March 2011, pp. 46–7; Alex Zane, '*Chalet Girl*', *The Sun*, 18 March 2011, p. 2.

113 Steve Pratt, '*Chalet Girl* Review', *The Northern Echo*, 17 March 2011, p. 29.

114 Tim Robey, 'McConaughey Back on the Case', *The Daily Telegraph*, 18 March 2011, p. 27.

115 Cadwalladr, 'Charmed, We're Sure'.

116 Brenda R. Weber, *Makeover TV: Selfhood, Citizenship and Celebrity* (London: Duke University Press, 2009), p. 25.

117 Woods, *British Youth Television*, p. 198.

118 Tamsin Egerton. 'Tamsin Egerton Interview', *View London*, n.d.

119 Gill, 'The Affective, Cultural, and Psychic Life of Postfeminism', p. 611.

120 Leonie Harthard, 'Interviews: Cast and Crew', *Chalet Girl on Set*, 4 November 2010.

121 Negra, *What a Girl Wants?*, p. 4.

122 Melanie Kennedy, '"Come on, [. . .] Let's Go Find Your Inner Princess":
     (Post-)feminist Generationalism in Tween Fairy Tales', *Feminist Media
     Studies*, 18:3 (2018), pp. 424–39, p. 429.

123 Weber, *Makeover TV*, p. 25.

124 Ibid.; Negra, *What a Girl Wants?*, p. 123.

125 Stacey, *Star Gazing*, p. 116.

126 Helen Warner, 'Style over Substance? Fashion, Spectacle and Narrative
     in Contemporary US Television', *Popular Narrative Media*, 2:2 (2009),
     pp. 181–93, p. 181.

127 Jamie Schwarz quoted in Brand Republic, 'Rom-com *Chalet Girl* Movie
     Gets Social Push', 18 February 2011.

128 Harris, *Future Girl*, p. 14.

129 Heywood, 'Producing Girls', p. 113.

130 Ibid., p. 114.

131 Kennedy, 'Come on, [. . .] Let's Go Find Your Inner Princess', p. 429.

132 Ibid.

133 Dr Suess, *Oh, The Places You'll Go* (London: Random House, 1960).

134 Colling, *The Aesthetic Pleasures of Girl Teen Film*, p. 28.

135 This was also evident in *Wild Child* as discussed in Chapter 1.

136 Sarah Gilligan, 'Performing Postfeminist Identities: Gender, Costume
     and Transformations in Teen Cinema' in Melanie Waters (ed.), *Women
     on Screen: Feminism and Femininity in Visual Culture* (Hampshire:
     Palgrave Macmillan, 2011), pp. 167–81, p. 167.

137 Negra, *What a Girl Wants*, p. 5.

138 John Vincent, John S. Hill, Andrew Billings, John Harris and C. Dwayne
     Massey, '"We are GREAT Britain": British Newspaper Narratives during
     the London 2012 Olympic Games', *International Review for the Sociology
     of Sport*, 53:8 (2017), pp. 895–923, p. 901.

139 Ibid.

140 '*Fast Girls* Production Notes', Optimum Releasing (2012), n.p.

141 Damian Jones quoted in '*Fast Girls* Production Notes', Optimum
     Releasing, n.p.

142 Graham Young, 'Fast Girls', *Sunday Mercury*, Features, 17 June 2012, p. 2.

143 Ashby, 'Postfeminism in the British Frame', p. 128.

144 Ibid., p. 130.

145 Ibid.

146 Matthew Bond, 'Fast Girls', *Mail on Sunday*, 17 June 2012, n.p; Keogh, 'Film Star's Olympic Hell', *Birmingham Evening Mail*, 22 June 2012, p. 6.

147 Valerie Walkerdine, 'Reclassifying upward Mobility: Femininity and the Neo-liberal Subject', *Gender and Education*, 15: 3 (2003), pp. 237–48, p. 239.

148 Bond, 'Fast Girls'; Graham Young, 'Girl Power Is Back on Track', *Wales on Sunday*, 17 June 2012, p. 6.

149 Williams, *Female Stars of British Cinema*, p. 197.

150 Skeggs, *Formations of Class and Gender*, pp. 99–100.

151 Beverley Skeggs, 'The Making of Class and Gender through Visualizing Moral Subject Formation', *Sociology*, 39:5 (2005), pp. 965–82, p. 973.

152 Ulrich Beck, *Risk Society: Towards a New Modernity* (London: Sage, 1992), p. 135; Skeggs, 'The Making of Class and Gender through Visualizing Moral Subject Formation', p. 974.

153 Wilks, '"Boys Don't Like Girls for Funniness"', p. 110.

154 Damian Jones quoted in '*Fast Girls* Production Notes', Optimum Releasing.

155 Cath Clarke, 'Fast Girls', *Time Out*, 14 June 2012, p. 66.

156 Keogh, 'Film Star's Olympic Hell', p. 6.

157 Regan Hall quoted in '*Fast Girls* Production Notes', p. 8.

158 For a fuller discussion of the construction of the athletic teen girl body in Hollywood cinema, see Colling, *The Aesthetic Pleasures of Teen Girl Film*, p. 77.

159 '*Fast Girls* Production Notes', Optimum Releasing.

160 Colling, *The Aesthetic Pleasures of Girl Teen Film*, p. 75; Lindner, 'Blood, Sweat and Tears: Women, Sport and Hollywood'.

161 Deborah Arthurs, '"I never compete without full make-up!" Olympic Star Jessica Ennis Reveals She Likes to Run in Style', *Daily Mail*, 2 April 2012.

162 '*Fast Girls* Production Notes', Optimum Releasing.

163 Ibid.

164 Lindner, 'Blood, Sweat and Tears: Women, Sport and Hollywood', p. 239.

165 Ibid., p. 244.

166 Ibid., pp. 242–3.

167 Colling, *The Aesthetic Pleasures of Girl Teen Film*, p. 89.

168 Gill, 'Postfeminist Media Culture', p. 151.

169 Bond, 'Fast Girls'.

170 Robbie Collin, '*Fast Girls* Review', *The Telegraph*, 14 June 2012.
171 The significance of the working-class protagonist's alternative knowledge of the city as a potential route to success and visibility is discussed in relation to *Kicks* in Chapter 3.
172 Boyd, 'Dance, Culture and Popular Film', p. 74.

Chapter 3

1 Winch, *Girlfriends and the Postfeminist Sisterhood*, p. 2.
2 Ibid.
3 Ibid., p. 9.
4 Mary Celeste Kearney, 'Girlfriends and Girl Power: Female Adolescence in Contemporary U.S. Cinema', in Frances Gateward and Murray Pomerance (eds.) *Sugar, Spice, and Everything Nice: Cinemas of Girlhood* (Detroit: Wayne State University Press, 2003), pp. 125–42, p. 130.
5 Valerie Hey, *The Company She Keeps: An Ethnography of Girls' Friendships* (Buckingham: Open University Press, 1997), p. 2.
6 Karen Hollinger, *In The Company of Women: Contemporary Female Friendship Films* (London: University of Minnesota Press, 1998).
7 Ibid., p. 12.
8 Bell and Williams, 'The Hour of the Cuckoo', p. 15.
9 Timothy Shary, *Generation Multiplex: The Image of Youth in American Cinema After 1980* (Texas: Texas University Press, 2014), p. 2.
10 Sandra Goldbacher, 'Best of Friends', *The Guardian*, 22 November 2001.
11 Hey, *The Company She Keeps*, p. 2.
12 Heidi Wyithe, 'Withnail and Eyeliner', *This Is Local London*, 17 December 2001, n.p.
13 Tom Charity, '*Me Without You* Film Review', *Time Out*, 22 November 2001, p. 88.
14 Ashley Franklin, 'Friel Film is a "Chick Flick"', *Derby Evening Telegraph*, 25 January 2001, p. 6.
15 Cosmo Landesman, 'Me Without You', *Sunday Times*, 25 November 2001.
16 Unattributed, 'Me Without You', *Birmingham Evening Mail*, 23 November 2001, p. 36.

17 Jason Solomons, 'Teenage Kicks Hit the Spot', *Mail on Sunday*, 25 November 2001, p. 72.
18 Charity, '*Me Without You*', p. 88.
19 Landesman, 'Me Without You'.
20 Unattributed, 'Pals' Well-observed Tale', *This Is Wiltshire*, 21 January 2002, n.p.
21 Franklin, 'Friel Film Is a "Chick Flick"', p. 6.
22 Ibid., Solomons, 'Teenage Kicks Hit the Spot', p. 72.
23 Allan Hunter, 'Spy Games and Me Without You', *Mail on Sunday*, 25 November 2001, p. 9.
24 Peter Bradshaw, '*Me Without You*', *The Guardian*, 23 November 2001.
25 BBC, 'Channel 4's Legacy of Controversy', 6 June 2007.
26 Solomons, 'Teenage Kicks Hit the Spot', p. 72.
27 Franklin, 'Friel Film Is a "Chick Flick"', p. 6.
28 Solomons, 'Teenage Kicks Hit the Spot', p. 72.
29 Hunter, 'Spy Games and Me Without You', p. 9.
30 Charity, '*Me Without You*', p. 88; Franklin, 'Friel Film Is a "Chick Flick"', p. 6; Hunter, 'Spy Games and Me Without You', p. 9.
31 Solomons, 'Teenage Kicks Hit the Spot', p. 72.
32 Charity, '*Me Without You*', p. 88.
33 Renold and Ringrose, 'Normative Cruelties and Gender Deviants', p. 585.
34 Hey, *The Company She Keeps*, p. 6.
35 Gill, 'Postfeminist Media Culture', p. 149.
36 Giddens, *Modernity and Society*; Rose, *Inventing Ourselves*.
37 Gill, 'Postfeminist Media Culture', p. 164.
38 Tasker and Negra, 'Introduction', p. 10.
39 Ringrose, *Postfeminist Education?*; Valerie Walkerdine, 'Shame on You! Intergenerational Trauma and Working-Class Femininity on Reality Television', in Beverley Skeggs and Helen Wood (eds.) *Reality Television and Class* (Basingstoke: Palgrave Macmillan, 2011), pp. 225–36.
40 Forrest, 'Better Things (Duane Hopkins, 2008) and New British Realism', p. 32.
41 Peter Bradshaw, 'Film of the Week: My Summer of Love', *The Guardian*, 22 October 2004.
42 Jonathan Romney, 'The Motor Scooter Diaries – Or How Summer Came at Last to British Film', *Independent on Sunday*, 24 October 2004.

43 Bradshaw, 'My Summer of Love', Romney, 'The Motor Scooter Diaries' Jeff Sawtell, 'Contender for Top Film of the Year: *My Summer of Love*, *Morning Star*, 22 October 2004, p. 9.

44 The 'lost girl' can be viewed as a development of the 'desperate girls' of 1990s British cinema in films such as *Under the Skin* (1997) and *Stella Does Tricks* (1996) who are often lost and made to undergo ambivalent and ambiguous emotional rites of passage. See Charlotte Brunsdon, 'Not Having It All: Women and Film in the 1990s' in Robert Murphy (ed.) *British Cinema of the 90s* (London: BFI, 2000), pp. 167–77.

45 Mayer, *Political Animals*, p. 79.

46 Ibid., p. 82.

47 Bradshaw, 'My Summer of Love'.

48 Natalie Press, quoted in Garth Pearce, 'Love Don't Cost a Thing', *The Sunday Times*, 3 October 2004, p. 6.

49 Pawel Pawlikowski quoted in Jen Foley, 'Pawel Pawlikowski: *My Summer of Love*', BBC, 28 October 2004.

50 Stanley Cohen, *Folk Devils and Moral Panics: The Creation of Mods and Rockers* (London: Routledge, 1972).

51 Ibid.

52 Andrea Arnold quoted in Artificial Eye, 'Production Notes', *Fish Tank Press Book*, p. 6.

53 Bradshaw, 'My Summer of Love'; Romney, 'The Motor Scooter Diaries'; Sawtell, 'Contender for Top Film of the Year', p. 9.

54 Walkerdine, 'Reclassifying Upward Mobility', p. 239.

55 Allen, '"Blair's children"', p. 761.

56 Harris, *Future Girl*, p. 25.

57 Monk, '"If You Can't Make a Good Political Film, Don't"', p. 497.

58 Tyler, 'Chav Mum, Chav Scum', p. 21.

59 Winch, *Girlfriends and the Postfeminist Sisterhood*, p. 22.

60 Joanna Rydzewska, 'Imagining Englishness: The Mapping of Identity in *My Summer of Love* (2004) by Pawel Pawlikowski', *New Cinemas: Journal of Contemporary Film*, 7:2 (2009), pp. 119–36, p. 123.

61 Monk, '"If You Can't Make a Good Political Film, Don't"', p. 499.

62 Winch, *Girlfriends and the Postfeminist Sisterhood*, p. 12.

63 Lindy Heymann, 'Extra Time', *Kicks* (UK: Drakes Avenue) [DVD].

64 Andrews, *Television and British Cinema*, p. 126.

65 Winch, *Girlfriends and the Postfeminist Sisterhood*, p. 20.

66 Anthony Mullen, 'Public Property: Celebrity and the Politics of New Labour', in David Forrest and Beth Johnson (eds.) *Social Class and Television Drama in Contemporary Britain* (London: Palgrave Macmillan, 2017), pp. 231–44.

67 Ibid., p. 131.

68 Ibid., p. 132.

69 Lindy Heymann, 'Director's Notes', n.d, kicksthemovie.com.

70 Ibid.

71 Colling, *The Aesthetic Pleasures of Teen Girl Film*, p. 49.

72 Projansky, *Spectacular Girls*, p. 6.

73 Ibid., p. 7.

74 Kennedy, *Tweenhood*, p. 13.

75 Winch, *Girlfriends and the Postfeminist Sisterhood*, p. 12.

76 Anna Smith, '*Kicks* Is an Enjoyable Insight into the World of Professional Footballers', *Metro*, 3 June 2010; Jason Solomons, 'Kicks', *Mail on Sunday*, 6 June 2010.

77 Giddens, *Modernity and the Society*, p. 76.

78 Winch, *Girlfriends and the Postfeminist Sisterhood*, p. 21.

79 Allen, 'Girls Imagining Careers in the Limelight', p. 149.

80 Barbara Follett quoted in Stephen Adams, 'Girls Just Want to Win The X Factor or Marry a Footballer, Says Minister', *The Telegraph*, 14 October 2008.

81 Leigh Campbell, 'About the Production', n.d., kicksthemovie.com.

82 Lindy Heymann quoted in Hermione Hoby, 'Review: Kicks', *The Observer*, 4 October 2009, p. 4.

83 Martin Beckford, 'Teenage Girls would Rather be WAGs than Politicians or Campaigners', *The Telegraph*, 18 November 2008.

84 Mendick et al., *Celebrity, Aspiration and Contemporary Youth*, p. 18.

85 Unattributed, 'Kicks', *The Glaswegian*, 11 November 2010, p. 3.

86 Sukhdev Sandhu, '*Kicks*, Review', *The Telegraph*, 3 June 2010.

87 Dave Calhoun, 'Kicks', *Time Out*, 1 June 2010.

88 Peter Bradshaw, 'Kicks', *The Guardian*, 3 June 2010.

89 Heymann, 'Extra Time'.

90 Ibid.

91 Solomons, 'Kicks'.

92 Unattributed, 'Kicks', p. 3.
93 Winch, *Girlfriends and the Postfeminist Sisterhood*, p. 5.
94 Ibid., p. 2.
95 Andrews, *Television and British Cinema*, p. 131.
96 Winch, *Girlfriends and the Postfeminist Sisterhood*, p. 2.
97 Colling, *Aesthetic Pleasures of Girl Teen Film*, p. 36.
98 Ibid., p. 60.
99 Levy, *Female Chauvinist Pigs*, p. 4.
100 Lindy Heymann quoted in Hoby, 'Kicks', *The Observer*, 4 October 2009, p. 4.
101 Ringrose, *Postfeminist Education?*, p. 47.
102 Niall MacCormick, 'Making Of', *Albatross*, dir. by Niall MacCormick (UK: Entertainment One, 2011) [DVD].
103 Andrew Ewart, 'Albatross', *The Sun*, 10 February 2011.
104 Alison Rowat, 'Albatross', *The Herald*, 21 June, 2011 p. 17.
105 Rafn, 'Making Of'.
106 Unattributed, 'Albatross', *The Glasgow Herald*, 13 October 2011, p. 18.
107 Allan Hunter, 'Albatross', Scottish *Express*, 14 October 2011; Chris Tookey, 'Albatross', *Daily Mail*, 14 October 2011.
    Albatross also gets linked to *An Education*, as both feature ambitious girls who are looking to escape and who have affairs with older men.
108 Marie-Alix Thouaille, *The Single Woman Author on Film: Screening Postfeminism*, PhD Thesis, (University of East Anglia, 2018).
109 Cosmo Landesman, 'Uncomfortably Numb', *Sunday Times*, 16 October 2011.
110 Anthony Quinn, 'Albatross', *Arts & Book Review*, 14 October 2011, n.p.
111 Sharon Lougher, 'Albatross', *Metro*, 9 February 2011, p. 61.
112 MacCormick, 'The Making of *Albatross*'.
113 Winch, *Girlfriends and the Postfeminist Sisterhood*, p. 2.
114 Ibid., p. 4.
115 Hollinger, *In the Company of Women*, p. 7.
116 Giddens, *Modernity and Society*, p. 75.
117 Justine Ashby, '"It's been Emotional": Reassessing the Contemporary British Woman's Film', in Melanie Bell and Melanie Williams (eds.) *British Women's Cinema* (Oxon: Routledge, 2010), p. 157.
118 Brunsdon, 'Not Having It All', p. 176.

Chapter 4

1   Claire Monk and Amy Sargeant, 'Introduction: The Past in British Cinema' in Claire Monk and Amy Sargeant (eds.) *British Historical Cinema* (London: Routledge, 2002), pp. 1–14, p. 1.

2   Jessica Taylor, 'Feminist Tropes: Corsetry and Rape in Saul Dibb's The Duchess', *Continuum*, 30:3 (2016), pp. 336–46, p. 339.

3   Yvonne Tasker, '*Enchnated* (2007) by Postfeminism: Gender, Irony and the New Romantic Comedy' in Hillary Radner and Rebecca Stringer (eds.) *Feminism at the Movies* (London: Routledge, 2001), pp. 67–79, p. 74; Kennedy, *Tweenhood*, p. 46.

4   Vidal, *Heritage Film*, p. 109.

5   Sukhdev Sandhu, 'Film Review: The Duchess', *The Telegraph*, 5 September 2008.

6   Kara McKechnie, 'Taking Liberties with the Monarch: The Royal Bio-pic in the 1990s' in Claire Monk and Amy Sargeant (eds.) *British Historical Cinema* (London: Routledge, 2002), pp. 217–36, p. 219.

7   Claire Monk, 'Sexuality and Heritage', *Sight and Sound*, 5:10 (1995), pp. 32–4.

8   James Chapman, *Past and Present: National Identity and the British Historical Film* (London: I.B. Tauris, 2005).

9   McKechnie, 'Taking Liberties with the Monarch', p. 221.

10   Andrew Higson, *English Heritage, English Cinema: Costume Drama since 1980* (Oxford: Oxford University Press, 2003), p. 220.

11   Ibid., p. 195.

12   Diane Negra and Yvonne Tasker, 'Introduction: Gender and Recessionary Culture' in Yvonne Tasker and Diane Negra (eds.) *Gendering the Recession: Media and Culture in an Age of Austerity* (London: Duke University Press, 2014), pp. 1–30, p. 10.

13   Biressi and Nunn, *Class and Contemporary British Culture*, p. 184.

14   Sukhdev Sandhu, 'The Other Boleyn Girl and Garage', *The Telegraph*, 7 March 2008.

15   Cosmo Landesman, 'It Could Do with a Bit of the Other', *The Sunday Times*, 9 March 2008, p. 12.

16   Peter Bradshaw, 'The Other Boleyn Girl', *The Guardian*, 7 March 2008.

17   Landesman, 'It Could Do with a Bit of the Other', p. 12.

18 Maggie Andrews, 'Fantasies, Factions and Unlikely Feminist Heroes in Contemporary Heritage Films' in Maggie Andrews and Sallie McNamara (eds.) *Women and the Media: Feminism and Femininity in Britain, 1900 to the Present* (London: Routledge, 2014), pp. 244–58, p. 249.

19 Dave Calhoun, 'Reviews: *The Other Boleyn Girl*', *Time Out*, 3 March 2008.

20 Taylor, 'Feminist Tropes', p. 336.

21 Gill, 'Postfeminist Media Culture', p. 149.

22 Harris, *Future Girl*.

23 Taylor, 'Feminist Tropes', p. 337.

24 Ibid.; Colling, *The Aesthetic Pleasures of Girl Teen Film*, p. 49.

25 Beck, *Risk Society*, p. 136.

26 Marina Gonick et al., 'Rethinking Agency and Resistance: What Comes after Girl Power?', *Girlhood Studies*, 2:2 (2009), pp. 1–9, p. 2.

27 Charlotte Brunsdon, 'Not Having It All: Women and Film in the 1990s', p. 167.

28 Louise Wilks, *Naughty Noughties? Depictions of Female Sexuality and the Body Politic in Contemporary British Cinema*, PhD Thesis, (University of Liverpool), p. 218.

29 Vidal, *Heritage Film*, p. 109.

30 Andrews, 'Fantasies, Factions and Unlikely Feminist Heroes in Contemporary Heritage Films', p. 246.

31 Ibid., p. 245.

32 Graham King, in GK Films, '*The Young Victoria* Production Notes' (2009), pp. 1–50, p. 5. See H.R.H. The Duchess of York, and Benita Stoney, *Victoria and Albert: Life at Osborne House* (London: Weidenfeld & Nicolson, 1991); H.R.H. The Duchess of York, Benita Stoney and Ben Matthews, *Travels With Queen Victoria* (London: Weidenfeld & Nicolson, 1993).

33 Peter Bradshaw, 'The Young Victoria', *The Guardian*, 6 March 2009.

34 Emily Blunt quoted in '*The Young Victoria* Production Notes', p. 9.

35 Marc Vallée quoted in '*The Young Victoria* Production Notes', p. 10.

36 Graham King in Edward Lawrenson, 'Fresh Heir: Director Jean-Marc Vallée and Producer Graham King on the set of The Young Victoria', *Screen International*, 2 November 2007.

37 Chris Hastings, 'Princess Diana and the Duchess of Devonshire: Striking Similarities', *The Telegraph*, 9 August 2008.

38 Graham King, quoted in Baz Bamigboye, 'Queen Vic Treatment for Rupert', *Daily Mail*, 6 July 2007, p. 55.

39 Emily Blunt quoted in '*The Young Victoria* Production Notes', p. 9.

40 Marc Vallée quoted in '*The Young Victoria* Production Notes', p. 8.

41 Julian Fellowes, quoted in '*The Young Victoria* Production Notes', p. 6.

42 Siobhan Synnot, 'The Young Victoria: Teen Queen's Search for a Prince', *Scotland on Sunday*, 1 March 2009, p. 8.

43 Derek Malcolm, 'No Sex Please, We're Victorians', *The London Evening Standard*, 5 March 2009.

44 Kennedy, '"Come on, [. . .] Let's Go Find Your Inner Princess"', p. 424.

45 Ibid.

46 Vidal, *Heritage Film*, p. 109.

47 Kennedy, '"Come on, [. . .] Let's Go Find Your Inner Princess"', p. 436.

48 Julia Kinzler, 'Visualising Victoria: Gender, Genre and History in *The Young Victoria* (2009)', *Neo-Victorian Studies*, 4:2 (2011), pp. 49–65, p. 52.

49 Barbara Scharff, 'Still Lifes – Tableaux Vivants: Art in British Heritage Films' in Eckart Voigts-Virchow (ed.) *Janespotting and Beyond: British Heritage Retrovisions Since the Mid-1990s* (Tübingen: Gunter Narr Verlag Tübingen 2004), pp. 125–34, p. 128.

50 Graham King quoted in '*The Young Victoria* Production Notes', p. 7.

51 Vidal, *Heritage Film*, p. 109.

52 Ibid., p. 105.

53 Harris, *Future Girl*, p. 32.

54 Kinzler, 'Visualising Victoria', p. 61.

55 Biressi and Nunn, *Class and Contemporary British Culture*, p.132.

56 Kim Allen, Heather Mendick, Laura Harvey and Aisha Ahmad, 'Welfare Queens, Thrifty Housewives, and Do-It-All Mums: Celebrity Motherhood and the Cultural Politics of Austerity', *Feminist Media Studies*, 15:6 (2015), pp. 907–25, p. 912.

57 Ibid., p. 913.

58 McRobbie, *The Aftermath of Feminism*, p. 72.

59 '*The Young Victoria* Production Notes', p. 3.

60 Benjamin Secher, 'Keira Knightley in *The Duchess*', *The Telegraph*, 30 August 2008, p. 5.

61 Laurence Phelan, 'The Duchess', *The Independent*, 6 September 2008, p. 22.

62 Saul Dibb quoted in Richard Saker, 'Observer Film Quarterly: New British Directors: Saul Dibb', *The Observer*, 27 July 2008, p. 29.

63 Andrews, 'Fantasies, Factions and Unlikely Feminist Heroes on Contemporary Heritage Films', p. 246.

64 Rob Driscoll, 'A Right Royal Affair', *The Western Mail*, 29 August 2008, p. 2; Hastings, 'Princess Diana and the Duchess of Devonshire: Striking Similarities'; Alison Rowat, 'It's All in the Best Possible Taste', *The Herald*, 4 September 2008, p. 18.

65 Gill, 'Postfeminist Media Culture', p. 150.

66 Projansky, *Spectacular Girls*, p. 6.

67 David Gritten, '18th Century It Girl', *The Telegraph Magazine*, 16 August 2008, p. 21.

68 Christina Lane and Nicole Richter, 'The Feminist Poetics of Sofia Coppola: Spectacle and Self-consciousness in *Marie Antoinette* (2006)' in Hilary Radner and Rebecca Stringer (eds.) *Feminism at the Movies: Understanding Gender and Contemporary Popular Culture* (Oxon: Routledge, 2011), pp. 189–202.

69 Fiona Handyside, *Sofia Coppola: A Cinema of Girlhood* (London: I.B. Tauris 2017), p. 147.

70 Charlotte O'Sullivan, 'War of the Devonshires', *The London Evening Standard*, 4 September 2008, p. 39.

71 Projansky, *Spectacular Girls*, p. 6; Vidal, *Heritage Film*, p. 107.

72 Keira Knightley quoted in Gritten, '18th Century It Girl', p. 21.

73 Rowat, 'It's All in the Best Possible Taste', p. 18.

74 Kevin Maher, 'A Very Fiennes Performance but Really Nothing to Di for', *The Times* (*Times2*), 4 September 2008, p. 15.

75 Peter Bradshaw, 'The Duchess', *The Guardian*, 5 September 2008.

76 Unattributed, *Nottingham Evening Post*, 29 August 2008, p. 15.

77 Sukhdev Sandhu, 'The Duchess', *The Telegraph*, 5 September 2008.

78 Taylor, 'Feminist Tropes', p. 341.

79 Saul Dibb quoted in Dave Calhoun, 'Hanoverian Success', *Time Out*, 21 August 2008, p. 77.

80 Taylor, 'Feminist Tropes', p. 344.

81 Amanda Foreman quoted in Henry Fitzherbert, 'Living in the Shadow of The Duchess', *Sunday Express*, 31 August 2008, p. 57.

82 See also Sarah Louise Smyth, '"I do not know that I find myself anywhere": The British Heritage Film and Spaces of Intersectionality in

Amma Asante's Belle (2014)', in Angela Daniel Matos et al. (eds.) *Yours, Mine and Ours: Intersectional Spaces on Screen* (Durham: Duke University Press, Forthcoming 2020).

83 Mayer, *Political Animals*, p. 98.
84 Scharff, 'Still Lifes – Tableaux Vivants', p. 132.
85 Robbie Collin, '*Belle* Review: A Vital Film', *The Telegraph*, 12 June 2014; Alistair Harkness, '*Belle*', *The Scotsman*, 14 June 2014, p. 22; Mark Kermode, '*Belle* Review – A Ripe Costume Drama with Teeth', *The Guardian*, 15 June 2014; Laurence Phelan, 'A Different Class of Costume Drama', *The Independent*, 12 June 2014; Brian Viner, 'What a Pretty Picture', *Daily Mail*, 13 June 2014.
86 Amma Asante, 'Director Amma Asante on the Inspiration behind Her Film Belle', *The Independent*, 7 July 2014.
87 Amma Asante quoted in '*Belle* Production Notes', Fox Searchlight Pictures (2013), p. 14.
88 Kermode, '*Belle* Review – A Ripe Costume Drama with Teeth'.
89 Henry Fitzherbert, 'Belle, Slave to Her Blinkered Society', *Sunday Express*, 13 June 2014.
90 Asante, 'Director Amma Asante on the Inspiration behind Her Film Belle'.
91 *Belle*'s success meant that Asante did not have to wait as long to release her next film. *A United Kingdom* (2016) is similarly based on a true story and explores issues of race within a period setting as it explores the romance between Seretse Khama (David Oyelowo) heir to the throne of Bechuanaland and his wife, Ruth Williams (Rosamund Pike).
92 Handyside, *Sofia Coppola*, p. 88.
93 Asante, '*Belle* Production Notes', p. 3.
94 Ibid.
95 '*Belle* Production Notes', p. 4.
96 Taylor, 'Feminist Tropes', p. 339.

Conclusion

1 Heymann, 'Director's Notes', n.d.
2 Samantha Lay, *British Social Realism: From Documentary to Brit Grit* (London: Wallflower Press, 2002).

3 Gill, 'The Affective, Cultural and Psychic Life of Postfeminism', p. 611.

4 Stacey, *Star Gazing*, p. 117.

5 Kearney, 'Sparkle', pp. 263–73.

6 Tasker and Negra, 'Introduction', p. 2.

7 Negra, *What a Girl Wants*, p. 123.

8 Ibid., p. 124.

9 Rachel Moseley, 'Glamorous Witchcraft: Gender and Magic in Teen Film and Television', *Screen*, 43:4 (2002), pp. 403–22, p. 406.

10 Samantha Colling, *The Aesthetic Pleasures of Girl Teen Film* (London: Bloomsbury Academic, 2017), p. 49.

11 Ibid., p. 36.

12 Damian Jones quoted in '*Fast Girls* Production Notes', p. 5.

13 Shelley Cobb, Linda Ruth Williams and Natalie Wreyford, 'Number Tracking', *Calling the Shots? Counting Women Filmmakers in British Cinema Today*, n.p.

14 Gill, 'The Affective, Cultural, and Psychic Life of Postfeminism', p. 611.

15 Ibid.

16 Ibid.

17 Tasker and Negra, 'Introduction', p. 1.

18 Williams, *Female Starts of British Cinema*, p. 7.

19 Peter Bradshaw, 'Wild Child', *The Guardian*, 15 August 2008.

Bibliography

Adams, Guy, 'St Trinian's Belles to Ring Once More', *The Independent*, 10 October 2006. Available at https://www.independent.co.uk/arts-enter tainment/films/features/st-trinians-belles-to-ring-once-more-419395.html (accessed 25 January 2019).

Adams, Mark, 'St Trin's… All Grins', *Sunday Mirror*, 16 December 2007, p. 52.

Adams, Mark, 'School's Pout', *Sunday Mirror*, 10 August 2008. Available at http://www.mirror.co.uk/lifestyle/going-out/film/film-of-the-week-wild -child-325853 (accessed 1 October 2015).

Adams, Mark, 'Flawless Dancers', *Sunday Mirror*, 16 May 2010. Available at http://blogs.mirror.co.uk/movies-mark-adams/2010/05/flawless-dancers-i n-streetdanc.html (accessed 5 January 2014).

Adams, Richard, 'Almost Half of All Young People in England Go on to Higher Education', *The Guardian*, 28 September 2017. Available at https://www.theguardian.com/education/2017/sep/28/almost-half-of-all-young-people-in-england-go-on-to-higher-education (accessed 24 January 2019).

Adams, Stephen, 'Girls Just Want to Win The X Factor or Marry a Footballer, Says Minister', *The Telegraph*, 14 October 2008. Available at https://www .telegraph.co.uk/sport/football/wags/3195308/Girls-just-want-to-win-The -X-Factor-or-marry-a-footballer-says-minister.html (accessed 26 January 2019).

Aftab, Kaleem, 'Fish Tank', *The Independent*, 14 May 2009. Available at http:/ /www.independent.co.uk/arts-entertainment/films/reviews/fish-tank-tbc -1684979.html (accessed 5 January 2014).

Allen, Kim, 'Girls Imagining Careers in the Limelight: Social Class, Gender and Fantasies of "Success"' in Su Holmes and Diane Negra (eds.) *In the Limelight and Under the Microscope: Forms and Functions of Female Celebrity* (London: Continuum, 2011), pp. 149–73.

Allen, Kim, '"Blair's Children": Young Women as "aspirational subjects" in the Psychic Landscape of Class', *The Sociological Review*, 62 (2014), pp. 760–79.

Allen, Kim, Heather Mendick, Laura Harvey and Aisha Ahmad, 'Welfare Queens, Thrifty Housewives, and Do-It-All Mums: Celebrity Motherhood and the Cultural Politics of Austerity', *Feminist Media Studies*, 15:6 (2015), pp. 907–25

Andrews, Hannah, *Television and British Cinema: Convergence and Divergence since 1990* (Hampshire: Palgrave Macmillan, 2014).

Andrews, Maggie, 'Fantasies, Factions and Unlikely Feminist Heroes in Contemporary Heritage Films' in Maggie Andrews and Sallie McNamara (eds.) *Women and the Media: Feminism and Femininity in Britain, 1900 to the Present* (London: Routledge, 2014), pp. 244–58.

Arthurs, Deborah, '"I never compete without full make-up!" Olympic Star Jessica Ennis Reveals She Likes to Run in Style', *Daily Mail*, 2 April 2012. Available at https://www.dailymail.co.uk/femail/article-2122884/London-2012-Olympics-star-Jessica-Ennis-reveals-likes-run-style.html (accessed 26 January 2019).

Artificial Eye, '*Fish Tank* Press Book' (2009), pp. 1–17. Available from http://www.artificialeye.com/database/cinema/fishtank/pdf/pressbook.pdf (accessed 12 December 2013).

Asante, Amma, 'Director Amma Asante on the Inspiration Behind Her Film Belle', *The Independent*, 7 July 2014. Available at http://www.independent.co.uk/arts-entertainment/films/features/director-amma-asante-on-the-inspiration-behind-her-film-belle-9549362.html (accessed 30 January 2015).

Ashby, Justine, 'Postfeminism in the British Frame', *Society for Cinema and Media Studies*, 44:2 (Winter 2005), pp. 127–33.

Ashby, Justine, '"It's been emotional": Reassessing the Contemporary British Woman's Film' in Melanie Bell and Melanie Williams (eds.) *British Women's Cinema* (Oxon: Routledge, 2010), pp. 153–69.

Ashby, Justine and Andrew Higson, 'Introduction' in Justine Ashby and Andrew Higson (eds.) *British Cinema, Past and Present* (Oxon: Routledge, 2000), pp. 1–19.

Bacon, Richard, 'Wild and Childish', *The Sunday People*, 10 August 2008.

Bamigboye, Baz, 'Queen Vic Treatment for Rupert', *Daily Mail*, 6 July 2007, p. 55.

Bamigboye, Baz, 'Teenage Angst and a Hilarious Kiss and Tell', *Daily Mail*, 4 July 2008.

Barber, Lynn, *An Education* (London: Penguin, 2009).

Barnes, Brooks, 'At the Box Office, It's No Longer a Man's World', *The New York Times*, 22 March 2015. Available at http://www.nytimes.com/2015/03/23/business/media/at-the-box-office-its-no-longer-a-mans-world.html?_r=0 (accessed 13 January 2019).

Bates, Laura, *Everyday Sexism* (London: Simon & Schuster, 2014).

BBC, 'Channel 4's Legacy of Controversy', 6 June 2007. Available at http://new
s.bbc.co.uk/1/hi/entertainment/6726693.stm (accessed 26 January 2019).

BBC, 'David Cameron's Plan to Fix "Broken Britain"', 31 March 2010.
Available at http://news.bbc.co.uk/1/hi/uk_politics/8596877.stm (accessed
24 January 2019).

Beaumont-Thomas, Ben, '*Guardian* Live: *The Guardian* Film Show', 28 April
2015. Available at https://www.theguardian.com/membership/2015/apr/28
/guardian-live-the-guardian-film-show (accessed 25 January 2019).

Beckford, Martin, 'Teenage Girls would Rather Be WAGs than Politicians or
Campaigners', *The Telegraph*, 18 November 2008. Available at http://www
.telegraph.co.uk/sport/football/wags/3479322/Teenage-girls-would-rather
-be-WAGs-than-politicians-or-campaigners.html (accessed 4 July 2015).

Beckwith, Gary, 'A Second-Class Comedy', *Newcastle Evening Chronicle*, 15
August 2008, pp. 4–5.

Bell, Emma, '*The Belles of St Trinian's*' in Emma Bell and Neil Mitchell (eds.)
Directory of World Cinema: Britain (Bristol: Intellect, 2012), pp. 113–15.

Bell, Melanie, 'Young, Single Disillusioned: The Screen Heroine in 60s British
Cinema', *The Yearbook of English Studies*, 42 (2012), pp. 79–96.

Bell, Melanie and Melanie Williams, 'The Hour of the Cuckoo: Reclaiming the
British Woman's Film' in Melanie Bell and Melanie Williams (eds.) *British
Women's Cinema* (Oxon: Routledge, 2010), pp. 1–18.

Berlant, Lauren, *The Female Complaint: The Unfinished Business of
Sentimentality in American Culture* (London: Duke University Press,
2008).

Berlant, Lauren, *Cruel Optimism* (Durham: Duke University Press, 2011).

BFI, 'BFI Obligates and Supports Lottery Funding Recipients to Reflect
Diversity in the UK', 30 November 2015. Available at https://www.bfi.org.
uk/news-opinion/news-bfi/announcements/bfi-obligates-supports-lottery-
funding-recipients-reflect-diversity-uk (accessed 24 January 2019).

BFI, 'New BFI Filmography Reveals Complete Story of UK Film 1911-2017',
20 September 2017. Available at https://www.bfi.org.uk/news-opinion
/news-bfi/announcements/bfi-filmography-complete-story-uk-film
(accessed 24 January 2019).

Biressi, Anita and Heather Nunn, *Class and Contemporary British Culture*
(Hampshire: Palgrave Macmillan, 2013).

Bolton, Lucy, 'A Phenomenology of Girlhood: Being Mia in *Fish Tank*
(Arnold, 2009)' in Fiona Handyside and Kate Taylor-Jones (eds.)

International Cinema and the Girl: Local Issues, Transnational Contexts (Hampshire: Palgrave Macmillan, 2016), pp. 75–84.

Bond, Matthew, 'Fast Girls', *Mail on Sunday*, 17 June 2012, n.p.

Boyd, Jade, 'Dance, Culture and Popular Film', *Feminist Media Studies*, 4:1 (2007), pp. 67–83.

Boyd, Jade, '"Hey, We're from Canada but We're Diverse, Right?": Neoliberalism, Multiculturalism, and Identity on So You Think You Can Dance Canada', *Critical Studies in Media Communication* 29:4 (2012), pp. 259–74.

Bradshaw, Peter, 'Me Without You', *The Guardian*, 23 November 2001. Available at http://www.theguardian.com/film/2001/nov/23/culture.pet erbradshaw1 (accessed 25 March 2013).

Bradshaw, Peter, 'Film of the Week: My Summer of Love', *The Guardian*, 22 October 2004. Available at http://film.guardian.co.uk/News_Story/Critic_ Review/Guardian_review/0,4267,1332467,00.html (accessed 20 March 2013).

Bradshaw, Peter, 'The Other Boleyn Girl', *The Guardian*, 7 March 2008. Available at https://www.theguardian.com/film/2008/mar/07/drama.roma nce (accessed 21 January 2019).

Bradshaw, Peter, '*Angus, Thongs and Perfect Snogging*', *The Guardian*, 25 July 2008. Available at https://www.theguardian.com/film/2008/jul/25/comedy (accessed 24 January 2019).

Bradshaw, Peter, 'The Young Victoria', *The Guardian*, 6 March 2009. Available at http://www.theguardian.com/film/2009/mar/06/the-young-victoria-film -review (accessed 25 January 2015).

Bradshaw, Peter, 'An Education', *The Guardian*, 29 October 2009. Available at https://www.theguardian.com/film/2009/oct/29/an-education-review (accessed 25 January 2019).

Bradshaw, Peter, 'Fish Tank', *The Guardian*, 10 September 2009. Available at http://www.theguardian.com/film/2009/sep/10/fish-tank-review (accessed 20 November 2018).

Bradshaw, Peter, 'Kicks', *The Guardian*, 3 June 2010. Available at https://ww w.theguardian.com/film/2010/jun/03/kicks-film-review (accessed 26 January 2019).

Bradshaw, Peter, 'Fast Girls - Review', *The Guardian*, 14 June 2012. Available at https://www.theguardian.com/film/2012/jun/14/fast-girls-review (accessed 26 January 2019).

Brand Republic, 'Rom-com *Chalet Girl* Movie Gets Social Push', 18 February 2011. Available at http://www.brandrepublic.com/news/1055707/Rom -com-Chalet-Girl-movie-gets-social-push/ (accessed 12 January 2014).

Brenner, Natalie, 'Once More with Ealing Interview' in *The Money Progamme*. [TV] BBC 2. 27 July 2007, 1900 hrs.

Brooks, Xan, 'Make More Films like Harry Potter, David Cameron Tells UK Film Industry', *The Guardian*, 17 November 2010. Available at https://www .theguardian.com/film/2010/nov/17/david-cameron-harry-potter-funding (accessed 24 January 2019).

Brunsdon, Charlotte, 'Not Having It All: Women and Film in the 1990s' in Robert Murphy (ed.) *British Cinema of the 90s* (London: BFI, 2000), pp. 167–77.

Buckingham, David, *Youth, Identity and Digital Media* (Cambridge, MA: MIT Press, 2008).

Butler, Jess, 'For White Girls Only? Postfeminism and the Politics of Inclusion', *Feminist Formations*, 25:1 (2013), pp. 35–58.

Cadwalladr, Carole, 'Charmed, We're Sure', *The Observer*, 20 February 2011. Available at http://www.theguardian.com/film/2011/feb/20/felicity-jones-c halet-girl-interview (accessed 12 December 2013).

Calhoun, Dave, 'Reviews: *The Other Boleyn Girl*', *Time Out*, 3 March 2008. Available at http://www.timeout.com/london/film/the-other-boleyn-girl -2007, (accessed 25 July 2013).

Calhoun, Dave, 'Hanoverian Success', *Time Out*, 21 August 2008, p. 77.

Calhoun, Dave, 'Fish Tank', *Time Out*, 23 March 2009. Available at http://www .timeout.com/london/film/fish-tank (accessed 8 January 2014).

Calhoun, Dave, '*Chalet Girl*', *Time Out*, 17 March 2011. Available at http://w02 .timeout.com/film/reviews/89535/chalet-girl.html (accessed 15 December 2013).

Campbell, Leigh, 'About the Production', n.d. Available at http://kicksthemovie .com/ (accessed 20 June 2015. Link no longer working).

Candy, Lorraine, 'Emma Watson, The December 2014 ELLE Cover Interview', *Elle*, 6 March 2015.

Cashmore, Ellis, *Sports Culture* (New York: Routledge, 2000).

Chapman, James, *Past and Present: National Identity and the British Historical Film* (London: I.B. Tauris, 2005).

Charity, Tom, 'Me Without You Film Review', *Time Out*, 22 November 2001, p. 88.

Christopher, James, 'Carry On Rampaging', *The Times*, 20 December 2007, p. 14.

Church Gibson, Pamela, 'From Dancing Queen to Plaster Virgin: *Elizabeth* and the End of English Heritage', *The Journal of Popular British Cinema*, 5 (2002), pp. 133–42.

Clarke, Cath, 'British Film's New It-Girl?', *Time Out*, 17 February 2011. Available at http://www.timeout.com/london/film/felicity-jones-british-films-new-it-girl-1 (accessed 12 December 2013).

Clarke, Cath, 'Fast Girls', *Time Out*, 14 June 2012, p. 66.

Cohen, Phil, 'Mods and Shockers: Youth Cultural Studies in Britain' in Andy Bennett, Mark Cieslik and Steve Miles (eds.) *Researching Youth* (London: Palgrave Macmillan, 2003), pp. 29–54.

Cohen, Stanley, *Folk Devils and Moral Panics: The Creation of Mods and Rockers* (London: Routledge, 1972).

Cojocaru, Alina, 'Revisiting "Cool Britannia": The Cinematic Construction of London as a Global City in Four British-Asian Films', *Altre Modernità*, 20 (2018), pp. 89–105.

Collin, Robbie, '*Chalet Girl*', *News of the World*, 13 March 2011, pp. 46–7.

Collin, Robbie, '*Fast Girls* Review', *The Telegraph*, 14 June 2012. Available at https://www.telegraph.co.uk/culture/film/filmreviews/9331840/Fast-Girls-review.html (accessed 26 January 2019).

Collin, Robbie, '*Belle* Review: "a vital film"', *The Telegraph*, 12 June 2014. Available at https://www.telegraph.co.uk/culture/film/filmreviews/10894373/Belle-review-a-vital-film.html (accessed 26 January 2019).

Colling, Samantha, *The Aesthetic Pleasures of Girl Teen Film* (London: Bloomsbury, 2017).

Connell, R. W., *Gender and Power: Society, the Person and Sexual Politics* (Cambridge: Polity, 1987).

Coughlan, Sean, 'The Symbolic Target of 50% at University Reached', *BBC News*, 26 September 2019. Available from https://www.bbc.co.uk/news/education-49841620 (Accessed 26 January 2020).

Deans, Jason, 'Jackson: I Got It Wrong with FilmFour', *The Guardian*, 22 September 2003. Available at https://www.theguardian.com/media/2003/sep/22/channel4.broadcasting (accessed 24 January 2019).

Douglas, Susan, *Enlightened Sexism: The Seductive Message that Feminism's Work Is Done* (New York: Times Books, 2010).

Doyle, Gillian, Philip Schlesinger, Raymond Boyle and Lisa W. Kelly, *The Rise and Fall of the UK Film Council* (Edinburgh: Edinburgh University Press, 2015).

Driscoll, Catherine, *Girls: Feminine Adolescence and Popular Culture and Cultural Theory* (New York: Columbia University Press, 2002).

Driscoll, Rob, 'A Right Royal Affair', *The Western Mail*, 29 August 2008, p. 2.

Driscoll, Rob, 'From Skiing Zero to Hero', *The Western Mail*, 11 March 2011. Available at http://www.walesonline.co.uk/lifestyle/showbiz/from-ski-ing-zero-to-hero-1845358 (accessed 28 November 2018).

Duarte, Maria, 'A Hit in 3D for Teen Dancers', *Morning Star*, 21 May 2010, n.p.

Dyer, Richard, *Stars* (London: BFI, 1998, 2nd edn).

Dyhouse, Carol, *Girl Trouble: Panic and Progress in the History of Young Women* (London: Zed Books, 2013).

Egerton, Tamsin, 'Tamsin Egerton Interview', *View London*, n.d. Available at http://www.viewlondon.co.uk/cinemas/tamsin-egerton-interview-feature-interview-3939.html (accessed 26 January 2019).

Ellen, Barbara, 'Katie Jarvis: "Walking down the red carpet, people screaming… madness!"', *The Observer*, 20 December 2009. Available at https://www.theguardian.com/film/2009/dec/20/faces-2009-katie-jarvis-fish-tank (accessed 25 January 2019).

Ewart, Andrew, '*Albatross*', *The Sun*, 10 February 2011, p. 3.

Fink, Janet and Penny Tinkler, 'Teetering on the Edge: Portraits of Innocence, Risk and Young Female Sexualities in 1950s' and 1960s' British Cinema', *Women's History Review*, 26:1 (2017), pp. 9–25.

Fitzherbert, Henry, 'Top of the Class for Jolly Japes', *Sunday Express*, 23 December 2007.

Fitzherbert, Henry, 'Living in the Shadow of The Duchess', *Sunday Express*, 31 August 2008, p. 57.

Fitzherbert, Henry, 'Winning Belles', *Sunday Express*, 10 February 2009, p. 21.

Fitzherbert, Henry, 'Yes, We have Serious British Talent', *Sunday Express*, 23 May 2010, p. 56–7.

Fitzherbert, Henry, 'Belle, Slave to Her Blinkered Society', *Sunday Express*, 13 June 2014. Available at http://www.express.co.uk/entertainment/films/482162/Belle-review-and-trailer (accessed 30 January 2015).

Foley, Jen, 'Pawel Pawlikowski: *My Summer of Love*', *BBC*, 28 October 2004. Available at http://www.bbc.co.uk/films/2004/10/11/pawel_pawlikowski_my_summer_of_love_interview.shtml (accessed 20 September 2015).

Foreman, Amanda, *Georgiana: Duchess of Devonshire* (London: Harper Perennial, 1998).

Forrest, David, 'Better Things (Duane Hopkins, 2008) and New British Realism', *New Cinemas: Journal of Contemporary Film*, 8:1 (2010), pp. 31–43.

Fox Searchlight Pictures, '*Belle* Production Notes' (2013). Available at http://webcache.googleusercontent.com/search?q=cache:CqcwAlA78GgJ:d97a3a d6c1b09e180027-5c35be6f174b10f62347680d094e609a.r46.cf2.rackcdn.c om/films/film/production_notes-a4ad4e58-0461-4f34-af78-e740073491 6b.docx+&cd=2&hl=en&ct=clnk&gl=uk (accessed 30 January 2015).

Franklin, Ashley, 'Friel Film Is a "Chick Flick"', *Derby Evening Telegraph*, 25 January 2001, p. 6.

French, Phillip, 'Fast Girls - Review', *The Observer*, 17 June 2012. Available at https://www.theguardian.com/film/2012/jun/17/fast-girls-review-lenora-crichlow (accessed 26 January 2019).

Galpin, Shelley Anne, 'Harry Potter and the Hidden Heritage Films: Genre Hybridity and the Power of the Past in the Harry Potter Film Cycle', *Journal of British Cinema and Television*, 13:3 (2016), pp. 430–49.

Gant, Charles, '*StreetDance 3D* Shimmies into First Place at UK Box Office', *The Guardian*, 25 May 2010. Available at https://www.theguardian.com/fi lm/filmblog/2010/may/25/streetdance-3d-box-office (accessed 23 January 2019).

Geraghty, Christine, 'Crossing over: Performing as Lady and a Dame', *Screen*, 43:1 (2002), pp. 41–56.

Geraghty, Christine, 'Women and 60s British Cinema: The Development of the "Darling" Girl' in Robert Murphy (ed.) *The British Cinema Book* (London: BFI, 2009), pp. 154–163.

Gerrard, Steven, *The Carry On Films* (London: Palgrave Macmillan, 2016).

Giddens, Anthony, *Modernity and Society: Self and Society in the Late Modern Age* (Cambridge: Polity Press, 1991).

Gilbey, Ryan, 'Fish Tank', *New Statesman*, 14 September 2009, p. 47.

Gill, Rosalind, 'Postfeminist Media Culture: Elements of a Sensibility', *European Journal of Cultural Studies*, 10:2 (2007), pp. 147–66.

Gill, Rosalind, 'The Affective, Cultural and Psychic Life of Postfeminism: A Postfeminist Sensibility 10 Years on', *European Journal of Cultural Studies*, 20:6 (2017), pp. 606–26.

Gilligan, Sarah, 'Performing Postfeminist Identities: Gender, Costume and Transformations in Teen Cinema' in Melanie Waters (ed.), *Women on*

Screen: Feminism and Femininity in Visual Culture (Hampshire: Palgrave Macmillan, 2011), pp. 167–81.

GK Films, '*The Young Victoria* Production Notes' (2009), pp. 1–50. Available at http://static.thecia.com.au/reviews/y/young-victoria-production-notes. pdf (accessed 26 January 2019).

Glynn, Stephen, *The British School Film: From Tom Brown to Harry Potter* (London: Palgrave Macmillan, 2016).

Goldbacher, Sandra, 'Best of Friends', *The Guardian*, 22 November 2001. Available at Available at http://www.theguardian.com/world/2001/nov/22/ gender.uk2 (accessed 23 November 2015).

Gonick, Marina, Emma Renold, Jessica Ringrose and Lisa Weems, 'Rethinking Agency and Resistance: What Comes after Girl Power?', *Girlhood Studies*, 2:2 (2009), pp. 1–9.

Gritten, David, '18th Century It Girl', *The Telegraph Magazine*, 16 August 2008, p. 21.

Hall, Stuart, 'Introduction' in Stuart Hall, Jessica Evans and Sean Nixon (eds.) *Representation* (Milton Keynes: Open University Press, 1997), pp. xvii– xxvi.

Hamad, Hannah and Anthea Taylor, 'Introduction: Feminism and Contemporary Celebrity Culture', *Celebrity Studies*, 6:1 (2015), pp. 124–7.

Handyside, Fiona, *Sofia Coppola: A Cinema of Girlhood* (London: I.B. Tauris, 2017).

Harkness, Alistair, 'Belle', *The Scotsman*, 14 June 2014, p. 22.

Harris, Anita, *Future Girl: Young Women in the Twenty-First Century* (London: Routledge, 2004).

Harthard, Leonie, 'Interviews: Cast and Crew', *Chalet Girl on Set*, 4 November 2010. Available at https://chaletgirlfilm.wordpress.com/interviews-cast-cr ew/ (accessed 26 January 2019).

Hastings, Chris, 'Princess Diana and the Duchess of Devonshire: Striking similarities', *The Telegraph*, 9 August 2008. Available at https://www.tel egraph.co.uk/news/uknews/theroyalfamily/2530446/Princess-Diana-an d-the-Duchess-of-Devonshire-Striking-similarities.html (accessed 26 January 2019).

Hattenstone, Simon, 'Julie Walters: "People like me wouldn't get a chance today"', *The Guardian*, 24 January 2015. Available at https://www.theguard ian.com/culture/2015/jan/24/julie-walters-people-like-me-wouldnt-get-a -chance-today (accessed 24 January 2019).

Hey, Valerie, *The Company She Keeps: An Ethnography of Girls'*
   Friendships (Buckingham: Open University Press, 1997).

Heymann, Lindy, 'Extra Time', *Kicks* (London: Drakes Avenue) [DVD].

Heywood, Leslie, 'Producing Girls: Empire, Sport and the Neoliberal Body' in
   Jennifer Hargreaves and Patricia Vertinsky (eds.) *Physical Culture, Power
   and the Body* (London: Routledge, 2006), pp. 101–20.

Higgings, Charlotte, 'How Row Set in Train Life-Changing Offer for *Fish
   Tank* Star', *The Guardian*, 14 May 2009. Available at http://www.theguardi
   an.com/film/2009/may/14/fish-tank-andrea-arnold-cannes-film-festival
   (accessed 5 January 2014).

Higson, Andrew, *English Heritage, English Cinema: Costume Drama since 1980*
   (Oxford: Oxford University Press, 2003).

Higson, Andrew, *Film England: Culturally English Filmmaking since the 1990s*
   (London: I.B. Tauris, 2011).

Hill, John, 'UK Film Policy, Cultural Capital and Social Exclusion', *Cultural
   Trends*, 13:2 (no. 50, June 2004), pp. 29–39.

Hill, John, 'British Cinema as National Cinema: Production, Audience and
   Representation' in Robert Murphy (ed.) *The British Cinema Book* (London:
   BFI, 2009), pp. 11–20.

Hill, Sarah, 'The Ambitious Young Woman and the Contemporary British
   Sports Film', *Assuming Gender*, 5:1 (2015), pp. 37–58.

Hill, Sarah, 'Young Femininity in Contemporary British Cinema: 2000-2015',
   PhD Thesis (University of East Anglia, 2015).

Hoby, Hermione, 'Review: Kicks', *The Observer*, 4 October 2009, p. 4.

Hoggard, Liz, 'Rising Starlet Is Top of the Class at St Trinian's', *Evening
   Standard*, 21 December 2007. Available at https://www.standard.co.uk/go/
   london/film/rising-starlet-is-top-of-the-class-at-st-trinians-6695770.html
   (accessed 25 January 2019).

Hollinger, Karen, *In the Company of Women: Contemporary Female Friendship
   Films* (London: University of Minnesota Press, 1998).

Holmes, Su, '"Reality Goes Pop!" Reality TV, Popular Music, and Narratives of
   Stardom in Pop Idol', *Television & New Media*, 5:2 (2004), pp. 147–72.

Hoyle, Ben, 'Instant Stardom for Girl from Tilbury Station', *The Times*, 15 May
   2009, p. 27.

H.R.H. The Duchess of York and Benita Stoney, *Victoria and Albert: Life at
   Osborne House* (London: Weidenfeld & Nicolson, 1991)

H.R.H. The Duchess of York, Benita Stoney and Ben Matthews, *Travels With
   Queen Victoria* (London: Weidenfeld & Nicolson, 1993).

Hunter, Allan, 'Spy Games and Me Without You', *Mail on Sunday*, 25 November 2001, p. 9.

Hunter, Allan, 'Albatross', *Scottish Express*, 14 October 2011, n.p.

Ince, Kate, *The Body and the Screen: Female Consciousness in Contemporary Cinema* (London: Bloomsbury Academic, 2017).

Jones, Glen, '"Down on the floor and give me ten sit-ups": British Sports Feature Film', *Film & History: An Interdisciplinary Journal of Film and Television Studies*, 35:2 (2005), pp. 29–40.

Jones, Glen, 'In Praise of an "invisible genre"? An Ambivalent Look at the Fictional Sports Feature Film', *Sport in Society*, 11:3 (2008), pp. 117–29, p. 12.

Kearney, Mary, 'Celeste, Girlfriends and Girl Power: Female Adolescence in Contemporary U.S. Cinema' in Frances Gateward and Murray Pomerance (eds.) *Sugar, Spice, and Everything Nice: Cinemas of Girlhood* (Detroit: Wayne State University Press, 2003), pp. 125–42.

Kearney, Mary, 'Sparkle: Luminosity and Post-girl Power Media', *Continuum: Journal of Media & Cultural Studies*, 29:2 (2015), pp. 263–73.

Keller, Jessalynn and Maureen Ryan, 'Call for Papers: Emergent Feminisms and the Challenge to Postfeminist Media Culture', Circulated 12 May 2015.

Kennedy, Melanie, '"Come on, […] Let's Go Find Your Inner Princess": (post-) Feminist Generationalism in Tween Fairy Tales', *Feminist Media Studies*, 18:3 (2018), pp. 424–39.

Kennedy, Melanie, *Tweenhood* (London: I.B. Tauris, 2019).

Kennedy, Tanya Ann, *Historicizing Post-Discourses: Postfeminism and Postracialism in United States Culture* (New York: State University of New York Press, 2017).

Keogh, Kat, 'Film Star's Olympic Hell', *Birmingham Evening Mail*, 22 June 2012, p. 6.

Kermode, Mark, '*Belle* Review – A Ripe Costume Drama with Teeth', *The Guardian*, 15 June 2014. Available at https://www.theguardian.com/film/2014/jun/15/belle-review-costume-drama-teeth-slavery (accessed 26 January 2019).

Kermode, Mark, 'Swoon with a View', *The Observer*, 26 April 2015. Available at https://www.theguardian.com/film/2015/apr/26/the-falling-carol-mo rley-maisie-williams-observer-film-review (accessed 25 January 2019).

Kinzler, Julia, 'Visualising Victoria: Gender, Genre and History in *The Young Victoria* (2009)', *Neo-Victorian Studies*, 4:2 (2011), pp. 49–65.

Klinger, Barbara, *Melodrama and Meaning: History, Culture, and the Films of Douglas Sirk* (Bloomington and Indianapolis: Indiana University Press, 1994).

Landesman, Cosmo, 'Me Without You', *Sunday Times*, 25 November 2001.

Landesman, Cosmo, 'We're, Like, So Over Jolly Hockey Sticks Now', *Sunday Times*, 23 December 2007.

Landesman, Cosmo, 'It Could Do with a Bit of the Other', *The Sunday Times*, 9 March 2008, p. 12.

Landesman, Cosmo, 'Uncomfortably Numb', *Sunday Times*, 16 October 2011, pp. 14–15.

Lane, Christina and Nicole Richter, 'The Feminist Poetics of Sofia Coppola: Spectacle and Self-consciousness in *Marie Antoinette* (2006)' in Hilary Radner and Rebecca Stringer (eds.) *Feminism at the Movies: Understanding Gender and Contemporary Popular Culture* (Oxon: Routledge, 2011), pp. 189–202.

Lawrence, Will, 'The St Trinian's Girls Go to Pot', *The Telegraph*, 14 December 2007. Available at https://www.telegraph.co.uk/culture/film/starsandstorie s/3669901/The-St-Trinians-girls-go-to-pot.html (accessed 25 January 2019).

Lawrenson, Edward, 'Fresh Heir: Director Jean-Marc Vallee and Producer Graham King on the Set of The Young Victoria', *Screen International*, 2 November 2007. Available at https://www.screendaily.com/fresh-heir-d irector-jean-marc-vallee-and-producer-graham-king-on-the-set-of-the-yo ung-victoria/4035635.article (accessed 26 January 2019).

Lay, Samantha, *British Social Realism: From Documentary to Brit Grit* (London: Wallflower Press, 2002).

Leggott, James, *Contemporary British Cinema: From Heritage to Horror* (London: Wallflower Press, 2008).

Levy, Ariel, *Female Chauvinist Pigs: Women and the Rise of Raunch Culture* (London: Zed Books, 2006).

Lindner, Katharina, 'Bodies in Action: Female Athleticism on the Cinema Screen', *Feminist Media Studies*, 11:3 (2011), pp. 321–45.

Lindner, Katharina, 'Spectacular (Dis-) Embodiments: The Female Dancer on Film', *Scope*, 20 (June 2011).

Lindner, Katharina, 'Blood, Sweat and Tears: Women, Sport and Hollywood' in Joel Gwynne and Nadine Muller (eds.) *Postfeminism and Contemporary Hollywood Cinema* (London: Palgrave Macmillan, 2013), pp. 238–55.

Lodderhose, Diana, 'St Trinian's', *Screen International*, 27 March 2008.

Lougher, Sharon, 'Albatross', *Metro*, 9 February 2011, p. 61.

MacCormick, Naill, 'Making Of', *Albatross*, dir. by Niall MacCormick (London: Entertainment One, 2011) [DVD].

MacKichan, Jane, 'Meet the Tribes of St Trinian's', *Daily Mail*, 6 December 2007. Available at https://www.dailymail.co.uk/tvshowbiz/article-500192/Meet-tribes-St-Trinians.html (accessed 25 January 2019).

Maher, Kevin, 'Ewww, Like, This Is Totally Gross', *The Times (Times 2)*, 24 July 2008, p. 17.

Maher, Kevin, 'A Very Fiennes Performance but Really Nothing to Di for', *The Times (Times2)*, 4 September 2008, p. 15.

Maher, Kevin, 'A Diamond in the Rough', *The Times*, 11 September 2009, p. 37.

Malcolm, Derek, 'No Sex Please, We're Victorians', *The London Evening Standard*, 5 March 2009. Available at https://www.standard.co.uk/go/londo n/film/no-sex-please-were-victorians-7439000.html (accessed 26 January).

Marshall, Elizabeth, 'Schooling Ophelia: Hysteria, Memory and Adolescent Femininity', *Gender and Education*, 19:6 (2007), pp. 707–28.

Mayer, Sophie, *Political Animals: The New Feminist Cinema* (London: I.B. Tauris, 2016).

McRobbie, Angela, *Feminism and Youth Culture* (London: Macmillan, 2000).

McRobbie, Angela, 'Top Girls?', *Cultural Studies*, 21:4–5 (2007), pp. 718–37.

McRobbie, Angela, *The Aftermath of Feminism: Gender, Culture and Social Change* (London: SAGE, 2009).

Mendick, Heatherand Kim Allen, Laura Harvey and Aisha Ahmad, *Celebrity, Aspiration and Contemporary Youth* (London: Bloomsbury Academic, 2018).

Mongrel Media, '*An Education* Press Kit' (2009), pp. 1–28.

Monk, Claire, 'Sexuality and Heritage', *Sight and Sound*, 5:10 (1995), pp. 32–4.

Monk, Claire, 'The British Heritage-Film Debate Revisited' in Claire Monk and Amy Sargeant (eds.) *British Historical Cinema* (London: Routledge, 2002) pp. 176–98, p. 178.

Monk, Claire, '"If You Can't Make a Good Political Film, Don't": Pawel Pawlikowski's Resistant Poetic Realism', *Journal of British Cinema and Television*, 9:3 (2012), pp. 480–501.

Monk, Claire and Amy Sargeant, 'Introduction: The Past in British Cinema' in Claire Monk and Amy Sargeant (eds.) *British Historical Cinema* (London: Routledge, 2002), pp. 1–14.

Moran, Albert, 'Global Franchising, Local Customizing: The Cultural Economy of TV Program Formats', *Continuum: Journal of Media & Cultural Studies*, 23:2 (2009), pp. 115–25.

Morley, Carol, 'Mass Hysteria Is a Powerful Group Activity', *The Observer*, 29 March 2016. Available at https://www.theguardian.com/film/2015/mar

/29/carol-morley-the-falling-mass-hysteria-is-a-powerful-group-activity
(accessed 29 January 2019).

Morris, Brorgan, '10 Great British Sports Films', *BFI*, 21 March 2018.
Available at https://www.bfi.org.uk/news-opinion/news-bfi/lists/10-great-
british-sports-films (accessed 25 January 2019).

Moseley, Rachel, 'Glamorous Witchcraft: Gender and Magic in Teen Film and
Television', *Screen*, 43:4 (2002), pp. 403–22.

Moseley, Rachel, 'Trousers and Tiaras: Audrey Hepburn, a Woman's Star',
Feminist Review, 71 (2002), pp. 37–51.

Muir, Kate, 'Extra House Points All Round', *The Times*, 24 April 2015, p. 43.

Mullen, Anthony, 'Public Property: Celebrity and the Politics of New Labour'
in David Forrest and Beth Johnson (eds.) *Social Class and Television
Drama in Contemporary Britain* (London: Palgrave Macmillan, 2017),
pp. 231–44.

Mulvey, Laura, 'Visual Pleasure and Narrative Cinema', *Screen*, 16:3 (Autumn
1975), pp. 6–18.

Mumsnet, 'Let Girls be Girls Campaign' (2010). Available at https://www
.mumsnet.com/campaigns/let-girls-be-girls (accessed 25 January 2019).

Negra, Diane, *What a Girl Wants: Fantasizing the Reclamation of the Self in
Postfeminism* (Oxon: Routledge, 2009).

Negra, Diane and Yvonne Tasker (eds.), *Gendering the Recession: Media and
Culture in an Age of Austerity* (London: Duke University Press, 2014).

Oakley, Ann, 'Foreword' in Valerie Hey, *The Company She Keeps: An
Ethnography of Girls' Friendships* (Buckingham: Open University Press,
1997), pp. vii–ix.

Optimum Releasing, '*Fast Girls* Production Notes'. Available at press.opti
mumreleasing.net/.../FAST%20GIRLS%20Production%20Note (accessed
12 December 2013).

Orenstein, Peggy, *Schoolgirls* (New York: Anchor Books, 1994).

O'Sullivan, Charlotte, 'War of the Devonshires', *The London Evening Standard*,
4 September 2008, p. 39.

Papadopoulos, Linda, 'Sexualisation of Young People Review', *UK Home
Office*, 25 February 2010. Available at https://dera.ioe.ac.uk/10738/1/sexu
alisation-young-people.pdf (accessed 25 January 2019).

Parkin, Damon, 'Are Schoolgirl Antics too Wild for Comfort', *Derby Evening
Telegraph*, 15 August 2008, p. 28.

Pearce, Garth, 'Love Don't Cost a Thing', *The Sunday Times*, 3 October 2004,
p. 6.

Phelan, Laurence, 'The Duchess', *The Independent*, 6 September 2008, p. 22.

Phelan, Laurence, 'A Different Class of Costume Drama', *The Independent*, 12 June 2014. Available at https://www.independent.co.uk/arts-entertainment /films/reviews/belle-film-review-amma-asantes-spirited-film-is-a-different -class-of-costume-drama-9532751.html (accessed 26 January 2019).

Pipher, Mary, *Reviving Ophelia: Saving the Selves of Adolescent Girls* (London: Penguin, 1994).

Polaschek, Bronwyn, *The Postfeminist Biopic* (London: Palgrave Macmillan, 2013).

Pratt, Steve, '*Chalet Girl* Review', *The Northern Echo*, 17 March 2011, p. 29.

Prince, Rosa, 'David Willets: Feminism has Held Back Working Men', *The Telegraph*, 1 April 2011. Available at https://www.telegraph.co.uk/educati on/educationnews/8420098/David-Willets-feminism-has-held-back-wor king-men.html (accessed 25 January 2019).

Projansky, Sarah, *Watching Rape: Film and Television in Popular Culture* (New York: New York University Press, 2001), p. 88.

Projansky, Sarah, *Spectacular Girls: Media Fascination & Celebrity Culture* (New York: New York University Press, 2014).

Quinn, Anthony, 'Albatross', *Arts & Book Review*, 14 October 2011, n.p.

Rees, Jasper, 'How History became Sexy', *The Telegraph*, 25 February 2008, p. 27.

Renold, Emma and Jessica Ringrose, 'Normative Cruelties and Gender Deviants: The Performative Effects of Bully Discourses for Girls and Boys in School', *British Educational Research Journal*, 36:4 (2010), pp. 573–96.

Ringrose, Jessica, *Postfeminist Education? Girls and the Sexual Politics of Schooling* (Oxon: Routledge, 2013).

Rivers, Nicola, *Postfeminism(s) and the Arrival of the Fourth Wave* (London: Palgrave Macmillan, 2017).

Roberts, Andrew, 'Back to School', *Sight & Sound*, August 2007. Available at http://old.bfi.org.uk/sightandsound/feature/49389 (accessed 24 January 2019).

Robey, Tim, '*StreetDance 3D* Review', *The Telegraph*, 21 May 2010. https://ww w.telegraph.co.uk/culture/film/filmreviews/7749404/Streetdance-3D-revi ew.html (accessed 6 January 2019).

Robey, Tim, 'McConaughey Back on the Case', *The Daily Telegraph*, 18 March 2011, p. 27.

Romney, Jonathan, 'The Motor Scooter Diaries – Or How Summer Came at Last to British Film', *Independent on Sunday*, 24 October 2004. Available at http://www.independent.co.uk/arts-entertainment/films/reviews/my-summer-of-love-15-30424.html (accessed 20 September 2015)

Rose, Nikolas, *Inventing Ourselves: Psychology, Power and Personhood* (Cambridge: Cambridge University Press, 1998).

Ross, Miriam, 'Spectacular Dimensions: 3D Dance Films', *Senses of Cinema*, 61 (December 2011). Available at http://sensesofcinema.com/2011/feature-articles/spectacular-dimensions-3d-dance-films/ (accessed 12 January 2014).

Rowat, Alison, 'It's All in the Best Possible Taste', *The Herald*, 4 September 2008, p. 18.

Rowat, Alison, 'Seduced by a Very Charming Man', *The Glasgow Herald*, 29 October 2009, p. 17.

Rowat, Alison, 'Albatross', *The Herald*, 21 June 2011, p. 17.

Ryall, Tom, 'New Labour and the Cinema: Culture, Politics and Economics', *Journal of Popular British Cinema*, 5:1 (2002), pp. 5–20.

Rydzewska, Joanna, 'Imagining Englishness: The Mapping of Identity in *My Summer of Love* (2004) by Pawel Pawlikowski', *New Cinemas: Journal of Contemporary Film*, 7:2 (2009), pp. 119–36.

Saker, Richard, 'Observer Film Quarterly: New British Directors: Saul Dibb', *The Observer*, 27 July 2008, p. 29.

Sandbrook, Dominic, *Never Had It So Good: A History of Britain from Suez to the Beatles* (London: Abacus, 2005).

Sandhu, Sukhdev, 'The Other Boleyn Girl and Garage', *The Telegraph*, 7 March 2008. Available at https://www.telegraph.co.uk/culture/film/filmreviews/3671648/Film-reviews-The-Other-Boleyn-Girl-and-Garage.html (accessed 21 January 2019).

Sandhu, Sukhdev, 'St Trinian's', *The Telegraph*, 18 December 2009, p. 33.

Sandhu, Sukhdev, 'Kicks, Review', *The Telegraph*, 3 June 2010. Available at http://www.telegraph.co.uk/culture/film/filmreviews/7801026/Kicks-review.html (accessed 1 July 2015).

Sawbrick, Susan, 'Royal Ascent', *The Glasgow Herald Magazine*, 7 March 2009, p. 6.

Sawtell, Jeff, 'Contender for Top Film of the Year: *My Summer of Love*', *Morning Star*, 22 October 2004, p. 9.

Sawtell, Jeff, 'St Trinian's' *Morning Star*, 21 December 2007.

Sawtell, Jeff, 'In Search of New Horizons', *Morning Star*, 11 September 2009.

Scharff, Barbara, 'Still Lifes - Tableaux Vivants: Art in British Heritage Films' in Eckart Voigts-Virchow (ed.) *Janespotting and Beyond: British Heritage*

Retrovisions since the Mid-1990s (Tübingen: Gunter Narr Verlag Tübingen 2004), pp. 125–34.

Schneider, Barbaraand David Stevenson, 'The Ambitious Generation', *Educational Leadership*, 57:4 (2000), pp. 22–5.

Secher, Benjamin, 'Keira Knightley in *The Duchess*', *The Telegraph*, 30 August 2008, p. 5.

Sewards, Lisa, 'The Tribes of St Trinian's', *Daily Mail*, 11 December 2009. Available at https://www.dailymail.co.uk/femail/article-1234941/The-St-Tr inians-tribes-The-characters-new-film-based-real-life-schoolgirls--YOUR -daughter.html (accessed 25 January 2019).

Shary, Timothy, *Generation Multiplex: The Image of Youth in American Cinema after 1980* (Austin: Texas University Press, 2014).

Singh, Anita, 'StreetDance 3D Tops UK Box Office with Record Takings', *The Telegraph*, 24 May 2010. https://www.telegraph.co.uk/culture/film/film -news/7760817/StreetDance-3D-tops-UK-box-office-with-record-takings .html (accessed 6 January 2019).

Skeggs, Beverley, *Formations of Class and Gender* (London: Sage, 1997).

Skeggs, Beverley, 'The Making of Class and Gender through Visualizing Moral Subject Formation', *Sociology*, 39:5 (2005), pp. 965–82.

Smith, Anna, '*Kicks* Is an Enjoyable Insight into the World of Professional Footballers', *Metro*, 3 June 2010. Available at http://metro.co.uk/2010/06 /03/kicks-is-an-enjoyable-insight-into-the-world-of-professional-footballe rs-353691/ (accessed 12 September 2015).

Smith, Damon, 'Fearsome Minxes? Not this Lot', *Herald Express*, 22 December 2007, p. 25.

Smyth, Sarah Louise, '"I do not know that I find myself anywhere": The British Heritage Film and Spaces of Intersectionality in Amma Asante's Belle (2014)' in Angel Daniel Matos et al. (eds.) *Yours, Mine and Ours: Intersectional Spaces on Screen* (Durham: Duke University Press, Forthcoming 2020).

Solomons, Jason, 'Teenage Kicks Hit the Spot', *Mail on Sunday*, 25 November 2001, p. 72.

Solomons, Jason, 'Kicks', *Mail on Sunday*, 6 June 2010, n.p.

Spigel, Lynn, 'Postfeminist Nostalgia for a Prefeminist Future', *Screen*, 54:2 (2013), pp. 270–8.

Stacey, Jackie, *Star Gazing: Hollywood Cinema and Female Spectatorship* (London: Routledge, 1994).

Street, Sarah, *British National Cinema* (Oxon: Routledge, 2009).

Suess, Dr, *Oh, The Places You'll Go* (London: Random House, 1960).

Synnot, Siobhan, 'The Young Victoria: Teen Queen's Search for a Prince', *Scotland on Sunday*, 1 March 2009, p. 8.

Tarr, Carrie, '"Sapphire", "Darling" and the Boundaries of Permitted Pleasure', *Screen*, 26:1 (1985), pp. 50–65.

Tasker, Yvonne, '*Enchnated* (2007) by Postfeminism: Gender, Irony and the New Romantic Comedy' in Hillary Radner and Rebecca Stringer (eds.) *Feminism at the Movies* (London: Routledge, 2001), pp. 67–79.

Tasker, Yvonne and Diane Negra, 'Introduction: Feminist Politics and Postfeminist Culture' in Yvonne Tasker and Diane Negra (eds.) *Interrogating Postfeminism: Gender and the Politics of Popular Culture* (Durham and London: Duke University Press 2007), pp. 1–25.

Taylor, Jessica, 'Feminist Tropes: Corsetry and Rape in Saul Dibb's The Duchess', *Continuum*, 30:3 (2016), pp. 336–46.

Thorpe, Vanessa, 'Hollywood Wakes Up to Girl Power: Teen Heroines Look Set to Reclaim Cinema Screens from Comic Book Superheroes', *The Observer*, 27 July 2008, p. 15.

Thouaille, Marie-Alix, *The Single Woman Author on Film: Screening Postfeminism*, PhD Thesis (University of East Anglia, 2018).

Tookey, Chris, 'Sorry Girls… Must Do Better', *Daily Mail*, 21 December 2007, p. 52.

Tookey, Chris, 'Public School Gets a Makeover', *Daily Mail*, 15 August 2008, p. 53.

Tookey, Chris, 'Let the Dancers Do Their Stuff', *Daily Mail*, 21 May 2010.

Tyler, Imogen, 'Chav Mum, Chav Scum: Class Disgust in Contemporary Britain', *Feminist Media Studies*, 8:1 (2008), pp. 17–34.

Unattributed, 'Me Without You', *Birmingham Evening Mail*, 23 November 2001, p. 36.

Unattributed, Pals, 'Well-Observed Tale', *This Is Wiltshire*, 21 January 2002, n.p.

Unattributed, 'Keira Knightley on *The Duchess*', *Nottingham Evening Post*, 29 August 2008, p. 15.

Unattributed, 'Dancing in the Street', *Wales on Sunday*, 13 May 2010. Available at https://www.walesonline.co.uk/lifestyle/showbiz/dancing-in-the-street-1919252 (accessed 26 January 2019).

Unattributed, 'Kicks', *The Glaswegian*, 11 November 2010, p. 3.

Unattributed, 'Albatross', *The Glasgow Herald*, 13 October 2011, p. 18.

Vaizey, Ed, 'The Future of the UK Film Industry', 29 November 2010. Available at https://www.gov.uk/government/speeches/the-future-of-the-uk-film-industry (accessed 24 January 2019).

Vertigo Films, '*StreetDance* Film Production Notes' (2010). Available at http://www.google.co.uk/url?sa=t&rct=j&q=&esrc=s&source=web&cd=10&ved=0CIIBEBYwCQ&url=http%3A%2F%2Fimg.fdb.cz%2Fmaterialy%2F3452-STREETDANCE-PROD-NOTES.doc&ei=F-DOUrWOJYLxhQegkYDACw&usg=AFQjCNEhQ-3YJz252zzVwK_NgW2CDFR_zw&bvm=bv.59026428,d.bGQ (accessed 12 December 2013).

Vidal, Belén, *Heritage Film: Nation, Genre and Representation* (Chichester: Wallflower, 2012).

Vincent, Alice, 'British Film Is Booming but not for Female Directors', *The Telegraph*, 24 July 2013. Available at http://www.telegraph.co.uk/culture/film/film-news/10197761/British-film-is-booming-but-not-for-female-directors.html (accessed 22nd November 2015).

Viner, Brian, 'What a Pretty Picture', *Daily Mail*, 13 June 2014. Available at http://www.dailymail.co.uk/tvshowbiz/article-2656769/What-pretty-picture-Inspired-painting-costume-drama-Belle-feast-eyes-not-just-corking-corsets.html (accessed 30 January 2015).

Walkerdine, Valerie, 'Reclassifying Upward Mobility: Femininity and the Neo-liberal Subject', *Gender and Education*, 15: 3 (2003), pp. 237–48.

Walkerdine, Valerie, 'Shame on You! Intergenerational Trauma and Working-Class Femininity on Reality Television' in Beverley Skeggs and Helen Wood (eds.) *Reality Television and Class* (Basingstoke: Palgrave Macmillan, 2011) pp. 225–36.

Warner, Helen, 'Style over Substance? Fashion, Spectacle and Narrative in Contemporary US Television', *Popular Narrative Media*, 2:2 (2009), pp. 181–93.

Weber, Brenda R., *Makeover TV: Selfhood, Citizenship and Celebrity* (London: Duke University Press, 2009).

Whelehan, Imelda, 'Remaking Feminism: Or Why Is Postfeminism so Boring?', *Nordic Journal of English Studies*, 9:3 (2010), pp. 155–72.

Wilks, Louise, '"Boys Don't Like Girls for Funniness": Raunch Culture and the British Tween Film', *Networking Knowledge*, 5:1 (2012), pp. 100–24.

Wilks, Louise, *Naughty Noughties? Depictions of Female Sexuality and the Body Politic in Contemporary British Cinema*, PhD Thesis (University of Liverpool, 2012).

Williams, Melanie, *Female Stars of British Cinema* (Edinburgh: Edinburgh University Press, 2017).

Winch, Alison, *Girlfriends and the Postfeminist Sisterhood* (Hampshire: Palgrave Macmillan, 2013).

Winship, Lindsay, 'Close Up: StreetDance 3D', *Time Out*, 20 May 2010, p. 69.

Wintour, Patrick, 'David Cameron Presents Himself as Leader of "aspiration nation"', *The Guardian*, 10 October 2012. Available from https://www.the guardian.com/politics/2012/oct/10/david-cameron-leader-aspiration-nati on (accessed 31 January 2020).

Woods, Faye, 'Teen TV Meets T4: Assimilating The O.C. into British Youth Television', *Critical Studies in Television*, 8:1 (2013), pp. 14–35.

Woods, Faye, *British Youth Television* (London: Palgrave, 2016).

Working Title Films, '*Wild Child* Production Notes', 2008, pp. 1–21.

Wyithe, Heidi, 'Withnail and Eyeliner', *This Is Local London*, 17 December 2001, n.p.

Young, Graham, 'A Headteacher's Headache', *Birmingham Evening Mail*, 18 December 2009, p. 43.

Young, Graham, 'Fast Girls', *Sunday Mercury*, Features, 17 June 2012, p. 2.

Young, Graham, 'Girl Power Is Back on Track', *Wales on Sunday*, 17 June 2012, p. 6.

Young, Toby, 'Top of the Class in Biology and Humanity', *The Times*, 30 October 2009, p. 13.

Zane, Alex, '*Chalet Girl*', *The Sun*, 18 March 2011, p. 2.

Filmography

Alterman, Robert. *Gosford Park*. 2001.

Anderson, Lindsay. *If*. 1968.

Arnold, Andrea. *Red Road*. 2006.

Arnold, Andrea. *Fish Tank*. 2009.

Arnold, Andrea. *Wuthering Heights*. 2011.

Asante, Amma. *A Way of Life*. 2004.

Asante, Amma. *Belle*. 2013.

Boyle, Danny. *Trainspotting*. 1996.

Branagh, Kenneth. *Cinderella*. 2015.

Buck, Chris and Jennifer Lee. *Frozen*. 2013.

Carter, Thomas. *Save the Last Dance*. 2001.

Cattaneo, Peter. *The Full Monty*. 1997.

Chadha, Gurinder. *Bahji on the Beach*. 1993.

Chadha, Gurinder. *Bend It Like Beckham*. 2002.

Chadha, Gurinder. *Angus, Thongs and Perfect Snogging*. 2008.

Chadwick, Justin. *The Other Boleyn Girl*. 2008.

Clarke, Noel. *Adulthood*. 2008.

Cole, Nigel. *Made in Dagenham*. 2010.

Columbus, Chris. *Harry Potter and the Philosopher's Stone*. 2001.

Coppola, Sofia. *Marie Antoinette*. 2006.

Curtis, Richard. *Love Actually*. 2003.

Daldry, Stephen. *Billy Elliot*. 2000.

Dante, Joe. *The Hole*. 2001.

Davies, Terence. *Of Time and City*. 2008.

Dearden, Basil. *Sapphire*. 1959.

Dibb, Saul. *Bullet Boy*. 2004.

Dibb, Saul. *The Duchess*. 2008.

Edwards, Blake. *Breakfast at Tiffany's*. 1961.

Fletcher, Anne. *Step Up*. 2006.

Gavron, Sarah. *Suffragette*. 2015.

Goldbacher, Sandra. *The Governess*. 1998.

Goldbacher, Sandra. *Me Without You*. 2001.

Gough, Lawrence. *Salvage*. 2008

Hall, Regan. *Fast Girls*. 2012.

Heckerling, Amy. *Clueless*. 1995.

Heymann, Lindy. *Kicks*. 2008.

Hooper, Tom. *The King's Speech*. 2010.

Huda, Menhaj. *Kidulthood*. 2006.

Hudson, Hugh. *Chariots of Fire*. 1981.

Ivory, James. *A Room with a View*. 1985.

Jackson, Pat. *Don't Talk to Strange Men*. 1962.

Jarrold, Julian. *Becoming Jane*. 2004.

Jarrold, Julian. *A Royal Night Out*. 2014.

Kapur, Shekhar. *Elizabeth*. 1998.

Kapur, Shekhar. *Elizabeth: The Golden Age*. 2008.

Kerrigan, Justin. *Human Traffic*. 1999.

Lee, Ang. *Sense and Sensibility*. 1995.

Lee, Kolton, *Freestyle*. 2010.

Leland, David. *Wish You Were Here*. 1987.

Lloyd, Phyllida. *Mamma Mia*. 2008.

Love, Nick. *The Football Factory*. 2004.

MacCormick, Niall. *Albatross*. 2011.

Madden, John. *Mrs Brown*. 1997.

Maguire, Sharon. *Bridget Jones's Diary*. 2001.

Marsh, James. *The Theory of Everything*. 2015.

Marshall, Gary. *The Princess Diaries*. 2001.

Maybury, John. *The Edge of Love*. 2008.

McGrath, Douglas. *Emma*. 1996.

Meadows, Shane. *This Is England*. 2006.

Moore, Nick. *Wild Child*. 2008.

Morley, Carol. *The Alcohol Years*. 2000.

Morley, Carol. *Dreams of a Life*. 2011.

Morley, Carol. *The Falling*. 2014.

Morton, Samantha. *The Unloved*. 2009.

Neame, Ronald. *The Prime of Miss Jean Brodie*. 1969.

Newell, Mike. *Four Weddings and a Funeral*. 1994.

Parker, Ol. *Mamma Mia: Here We Go Again*. 2018.

Parker, Oliver and Barnaby Thompson. *St Trinian's*. 2007.

Parker, Oliver and Barnaby Thompson. *St Trinian's 2: The Legend of Fritton's Gold*. 2009.

Pasquini, Dania and Max Giwa. *StreetDance*. 2010.

Pawlikowski, Pawel. *Last Resort*. 2000.

Pawlikowski, Pawel. *My Summer of Love*. 2004.

Potter, Sally. *Orlando*. 1992.

Potter, Sally. *Ginger and Rosa*. 2012.

Ramsay, Lynne. *Morvern Callar*. 2002.

Richardson, Tony. *A Taste of Honey*. 1961.

Romanek, Mark. *Never Let Me Go*. 2010.

Ross, Gary. *The Hunger Games*. 2012.

Rozema, Patricia. *Mansfield Park*. 1999.

Scherfig, Lone. *An Education*. 2010.

Scherfig, Lone. *Their Finest*. 2017.

Schlesinger, John. *Darling*. 1965.

Scott, Jordan. *Cracks*. 2009.

Seidelman, Susan. *Desperately Seeking Susan*. 1985.

Spiers, Bob. *Spice World: The Movie*. 1997.

Taylor-Johnson. *Fifty Shades of Grey*. 2015.

Traill, Phil, *Chalet Girl*. 2011.

Vallée, Jean-Marc. *The Young Victoria*. 2009.

Waters, Mark. *Mean Girls*. 2004.

Weir, Peter. *Picnic at Hanging Rock*. 1975.

West, Simon. *Tomb Raider*. 2001.

Wilcox, Herbert. *Victoria the Great*. 1937.

Wright, Joe. *Pride and Prejudice*. 2005.

Wright, Joe. *Anna Karenina*. 2012.

Teleography

Ally McBeal (1997–2001) Fox.
Boys from the Blackstuff (1982) BBC Two.
Bleak House (2005) BBC One.
Britain's Got Talent (2007–) ITV.
British Film Forever (2007) BBC Two.
Brookside (1982–2003) Channel Four.
Buffy the Vampire Slayer (1997–2003) Fox.
Cribs (2000–) MTV.
Dawson's Creek (1998–2003) Channel Four.
Downton Abbey (2010–2015) ITV.
Fawlty Towers (1975–1979) BBC One.
Gossip Girl (2007–2011) CWTV/ITV.
Hannah Montana (2006–2011) Disney Channel.
Made in Chelsea (2011–) E4.
Margaret Thatcher: The Long Walk to Finchley (2008) Channel Four.
My Super Sweet 16 (2005–) MTV.
Pop Idol (2001–2003) ITV.
Pride and Prejudice (1995) BBC One.
Sex and the City (1998–2004) HBO.
The Crown (2016–) Netflix.
The O.C. (2003–2007) CTV/E4.
The Tudors (2007–2010) HBO.
X Factor (2004–) ITV.

Music

'California Dreamin'' (1968, written by John Phillips, Michelle Phillips, performed by Bobby Womack).

'Dance of the Knights' (1935, written by Sergei Prokofiev).

'Life's a Bitch' (1994, written by Ronnie Wilson, Oliver Scott, Nasir Jones and Anthony Cruz, performed by Nas).

'On the Rebound' (1961, written by Floyd Cramer, Floyd Cramer, Duke Ellington, Barney Bigard and Irving Mills).

'One in a Million' (2010, written by P. Neil, S. Naqui and K. Qazzaz, performed by Swiss Feat. Music Kidz).

'Três Caravelas' (1968, written by Gilberto Gil and Caetano Veloso, performed by Gilberto Gil and Caetano Veloso).

'Voyage of the Moon' (1969, written by Donavan, performed by Mary Hopkin).

Index

Illustrations in bold

www.ingramcontent.com/pod-product-compliance
Lightning Source LLC
Chambersburg PA
CBHW050420280326
41932CB00013BA/1931